The ASTD Trainer's WorkShop Series

◆

The ASTD Trainer's WorkShop Series is designed to be a practical, hands-on road map to help you quickly develop training in key business areas. Each book in the series offers all the exercises, handouts, assessments, structured experiences, and ready-to-use presentations needed to develop effective training sessions. In addition to easy-to-use icons, each book in the series includes a website with PowerPoint presentations and electronic copies of all supporting material featured in the book.

ASTD Trainer's WorkShop Series

Coaching Employee Engagement TRAINING

Peter R. Garber

ASTD
WORKPLACE LEARNING & PERFORMANCE
PRESS

ASTD Press is an internationally renowned source of insightful and practical information on workplace learning and performance topics, including training basics, evaluation and return-on-investment (ROI), instructional systems development (ISD), e-learning, leadership, and career development.

Ordering information: Books published by ASTD Press can be purchased by visiting our website at store.astd.org or by calling 800.628.2783 or 703.683.8100.

Library of Congress Control Number: 2011943177

ISBN-10: 1-56286-819-5
ISBN-13: 978-1-56286-819-2

ASTD Press Editorial Staff:

Production Manager: Larry Fox
Community of Practice Manager, Human Capital: Kristin Husak
Developmental Editor: Mark Morrow
Associate Editor: Heidi Smith
Copyeditor: Heidi Smith
Indexer: Linda Buskus
Proofreader: Kim Husband
Interior Design and Production: Abella Publishing Services, LLC
Cover Design: Ana Ilieva Foreman
Cover Illustrator: Ken Condon, www.illustrationsource.com

Printed by Versa Press, Inc., East Peoria, Illinois, www.versapress.com

Contents

◆

P r e f a c e

◆

We hear a great deal about employee engagement today, but the concept is not always clearly understood. Simply, employee engagement means that employees feel a sense of ownership for their work and their contributions to the organization as a whole.

The effectiveness of the leadership in the organization plays a very significant role in creating and maintaining this workplace culture of employee engagement. Each of the lessons and activities in this Training WorkShop has been designed to help create a workplace supportive of employee engagement and to help participants become more effective coaches in their supervisory roles, regardless of their experience leading others.

Those who lead others today have one of the most important and challenging jobs in the organization. The future success of the organization depends largely on the ability of these individuals to motivate employees. The climate and culture of the organization are dependent on their ability to create a work atmosphere that is supportive of the concepts of employee engagement.

To create such a work environment, leaders need to earn the respect and trust of those they lead. Creating a more engaged workplace is really a matter of becoming familiar with the basics of motivating and leading people. A leader who becomes comfortable implementing these basic skills is the first step toward creating an engaged workplace.

◆

Introduction: How to Use This Book Effectively

Why a Coaching Approach

It has been found that the primary reason employees quit jobs is not so much based on the organization or the job itself, but rather is based on her relationship with her supervisor. To the employee, the supervisor is the face of the company.

A supervisor typically determines or at least influences the following: what the employee works on each day, the amount of feedback and recognition the employee receives, the type of promotional opportunities made available to the employee, the amount of raises the employee receives, or any discipline or other sanctions that may be imposed on the employee. Obviously, becoming a more effective supervisor or coach is a worthwhile goal of anyone in a leadership role on any level in the organization. The bottom line in any situation involving people at work is that leadership and, more specifically, the role of the coach, is undoubtedly the most important factor in any employee's work life.

Each of the lessons and activities included in this workbook is designed to address one aspect of becoming a better coach. There is no magic formula to becoming a better coach—it is mostly about these basic principles of leadership. Just putting forth the effort to become a better coach can be a big step toward achieving this objective. Paying attention to the "soft" skills of leadership can pay great dividends. These soft skills include: becoming a better communicator, paying attention to employees' feelings, giving feedback on performance, providing recognition and rewards when deserved, and encouraging participation and teamwork, all of which are covered in this workbook.

Utilizing This Workbook

You will find that this workbook is rich in content on the subject of coaching employee management. It contains 50 different content modules on this important topic, which can help you teach others how to be better coaches and leaders of engaged employees. Presenting these materials has been made easy for you as a facilitator. These lessons and activities have been organized with step-by-step instructions and guidance. Participant materials including handouts, assessments, and PowerPoint slides are available online at www. astd.org/coachingemployeeengagementtraining. In addition to the various presentation format options outlined in this workbook, these materials could also be utilized to supplement your current training programs or objectives or simply be used as coaching tools for specific challenging situations a coach or supervisor may find.

This workbook presents a number of different ways and formats that these materials can be utilized including a multiday training program, a one-and-a-half-day program, half-day program, and a brief two-and-a-half hour overview program. Included also is guidance on how to use many of these materials on an individualized basis as part of a consulting or even coaching process to help individuals deal more effectively with the many leadership challenges they may face on the job. Each of these plans is clearly explained and detailed to provide you with an easy path forward to helping understand and practice the skills taught in these programs.

You will find that these materials can serve as an invaluable resource not only for designing and presenting your training objectives but also for providing direction and guidance on an ongoing basis.

Definition of Terms

There are a number of terms utilized throughout this workbook that may need to be more clearly defined concerning their application and usage in this program. These definitions are not intended to change or modify any definitions that may be applied in other situations but merely to explain their intent in this book.

Many of these terms may be perceived or utilized differently in other contexts, and this is fine. What is most important is that the principles and concepts being presented are understood as applied in this workbook and for the purpose of better understanding the concepts of employee engagement.

COACH

The term *coach* often is associated with one who plays a supportive or even mentoring role for others, especially when this concept is applied in the workplace. Coaching employees has proven to be an extremely effective way to motivate employees to perform at their highest level and greatest potential.

SUPERVISOR

The term *supervisor* often implies more of a traditional or directive role in leading employees at work.

COACH OR SUPERVISOR

Neither description should be considered to be better or worse than the other but merely descriptive of the many roles and responsibilities of those who lead others in today's workplace.

SUPERVISING AND COACHING

The concepts of supervising and coaching, for purposes of this book, are closely aligned and often used interchangeably. A supervisor can be a coach and a coach can be a supervisor. To be an effective leader, you must be able to be both a supervisor and a coach to employees, depending on the situation.

EMPLOYEE ENGAGEMENT

Engagement can be defined as creating an environment in which employees on all levels of the organization feel a greater sense of ownership for their work and commitment to the success of the organization.

CONFLICT

Conflict includes the different viewpoints, thoughts, and ideas that employees may feel and express while they are working together. Some conflict is inevitable in just about any situation in which people are working together, but it is not necessarily bad if managed properly, as it can allow new or different ideas to be expressed and adapted.

EMPATHY

Empathy means that you try to understand how someone else feels. Empathy is different than agreement and is nonjudgmental. Empathy is conveying to another person, "I know how you feel," and simply means that you are trying to understand how a person is feeling and what she is experiencing at the moment.

COMPLAINT

A *complaint* is any condition an employee thinks or feels is unjust or inequitable from her perspective. Even though a complaint may be seen from a very different perspective by other people, including the coach or supervisor, this does not diminish the importance of it to the person who has the complaint.

FEEDBACK

Feedback is information communicated to an employee concerning how she is currently performing her job. Feedback is the key to learning and improving performance. Providing feedback to employees allows them to grow and develop in their jobs.

RECOGNITION

Recognition is positive feedback about a person's job performance and can be either formal or informal. The ultimate goal of recognition is not only to acknowledge an employee's good work but also to reinforce these behaviors so that good work will be repeated in the future.

CONSENSUS

Consensus means that all team members support a decision or path forward even though it may not have been their idea or they might not personally agree. Consensus expressed would sound like, "This decision was not my idea or even my first choice concerning the decision of the team, but I do agree to support and work toward the success of this decision just as if it were my own."

SYNERGY

Synergy is the blending of different human skills, talents, and experiences to produce a total effect greater than the sum of the individual team member's skills, talents, and experiences alone.

Content of the Training

The training designs in this workbook are intended to address the full range of topics associated with coaching for employee engagement. Below is a listing of the modules along with a brief description.

Content Module 9.1—The Importance of Communication

Content Module 9.2—Coaching Communication Model

Content Module 9.3—Listening for Better Coaching

Content Module 9.4—Silent Messages

Content Module 9.5—Phrases That Kill Ideas

Content Module 9.6—3 Levels of Coaching Communication

Content Module 9.7—Communicating Assignments Quiz

Content Module 9.8—Rumors

Content Module 9.9—14 Commitments for Effective Coaching

Content Module 9.10—Basic Coaching Principles

Content Module 9.11—Engaged Coaching

Content Module 9.12—The Real Experts

Content Module 9.13—Helping Employees Contribute

Content Module 9.14—Spending Time With Employees

Content Module 9.15—Supervisor Ask/Tell Model

Content Module 9.16—Positive Conflict

Content Module 9.17—Causes of Conflict at Work

Content Module 9.43—When Teams Are Most Effective

Content Module 9.44—Reaching Consensus

Content Module 9.45—Synergy

Content Module 9.46—Designing Engagement Into Your Organization

Content Module 9.47—Helping Teams Get Things Done

Content Module 9.48—Dealing With Difficult Team Members

Content Module 9.49—Characteristics of an Engaged Team Player

Content Module 9.50—Creating a Team Project Plan

How the Book Is Organized

This book contains content perfectly suited to be combined with your own training programs and designs for a wide variety of learning situations. The materials include:

- ◆ **effectively assessing needs and customizing training** for your learners and participants in your programs (chapter 2)

- ◆ **evaluating methodologies** for determining the effectiveness and appropriateness of your training programs (chapter 3)

- ◆ **designing and facilitating techniques** and tips to ensure you build interactive and engaging training (chapter 4)

- ◆ **content modules** you can use as they are or modify to meet your particular training needs (chapter 9)

- ◆ **structured experiences** that include role plays and other interactive participant experiences to enhance training (chapter 11)

- ◆ **assessments** that you can use to supplement and enhance the training experiences of your learners and increase applicability

- ◆ **Microsoft Word documents** so that you can customize participant materials (online materials)

- ◆ **Microsoft PowerPoint presentations** to use in your presentations or customize to your particular needs

 ◆ **bibliography** of additional resources you can use to support your training program.

Icons

 Assessment: Appears when an agenda or learning activity includes an assessment, and it identifies each assessment presented.

 **Website:** Indicates the online materials accompanying this workbook.

 Clock: Indicates recommended timeframes for specific activities.

 Discussion/Debrief: Points out discussion or debriefing activities you can use to explore specific ideas associated with training.

 Handouts: Indicates handouts that you can print or copy and use to support training activities (online).

 **Key Points:** Alerts you to key points that you should emphasize as part of a training activity

 PowerPoint Slide: Indicates PowerPoint presentations and slides that can be used in your training. Thumbnails of the slides associated with each training program are reprinted at the end of each associated chapter. Instructions for using PowerPoint slides and the online material are in the Appendix.

Structured Experience: Introduces structured experiences (participant exercises), which are included in chapter 11.

Training Assessments and Instruments: Identifies specific tools and assessments that you can use during your training programs.

What to Do Next: Highlights recommended actions that will help you make the transition from one section of this workbook to the next, or from one activity to the next.

What to Do Next

- ◆ Study the entire contents of the book to get an overview of the resources provided.

- ◆ Review the content of the online materials so that you can understand how it relates to the material in the printed book. Open the files in Microsoft Word, PowerPoint, and Adobe Acrobat Reader so you are able to determine how to make copies of the forms you will need to print and the presentations you may use to enrich the material. This step should include a careful reading of the Appendix "Using the Online Materials."

- ◆ Study and apply the strategies outlined in chapter 2, "Assessing the Needs of Learners," to ensure that your sessions with learners are relevant and timely.

- ◆ When you have absorbed the information you discover while assessing your training needs, proceed to chapter 3. Design your session to meet the specific learning needs your potential participants have expressed. Carefully consider modifying the designs in this book as you formulate your plan to facilitate the learning of your client audience. You can use the sample designs in chapters 5 through 8 or modify them as your needs analysis suggests. The content modules in chapter 9 are detailed. You can plan to use them as they are or modify them. Chapters 10 and 11 contain the structured experiences, assessments, and modules required. Because each of these is also a stand-alone item, you can easily incorporate any or all of them into your existing training designs.

◆ Prepare to facilitate your training by studying the approaches in chapter 3. Each of your sessions should improve on the previous ones, and chapter 3 contains tips on how you can make sure that you learn along with your trainees. You will become a highly effective facilitator; the trainees will become highly effective supervisors/coaches.

◆ Plan to evaluate each of your training sessions. Chapter 5 tells you why this is important and gives you steps to gain insight into the payoffs of your supervisor training. Outline the steps you will take to gather and analyze evaluation data, and modify your training design as a result.

Chapter 2

Assessing the Needs of Learners

- The need for assessment
- How to determine specific training needs
- Using the Needs Assessment Model

Why Use Assessments

There are several factors to consider when designing and implementing any training program. When considering these factors, it becomes clear that you must also think about how much should realistically be invested in employee training. An organization cannot continue to provide resources to a function without some measure of the value received from the investment. A business case must be made in order to justify the investment of training employees.

You need to assess just how much training is necessary to ensure that employees have the appropriate skills and knowledge to perform the job or tasks they will be assigned. It is not fair to expect someone to do a job for which she has not received adequate training. However, the cost of training can be high. When considering training for any employee, you need to ensure that the training provided is necessary and job related.

The Right Questions to Ask

The question that should be asked when thinking about providing training is, "What do employees need to know in order to perform their job to the organization's expectations?" Starting from this question and working back will help you better determine exactly what training needs to be provided for employees and how to utilize the materials included in this workbook.

Organizations invest considerable resources by allowing participants time away from their important work and busy schedules to attend training. Spending time thinking about how to most effectively and efficiently present your training program is certainly worthwhile. The dilemma is always how much training is enough and how much is too much?

You want to make sure that you adequately cover the materials you want participants to learn, but you don't want to overwhelm them with more information than they can realistically learn in the time allotted. You want participants to be stimulated and challenged, but at the same time learn at a pace that is comfortable and supportive of learning. And perhaps most importantly, you want to make sure that you are meeting the expectations of the sponsor or sponsors of this training. The following model can help you make these important determinations.

Using the Training Objectives Matrix

You have many options in deciding how to develop your training program to use these materials. The workbook offers suggested formats for various schedules and timetables for presenting these materials. To more effectively determine your training needs, the Training Objectives Matrix (See Table 2-1) provided will help you assess specific needs for any training intervention.

You use the Training Objectives Matrix to assess your training on four different levels:

- ◆ resource commitment for the training by the organization

- ◆ how participants are expected to change as a result of the training experience

- ◆ the goals and objectives expected by the organization or sponsors as a result of the training

- ◆ the cultural change expected to occur as a result of the training.

Table 2–1 Training Objectives Matrix

	Low Importance	Moderate Importance	High Importance	Critical Objective
Resource Commitment				
Time Investment				
Support				
Follow-up				
Accountability				
Participant Training Objectives				
Inform				
Teach				
Change Perceptions				
Create Behavioral Change				
Organizational Training Objectives				
Educate				
Reach Organizational Goals				
Cultural Change				
Support Cultural Change				

The Training Objectives Matrix can help you develop more accurate assessments of your organization's training needs. Use each of the factors as a basis to assess the need for any of the training you develop using this book or any other training you develop in your organization.

Resource Commitment

♦ **Time**—The amount of time either in hours or days that the organization is willing to commit for the training.

*Note: For purposes of the matrix presented, assume that *Low Importance* indicates the organization is unwilling to commit significant amounts of time for training and that *Critical Objective* means the organization is willing to invest larger amounts of time for these training objectives.

- ◆ **Support**—The level of support in the organization not only for resourcing the training but also for encouraging that concepts presented should be used by participants.

- ◆ **Follow-up**—The commitment the organization is willing to make to ensure that the materials presented in the training program are utilized by participants following the training.

- ◆ **Accountability**—The degree to which participants are held accountable for utilizing the training they receive.

Participant Training Objectives

- ◆ **Inform**—Provide information to participants that is important to performing their jobs better.

- ◆ **Teach**—Help participants learn new methods, techniques, approaches, and more for performing their jobs.

- ◆ **Change Perceptions**—Help participants understand and view their roles in new and different ways based on insights, they gain during the training experience.

- ◆ **Create Behavioral Change**—Teach and motivate participants to perform their jobs differently based on the information, insights, and changed perceptions resulting from the training experience.

- ◆ **Educate**—Provide information to participants that is important and pertinent to their jobs.

- ◆ **Reach Organizational Goals**—Provide concepts and skills training to participants to help enable organizational goals to be reached.

- ◆ **Support Cultural Change**—Training intended to support an organization's cultural change initiatives by teaching participants any new philosophies, expectations, and skills that are introduced.

Matrix Rating Guide

The Training Objectives Rating Guide provides a cross-reference between how you evaluated your specific training needs above as they relate to each of the factors on this matrix. To use this guide, simply look at how you rated your particular training on the matrix above and find the specific content module(s) that best meets this factor.

To help you identify this information, you will find a Training Objectives Matrix Rating Guide online (www.astd.org/coachingemployeeengagement-training) based on how that particular content module addresses each of the Matrix's factors. Table 2–2 is an example of the completed Matrix for Content Module 9.3—Listening Tips.

Table 2–2 Content Module 9.3—Listening Tips

	LOW	MODERATE	HIGH	CRITICAL OBJECTIVE
Resource Commitment				
Time Investment	X			
Support	X			
Follow-up	X			
Accountability	X			
Participant Training Objectives				
Inform		X		
Teach			X	
Change Perceptions			X	
Create Behavioral Change			X	
Organizational Training Objectives				
Educate			X	
Reach Organizational Goals		X		
Cultural Change				
Support Cultural Change			X	

Other Assessment Methods

Many strategies determine what potential training participants need to learn. Some are more time consuming than others, but here are five that are used frequently:

◆ **Existing data**—This can include benchmarking reports, performance appraisals, strategic plans, competency models, financial reports, job descriptions, mission statements, and annual reports. The advantage of this method is that the information is readily accessible from the organization and provides hard, reliable data and measures. Because this information is typically gathered for purposes other than training, it is necessary to make inferences from it to determine whether training issues are present.

◆ **Surveys**—Participants answer a series of focused questions, typically by a deadline; results are easy to tally and analyze. This method is usually an inexpensive way for respondents to provide information quickly and easily, either via an electronic tool or a paper-and-pencil questionnaire. It is important, however, to word the questions carefully so that you get the desired data and the questions mean the same thing to each respondent.

◆ **Interviews**—Interviews are one-on-one discussions, either face to face or over the phone, to gather data about individual learner and business needs. Plan interview questions ahead, record the session (with the interviewee's permission), and take notes. Although this is a time-consuming method, it can provide great detail and draw out information that is difficult to obtain from a survey. The interviewer must objectively record responses and not add her interpretation to what is said.

◆ **Focus groups**—A facilitator conducts a group interview, which can provide information about learners' skill and performance levels, the work environment, culture, and perceptions of potential training participants. An advantage to this data-collection method is that all participants can hear and build on each other's' ideas. It can also be time consuming, and it may be beneficial to have more than one facilitator conduct a focus group session.

♦ **Observation**—The observer visits the organization to watch learners do their jobs, then records information regarding such items as behavior patterns, task performance, interactions with others, and use of time. Although this method is helpful to assess training needs and skill levels for individual learners, the observer cannot typically assess mental processes. Individuals may also behave differently around an observer than they would under normal circumstances.

What to Do Next

♦ Choose an assessment method outlined in this chapter, either using the provided Matrix or following one of the traditional methods noted above. Review the Training Objectives Matrix online to understand how the matrix is applied at www.astd.org/coachingemploy-eeengagementtraining.

♦ Gather pertinent data from key stakeholders or others for whom the training program is being developed.

♦ Choose your assessment tool to help you carry out your assessment as part of your training design process.

◆

Designing and Facilitating Engagement Training

What's in This Chapter

- ◆ Designing learner-centered training
- ◆ Basic training theory
- ◆ Top factors for successful training
- ◆ Successful training facilitation

Design a Learner-Centered Training Program

You should have a vision of the training you are intending to create and a blueprint to help you build it correctly. As you design your training programs, always keep in mind the needs of the learner. Your training design should be *learner-centered* or, in other words, you should keep the needs of the participants as your most important objective during the entire training experience.

Ask yourself, "What is it that each person needs to know and learn in order to practice the concepts presented?" Keep your training design both interesting and relevant to the needs of the learner. This workbook will give you many different options and alternatives to your training design so you can be as flexible as possible in developing your programs.

Basic Adult Learning Principles

Malcolm Knowles (1998) first introduced the term *andragogy* to refer to the science of teaching adults. He identified facets of adult learning that affect how training is designed. You should keep the following principles in mind when you design training:

◆ Adults need to know why they must learn something before they learn it. It is the facilitator's responsibility to explain why the learning is of value and how the training will help the participants improve their coaching skills.

◆ Adults need to feel that others consider them able to make their own decisions and direct their own lives. They may fear that training will be similar to their school experiences and thus resist participation. Trainers must create learning experiences that help adults make the transition from dependent to independent learners by providing them with useful strategies and tools.

◆ The richest resources for adult learning are in the learners themselves. All adults have unique experiences to share, as well as varied backgrounds, motivations, learning styles, interests, and needs. It will be most effective for the facilitator to use the participants' experiences with supervising and coaching during the training session.

◆ Learning must be authentic, as adults are ready to learn to cope with real-life situations. It is also important that the learning coincide with a participant's development and be appropriate for the learner's skill and knowledge levels. To ensure that the training meets the needs of all learners, facilitators can use a variety of structured experiences and can share information that directly addresses coaching and supervising issues.

◆ Adults are motivated to learn if they believe that the training will help them on the job and in their relationships. The most effective training helps individuals perform tasks and handle problems that they confront in their everyday lives. Participants in an effective coaching training session should be allowed to influence the learning approach. Facilitators should use interactive training methods that focus on how participants can apply the learning and change their behavior.

◆ Adults are strongly motivated by internal pressures: quality-of-life issues, job satisfaction, or respect in the workplace. Each person's type and level of motivation is different, so the trainer must identify those motivators and decide the best way to incorporate them into the training, which can be challenging.

◆ Adult learners are goal oriented with little time and a finite capacity to absorb information. Limit lecture time for delivering information to allow a free flow of discussion and opinions to be expressed.

Factors That Drive Successful Training

Your objective in any training program should always be to have participants leave thinking, "That was a really valuable and worthwhile experience." Considering the fact that a great deal of resources including everyone's time are invested in any training program, this is a reasonable expectation and standard to strive to achieve.

But what makes the difference between participants just sitting through a training program as required by their employer and really connecting with them and having them leave the experience excited about what they have learned and better equipped to meet the challenges of their jobs? The following factors can help you create and present training programs that will result in participants experiencing more of this "wow" factor and less of the feeling that the training was just going through the motions of presenting required materials.

TRAINING FACILITY AND RESOURCES

Although you may not have much—or any—control over where the training takes place, you should try as much as possible to ensure that the actual physical facility is adequate for the training you are going to present. Factors such as the size of the facility, air-conditioning or heating systems, audio/visual resources, technical support, privacy, restrooms, food and beverage service or availability, accessibility, security clearances, directions, even the availability of tables and chairs should all be checked into before the start of the training program. If not, you could be delayed in running the program if these factors are not taken care of, which then detracts from the effectiveness of your program.

TIMING

Getting the timing right concerning a training program is not always easy. You need to have enough time to allow you to adequately cover the subject matter, but you don't want to belabor the topic to the point that participants don't feel that their time is being utilized beneficially. Give thought to the timing of your presentation, considering realistically how long it will take to cover each topic or activity you plan on presenting. Be time efficient in your training design by expecting that most things take more time than you may at first estimate.

You need to allow for questions and responses along the way from participants. You don't want to find yourself rushing participants through materials that they have a great interest in exploring. You may want to develop optional materials to use if you find that your timing expectations were too conservative and you are ahead of your training schedule, although this isn't necessarily a bad thing.

Part of your timing planning should also take into consideration what activities you plan at different times during your presentation. For example, if you are conducting a day-long program, you should think about what activities would be best after lunch or in the middle of the afternoon, as everyone (including yourself) may begin to fatigue. Planning an interactive activity during these times can help reenergize everyone.

Present the Right Subject Matter

Obviously, training needs to be focused on the needs of the learner. Ensuring that your subject matter pertains specifically to your training audience is critically important. You can have excellent training material, but if it is not appropriate for a particular group, then it will not be useful to participants. This also applies to inviting the right audience to attend the training.

Sometimes it may be tempting to include someone in a training program for reasons other than their need to learn the subject matter that is being presented. Ensure that you are delivering the right training program to the right people.

MAKE IT INTERACTIVE

It is always best to make training as interactive as possible. Interactive training means that participants do more than simply sit and listen to the facilitator lecture. Interactive training includes getting the participants involved in the training through discussion, exercises, activities, group discussions, and so forth. This creates a better learning environment as well as a more interesting and enjoyable experience for everyone. Finding the right mix of instruction and interaction is usually the key to effective training design and delivery. This workbook will give you a number of different options to find the right balance for your audience.

STICK TO YOUR AGENDA

It is always desirable to develop a training agenda that outlines what is to be included in a training program and lists the timing of each section or module that will be presented. It is important to stick to the agenda as closely as possible to ensure that all of the material included in the program is covered and according to schedule. It is frustrating for participants to be told that certain skills will be taught, and at the end of the program, to find these materials have not been covered. Spending too much time on the earlier parts of the agenda at the expense of the later topics is not an effective way to present any training program.

MONITOR INTEREST LEVEL

Pay attention to the responses of participants in your training program and make any necessary adjustments based on their interest in the materials you are presenting. Put yourself in the participants' chairs and envision what it would be like if you were sitting in on your presentation. It is important to stay on topic and stick to the agenda, but when participants experience fatigue, sometimes moving an activity or group exercise to an earlier time can reenergize the group and ensure they are getting the most out of the program. Remember, most participants are not used to sitting for long periods as they do during a training program, and this can be tiring. Getting participants on their feet or taking an extra brief break can help relieve some of this fatigue.

END ON TIME

People have busy schedules and should not be expected to stay in a training session longer than the announced end time. Again, this is a matter of sticking to the agenda and subject matter throughout the program so the facilitator doesn't find at the end of the day that she is trying to cram too much information into not enough time to adequately cover the materials. It is important to both start and end the program on time.

EVALUATE

Ask participants to complete an evaluation on the training, which can provide you with invaluable feedback on how effective the program was in meeting its objectives, as well as how it might be improved in the future. Sometimes this can be difficult. Participants will usually tell you exactly how they felt about the training. You need to accept this information as constructive feedback that can help you improve the training program in the future. Don't expect to get your training perfect the first time. Like anything else, effective training design and delivery are often matters of trial and error. The biggest mistake you can make as a provider of training is to not pay attention to this feedback and fail to continuously improve the learning experience for participants in your future programs.

10 Tips for Better Presentations and Facilitation

There is no doubt that visual aids can improve the quality of the training experience for participants, and this program provides you with a number of these training tools. However, there is a very important training principle that you need to always keep in mind: You are still the most important visual in your training presentation.

You are what the audience will spend the majority of its focus on during the training. You can either enhance or detract from your other visual training aids. How you deliver materials will ultimately make the difference between your audience benefiting from the materials you present or not paying very much attention to what you present. The following are 10 tips for better presentations that can help you become a better presenter in the future:

1. **Look the part**—You don't have to look like a model or movie star to play the role of a trainer, but you do need to look the part. You should dress appropriately for the audience and environment. For instance, if the training is at a resort, your attire should reflect what is appropriate for the situation. However, if you are at the corporate offices where business attire is expected, you should dress accordingly. You need to make sure that your grooming is not distracting to the audience. Obviously, you need to make sure your hair is combed or brushed, your clothing is properly worn, and so forth. By nature of the profession, trainers often come in contact with felt-tipped markers. If you find yourself handling these writing instruments, make sure you don't put colored marks on your face that may distract the audience from your presentation.

2. **Pay attention to your nonverbal behaviors**—This means the way you communicate to your audience in ways other than with your words. This is often called your body language. You need to ensure that your body language is consistent with your verbal message. If not, you

will instantly lose credibility with your audience. For instance, if you make a statement about how important a particular point is but your body language is too casual or relaxed, the real message you may be presenting is that the point is not very important at all. Similarly, your vocal inflections also provide subtle messages that may be inconsistent with your verbal message. If you say you feel strongly about something but say it in such a way that it sounds like you don't really care about the point, the audience will get a mixed message.

3. **Get your voice heard**—The participants need to be able to comfortably hear what you say. If you need to use a microphone in order to be clearly heard, don't be reluctant to use one, preferably a wireless microphone that can be clipped on. If you have to use a hand-held microphone, make sure you keep it close to your mouth so that the amplification of your voice doesn't vary. Also, before you begin the presentation, test the sound to make sure that you are coming across clearly and not too loud or soft for those near or far from the speakers.

4. **Practice "stage presence"**—The best entertainers in show business typically have the best stage presence. Stage presence is how you are seen by the audience watching you. When presenting, you should think about yourself as if you were an entertainer on stage. How you walk, where you position yourself, and how you move on this stage will all have an impact on your audience. Watch your favorite entertainers and emulate some of their stage presence techniques. Some move around, some interact more with the audience, some use certain gestures, some use "props" to help them keep the audience's attention. One thing you need to be careful of is creating distractions, such as fiddling with something in your hands, picking at yourself, constantly adjusting your clothing, and so forth, as these all create "noise in the channel" that can be very distracting.

5. **Take a lesson from the weatherman**—Watch weather forecasters on television and you will see them touch, turn, and talk as they deliver the weather forecast. They touch (or point) to the weather map, focusing their attention and yours on what is being displayed, they turn to the camera, and then they talk to the viewing audience. Avoid talking to your visual aids and not to your audience.

6. **Relate to the audience**—Remember what it is like to be sitting in the audience. What makes the difference between a training experience that is totally enjoyable or one that is a boring or even punishing experience? Often this difference is determined by the design and delivery of the training. The best training is a program in which the presenter really thought about what the participants would be experiencing. The presenter should have considered the main points she wants to convey to the audience, what knowledge the participants would take from the training experience, and how the audience may feel at various times during the training schedule (ready to participate early in the day or feeling sluggish after lunch, for example) and designed the program accordingly.

7. **Pay attention to the environment**—You need to make sure the room isn't too hot or cold, too stuffy or breezy (fans, air-conditioning blowing), too noisy, or too messy. Let light in from the outside if possible. Ask participants if they are comfortable with the room's climate, noise, and so on. If an issue arises, take the time to correct any problems that you can.

8. **Be a variety show**—Again, think about your audience and what their learning experience is like. No matter how effective it is, using one presentation style or method can get tedious, particularly if the program lasts all day. Utilize as many different learning approaches as possible, such as multiple presenters, audio/visuals, group discussions, breakout sessions, questions and answers, and more.

9. **Entertain the audience**—Don't be afraid to be entertaining in your training. This will make you an even better visual aid to the audience. An occasional joke or funny story helps break up the presentation and provides some comic relief. People like to hear personal stories or experiences that generally relate to the topic being presented. This makes the material seem more practical and is easier to relate to and understand.

10. **Make them wish you had talked longer**—The point is not to push the time of your presentation beyond what the subject requires or what the audience will comfortably tolerate. Many potentially excellent presentations are ruined by going on too long. If they had only

been shorter, the audience would have gotten a great deal more out of the presentation. Don't irritate your audience by over-presenting the information you have to share.

What to Do Next

♦ Determine how you will incorporate basic learning principles and practices into your training session.

♦ Incorporate the training design, facilitation, and presentation techniques outlined in this chapter.

♦ Get feedback from others about your training design and planned workshop activities.

◆

Chapter 4

Evaluating Effectiveness

- ◆ Importance of evaluation
- ◆ Basic training evaluation methodology
- ◆ Tips on evaluating coaching employee engagement
- ◆ Tips on successful evaluation

Why Evaluation Is Important

Evaluating training can be extremely beneficial to both the trainer and the organization. If you do not do some kind of evaluation, it is very difficult to know whether your training efforts have been effective. First, without bothering to do some kind of evaluation, you don't even know if your participants liked sitting in your class, much less whether they learned anything. More importantly, you have no idea if your training efforts benefitted the organization in any way.

This chapter's purpose is to cover some basic evaluation techniques, since a comprehensive look at evaluation would fill the pages of many books. The *For Further Reading* section at the end of this book offers up some basic sources on the topic of evaluation if you want to explore the topic further.

Benefits of Evaluation

To begin thinking about the evaluation process, you'll need to ensure that the learning needs of your participants discussed in chapter 2 are matched up with expected training outcomes you had at the time of training. A basic question is how well the participants liked the training (sometimes called the smile factor). You also need to know if your participants learned the content provided and, more importantly, if your participants applied what they learned on the job.

This is the gold standard of training—whether the participants used what they learned on the job. Clearly, this is the hardest question to answer and is classically referred to as *results*. Some organizations insist on an even more direct payback to the organization for your training efforts referred to as return on investment. Quantifying this organizational impact as a result of your training program is a complex process and not discussed here. For more on the topic, see the *For Further Reading* section in this book.

Classic Training Evaluation Levels

Most trainers rely on an evaluation methodology developed by Donald Kirkpatrick (2006) consisting of four levels. The levels range from measures that are easy to determine to measures that are more difficult to obtain, such as application on the job (results). Here is a listing and description of these training levels:

- ◆ **Level I—Reaction:** This is a measure of the reaction of participants to the training. Often referred to as smile sheets, this level lets you know if your participants at least liked what you presented. Level 1 evaluation does not mean that the participants learned anything, but level 1 can impact participant learning because learning is hard when the participant is bored, confused, or overwhelmed. Level 1 can also help you decide whether to offer the same training again.

- ◆ **Level 2—Learning:** Lets you know if learning objectives were achieved. Level 2 will let you know if your participants increased their knowledge or improved their skills or attitudes as a result of training.

- ◆ **Level 3—Behavior:** If you are interested in how much your training has changed the actual behavior of your participants within the organization, then level 3 measurement is useful.

- ◆ **Level 4—Results:** As noted earlier, this is the most difficult measure of Kirkpatrick's model since you are trying to quantify behavioral changes that happened as a result of training.

A Few Four-Level Details

Level 1 evaluation calls for short reaction surveys (smile sheets) that use Likert scales to measure the effectiveness of the training content and delivery. Participants answer questions about enjoyment or value and are offered space to write comments. If you follow some of the basic advice given in chapter 3 of this book, you are likely to get positive survey results. Unfortunately, smile sheets do not mean you have helped the participants apply their learning or have changed their behavior in a positive way.

Organizations like level 1 evaluations because they are easy to do and track. That's why the use of the higher levels of evaluation (levels 2, 3, and 4) are ignored by many organizations—especially level 4 and certainly ROI (sometimes referred to as level 5). As a trainer, it is good to remember that the more information you have about the impact of your training efforts, the better. If your organization will support higher levels of evaluation, then take the extra time and effort to perform these more thorough evaluations.

You can take some proactive steps toward higher levels of evaluation by including pretests and posttests in your training design that link to level 2 evaluation. You might also take the time to interview your participants and their supervisors to obtain specific information on behavior change related to level 3 evaluation. Finally, you might look at sales figures and performance measures before training and compare these figures to current, after-training metrics. Taking this step provides the basis for a level 4 evaluation. See *For Further Reading* at the back of this book for additional resources on training measurement and evaluation.

What to Do Next

- **Decide on an evaluation strategy**—Decide what evaluation method is most suited to the coaching employee engagement training you decide to design. Establish a clear plan that outlines how you will implement this strategy.

- **Gather feedback**—Once you have completed your training, get the appropriate data from participants and any other individuals relevant to the process. Use the basic information in this chapter to get started.

◆ **Analyze results**—Analyze the responses you received as a result of your chosen evaluation method. You should try to be objective during this process since it is natural to use the data to validate your own opinions and beliefs.

◆ **If necessary, change your training**—You should use your evaluation to strengthen your program and improve delivery and content.

◆

Short Program Training—2.5 Hours

What's in This Chapter

- ◆ Advice on how to work efficiently in a 2.5-hour format
- ◆ How to choose the right content
- ◆ Step-by-step preparation and training delivery instructions
- ◆ Sample agendas

There are many occasions when you may be asked to provide a brief training program or instruction to a group as part of another program, meeting, seminar, or other initiative where these types of materials could be beneficial and appropriate for attendees. This may be to supplement a meeting, present at a conference, or be part of another training initiative.

This chapter provides you with suggestions on presenting a short-format program in the most effective manner to meet this type of request. There are, of course, limitations on how much you can cover in such a short format, but there can still be many benefits to participants who attend even this brief program.

Training Objectives

The objective of the 2.5-hour program is to present as much information as possible in a very short time while still maximizing the learning experience for the participant. However, you need to make sure that you choose the right materials given the relatively brief amount of time you have to provide attendees with meaningful training on coaching employee engagement.

There are several key factors to keep in mind when designing a short training program:

- ◆ Concepts presented should be kept simple and to the point.

- ◆ Don't try to accomplish more than the time allotted will allow.

- ◆ Your goal should be to have participants leave with an understanding of several key learning points that they can use in the future at their jobs. Providing participants with a handout or some other written reference with these learning points can greatly enhance your ability to achieve this objective.

 You will find detailed instructions for presenting each of these activities along with their corresponding slides, which can be shown and possibly provided to participants as "takeaway" references to reinforce the learning points presented. All of these materials are available on the website (www.astd.org/coachingemployeeengagementtraining) for easy accessibility, reference, and use in designing this short program.

Choosing the Content

This short program is principally about the role of communication and effective coaching. The material covers how leaders and supervisors deal with good job performance as well as unacceptable performance in the workplace. In addition, you will find material here that gives accurate and meaningful feedback about how employees are performing their jobs, an important task for any supervisor or coach at work. The content also stresses the importance of teamwork and what makes someone an effective team player. The appropriate content modules for this 2.5-hour session are found in chapter 9.

 TIME

- ◆ 2.5 Hours

MATERIALS

For the instructor:

- ◆ Content Module 9.1—The Importance of Communication

- ◆ Content Module 9.3—Listening for Better Coaching

◆ Content Module 9.10—Basic Coaching Principles

◆ Content Module 9.15—Supervisor Ask/Tell Model

◆ Content Module 9.28—Causes of Poor Performance

◆ Content Module 9.29—5-Step Performance-Correction Process

◆ Content Module 9.30—Setting Performance Standards

◆ Content Module 9.36—A World Without Feedback

◆ Content Module 9.37—Formal and Informal Feedback

◆ Content Module 9.49—Characteristics of a Team Player

◆ PowerPoint presentation: Coaching Employee Engagement Training.
To access slides for this program, open the files *2 Hour Program.ppt* in
the online materials. Facsimiles of the slides for this training session
are included at the end of this chapter (Slides 5.1 through 5.19).

For the participants:

◆ none for this program

Sample Agenda

8:00 A.M.   Introduction (5 minutes)

8:05 A.M.   Content Module 9.1—The Importance of Communication
(chapter 9) (10 minutes)

Objective: Understand how important communication is
in the supervisor/employee relationship to becoming an
effective coach and creating an engaged workplace.

8:15 A.M.   Content Module 9.3—Listening for Better Coaching
(chapter 9) (15 minutes)

Objective: To help participants become better listeners.

8:30 A.M.   Content Module 9.10—Basic Coaching Principles (chapter
9) (15 minutes)

Objective: To give participants basic principles they can
use to engender greater trust and respect from those they
supervise.

8:45 A.M.　Content Module 9.15—Supervisor Ask/Tell Model (chapter 9) (20 minutes)

Objective: To find applications for a Supervisor Ask/Tell model which measures the extent that a supervisor engages in either *asking* or *telling* employees about the performance of their jobs, and based on each person's experience and skill level.

9:05 A.M.　Content Module 9.28—Causes of Poor Performance (chapter 9) (15 minutes)

Objective: To explore strategies for addressing the three major reasons for poor performance, including lack of communication, lack of conditions, and lack of consequences.

9:20 A.M.　Content Module 9.29—5-Step Performance-Correction Process (chapter 9) (15 minutes)

Objective: To discuss and learn to apply a 5-step performance-correction process model that helps supervisors understand how to proceed when dealing with an employee's performance problem.

9:35 A.M.　Content Module 9.30—Setting Performance Standards (chapter 9) (10 minutes)

Objective: To explore the real organizational costs of allowing poor employee performance to go unchallenged or unaddressed.

9:45 A.M.　Content Module 9:36—A World Without Feedback (chapter 9) (15 minutes)

Objective: To explore the importance of feedback using a sports analogy in which participants are asked to envision participating in a sport without any feedback on their performance. Different levels of feedback are presented and discussed.

10:00 A.M.　Content Module 9.37—Formal and Informal Feedback (chapter 9) (10 minutes)

Objective: To discuss and explore formal and informal feedback with guidance provided on when each type of feedback may be most applicable and beneficial.

10:10 A.M.   Content Module 9.49—Characteristics of a Team Player
(chapter 9) (20 minutes)

Objective: To discuss and explore a list of 10 characteristics
of an engaged team player and to find practical applications for team leaders and team members.

10:30 A.M.   Close

Step-by-Step Instructions

◆ Arrive at the facility early.

◆ Set up and test any technology (such as a laptop or digital project
connections).

◆ Prepare the room and check on refreshments (if any).

◆ Welcome participants to the training program. It is best to keep your
welcome and introductions simple and relatively brief. Although everyone should know what the subject matter of the program will be
and why they are attending, it still is a good idea to restate this in the
opening remarks and welcome. If possible, it is also a good idea to
have the sponsor of the training program or some other member of
the management of the organization greet participants and introduce
the program to show support and add emphasis to its importance.

◆ Explain that in these next few hours, a number of communication
tips and tools will be presented. It is important for those in leadership
and supervisory roles to be able to deal with good job performance
as well as unacceptable performance, and both of these topics will be
covered in this program.

◆ Also explain that being able to provide employees with accurate and
meaningful feedback about how they are performing their jobs is also
an important responsibility of any supervisor or coach at work and
that this important topic will also be covered.

◆ As facilitator, you should encourage participants to ask questions,
share their thoughts and experiences, and participate in the discussions you will lead on each of these various topics, as there has been
time built into this agenda for these interactive activities.

◆ Conclude the program by again emphasizing the importance of communication in becoming an effective coach and engaging employees. Encourage participants to utilize the principles and tools they learned during this program. Ask participants what they felt were the most important lessons they learned during the program in order to become better coaches and to engage their employees.

◆ Suggest that participants try to use at least one of the concepts reviewed during this program on a daily basis.

What to Do Next

◆ Identify the participants and assess the training most needed by the group.

◆ Identify the time available for training.

◆ Select appropriate training modules.

◆ Schedule the session and arrange a training room or other facility.

◆ Send training reminders to participants and include an agenda or any work to be done before the session.

◆ Prepare your training materials, including handouts, slide presentations, and supplies.

Slide 5-1

Employee Engagement Training

Slide 5-2

Most problems at work are a result of poor communication.

Slide 5-3

Communication is an Art, Not a Science

There is no absolute right or wrong way to communicate effectively. What is most important is that you communicate in a manner and style most comfortable and effective for you.

Slide 5-4

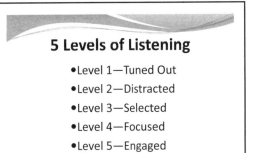

5 Levels of Listening

- Level 1—Tuned Out
- Level 2—Distracted
- Level 3—Selected
- Level 4—Focused
- Level 5—Engaged

Slide 5-5

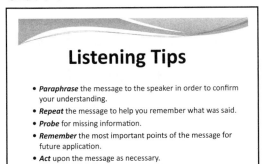

Listening Tips

- *Paraphrase* the message to the speaker in order to confirm your understanding.
- *Repeat* the message to help you remember what was said.
- *Probe* for missing information.
- *Remember* the most important points of the message for future application.
- *Act* upon the message as necessary.

Slide 5-6

Basic Supervisory Principles
FIRM

- Adhering to company policies and procedures
- Meeting job requirements
- Insisting on job excellence
- Expecting the best at all times

Slide 5-7

Basic Supervisory Principles

FAIR

- In using discretion with employees
- In assigning work
- In providing training and growth opportunities
- In promoting employees

Slide 5-8

Basic Supervisory Principles

CONSISTENT

- In applying rules and policies
- In utilizing discipline
- In setting a personal example
- In your decision-making process

Slide 5-9

Basic Supervisory Principles

RESPECTFUL

- Treat everyone with dignity regardless of the situation.
- Listen, ask, explain.
- Follow up with answers to questions.

Slide 5-10

Supervisor ASK/TELL Model

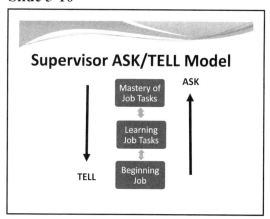

Slide 5-11

Reasons for Poor Performance

- Lack of communication
- Lack of conditions
- Lack of consequences

Slide 5-12

5 Step Performance Correction Process

- Step 1—Observe
- Step 2—Discuss
- Step 3—Correct
- Step 4—Advise
- Step 5—Confirm

Slide 5-13

2 Basic Rules About Managing Performance

1. Always expect excellent performance.
2. Never let poor work go unnoticed or performance issues go unchallenged.

Slide 5-14

Levels of Feedback

- None at all
- Negative only
- Positive only
- Balanced

Slide 5-15

The Default Performance Feedback System

"If you don't hear anything, you are doing just fine but if you screw up we'll let you know!"

Slide 5-16

Types of Feedback

- **Formal**—documented annual/ semiannual performance review
- **Informal**—day-to-day communication and feedback about performance

Slide 5-17

Types of Difficult Team Members

- The reluctant team member
- The defiant team member
- The dominant team member
- The absentee team member
- The vacationer team member

Slide 5-18

Characteristics of an Engaged Team Player

1. Openly shares feelings, opinions, thoughts, and perceptions about problems and issues relating to the team.
2. When listening, attempts to hear and interpret communication from sender's point of view.
3. Utilizes resources, ideas, and suggestions of other team members.
4. Trusts and supports other team members, encouraging their growth and development.
5. Understands and is committed to team objectives.

Slide 5-19

Characteristics of an Engaged Team Player (Cont.)

6. Acknowledges and works through conflict openly, by respecting and being tolerant of individual differences.
7. Makes decisions based on information only, rather than being influenced by peer pressure.
8. Provides ideas and suggestions to the team leader that are helpful to the team.
9. Always strives for a win/win solution.
10. Strives for consensus on team decisions.

Half-Day Training

What's in This Chapter

- Advice on how to work efficiently in a half-day format
- How to choose the right content
- Step-by-step preparation and training delivery instructions
- Sample agendas

Having most of a day for presenting training provides you with greater opportunities to develop a more comprehensive program. In this suggested format, you have the chance to develop a program that covers in more detail a number of different topics. In this format, you can present the program to cover the general topics of:

1. Communication

2. Building trust

3. Managing conflict

4. Complaint handling

5. Managing performance problems

6. Feedback and recognition

7. Leading engaged teams

Presenting Longer Programs

Each of these module topics is important to teaching participants how to become more effective coaches of engaged employees. The lessons found in each module are designed to teach a specific skill or concept relating to the topic covered. This format also gives you the opportunity to supplement the training with materials or communication specific to the organization and participants and still stay within a one-day time period.

It is important to keep in mind when presenting longer training programs that it is likely participants are not used to sitting for most of the day, as their jobs likely keep them active throughout their workday. Giving frequent breaks, including brief stand-up stretches, will help participants stay focused on the presentation. Also, keeping participants actively involved in the presentations by asking for their opinions, input, reactions, and so forth to subject matter and topics makes the learning experience more enjoyable and beneficial. Each of the lessons included in this program has been designed to stimulate this type of participant interaction to help you achieve this objective.

Training Objectives

The objective of this program is to present as much information as possible in a short time while still maximizing the learning experience for the participant. However, you need to make sure that you choose the right materials given the relatively brief amount of time you have to provide attendees with meaningful training on coaching employee engagement.

You will find detailed instructions for presenting each of these activities along with their corresponding slides, which can be shown or provided to participants as "takeaway" references to reinforce the learning points presented. All of these materials are available on the website (www.astd.org/coachingemployeeengagementtraining) for easy accessibility, reference, and use in designing this program.

Choosing the Content

While relatively short, this program still covers a good deal of material, including sections about the role of communication and some basic concepts about effective coaching. The material also covers how leaders and supervisors build trust, manage conflict, handle complaints, and manage performance issues. As in the 2.5-hour option, you will find material here covering the topic of giving accurate and meaningful feedback about how employees are performing their jobs. Feedback and recognition are also covered. Again, the importance of teamwork and what makes someone an effective team player are discussed. The appropriate content modules for this session are found in chapter 9.

TIME

◆ a half-day

MATERIALS

For the instructor:

- ◆ Content Module 9.1—The Importance of Communication

- ◆ Content Module 9.2—Coaching Communication Model

- ◆ Content Module 9.3—Listening for Better Coaching

- ◆ Content Module 9.7—Communicating Assignments Quiz

- ◆ Content Module 9.10—Basic Coaching Principles

- ◆ Content Module 9.11—Engaged Coaching

- ◆ Content Module 9.13—Helping Employees Contribute

- ◆ Content Module 9.15—Supervisor Ask/Tell Model

- ◆ Content Module 9.16—Positive Conflict

- ◆ Content Module 9.17—Causes of Conflict at Work

- ◆ Content Module 9.18—Conflict Strategies

- ◆ Content Module 9.22—Dealing With Upset Employees

- ◆ Content Module 9.23—Definition of a Complaint

- ◆ Content Module 9.28—Causes of Poor Performance

- ◆ Content Module 9.29—5-Step Performance-Correction Process

- ◆ Content Module 9.30—Setting Performance Standards

- ◆ Content Module 9.32—Documentation

◆ Content Module 9.36—A World Without Feedback

◆ Content Module 9.37—Formal and Informal Feedback

◆ Content Module 9.41—Recognition

◆ Content Module 9.43—When Teams Are Most Effective

◆ Content Module 9.47—Helping Teams Get Things Done

◆ Content Module 9.49—Characteristics of a Team Player

◆ PowerPoint presentation: Coaching Employee Engagement Training. To access slides for this program, open the file *Six Hour Program.ppt* available in the online materials.

Copies of this training session's slides are included at the end of this chapter (Slides 6–1 through 6–35).

For the participants:

◆ Assessment 10.1—Communicating Assignments Quiz (chapter 10)

◆ Handout 11.3—Conflict Strategies Role Play

◆ Structured Experience 11.3

◆ Writing instruments

◆ Blank paper

Sample Agenda

8:00 A.M.   Introduction (5 minutes)

8:05 A.M.   Content Module 9.1—The Importance of Communication (chapter 9) (10 minutes)

Objective: Understand how important communication is in the supervisor/employee relationship to becoming an effective coach and creating an engaged workplace.

8:15 A.M.   Content Module 9.2—Coaching Communication Model (chapter 9) (15minutes)

Objective: Presents a communication model for coaches to follow when communicating with employees.

8:30 A.M.   Content Module 9.3—Listening for Better Coaching (chapter 9) (15 minutes)

Objective: To help participants become better listeners.

8:45 A.M.   Content Module 9.7—Communicating Assignments Quiz (chapter 9) (15 minutes)

Objective: To assess each participant's own level of communication acumen using a 10-question Communicating Assignments Quiz.

9:00 A.M.   Content Module 9.10—Basic Coaching Principles (chapter 9) (15 minutes)

Objective: To give participants basic principles to use that engender greater trust and respect from those they supervise.

9:15 A.M.   Content Module 9.11—Engaged Coaching (chapter 9) (15 minutes)

Objective: To build understanding of the two leadership philosophies most people use and to explore the benefits of a more supportive supervisory model.

9:30 A.M.   Content Module 9.13—Helping Employees Contribute (chapter 9) (10 minutes)

Objective: To explore the power of creating a work climate that supports employee contribution to the overall success of the organization.

9:40 A.M.   Content Module 9.15—Supervisor Ask/Tell Model (chapter 9) (15 minutes)

Objective: To find applications for a Supervisor Ask/Tell model tht measure the extent a supervisor engages in the *asking* or *telling* employees about their performance of their jobs, and based on each person's experience and skill level.

BREAK (10 minutes)

10:05 A.M.   Content Module 9.16—Positive Conflict (chapter 9) (15 minutes)

Objective: To discover the positive outcomes possible as a result of conflict and to discuss direct applications to the workforce.

10:20 A.M. Content Module 9.17—Causes of Conflict at Work (chapter 9) (15 minutes)

Objective: To explore the reasons that conflict may exist in the workplace and how to mitigate the impact.

10:35 A.M. Content Module 9.18—Conflict Strategies (chapter 9) (15 minutes)

Objective: To discuss and explore commonly used strategies for dealing with conflict in the workplace and to evaluate their effectiveness.

10:50 A.M. Content Module 9.22—Dealing With Upset Employees (chapter 9) (15 minutes)

Objective: To understand the importance of acknowledging the feelings of an upset employee at that moment, and how to demonstrate empathy for the employee.

11:05 A.M. Content Module 9.23—Definition of a Complaint (chapter 9) (15 minutes)

Objective: To explore key aspects of an employee complaint and how to use a set of tips to deal with employee complaints more effectively.

11:20 A.M. Content Module 9.28—Causes of Poor Performance (chapter 9) (15 minutes)

Objective: To explore strategies for addressing the three major reasons for poor performance including lack of communication, lack of conditions, and lack of consequences.

11:35 A.M. Content Module 9.29—5-Step Performance-Correction Process (chapter 9) (15 minutes)

Objective: To discuss and learn to apply a 5-step performance-correction process model that helps supervisors understand how to proceed when dealing with an employee's performance problem.

11:50 A.M. Content Module 9.30—Setting Performance Standards (chapter 9) (10 minutes)

Objective: To explore the real organizational costs of allowing poor employee performance to go unchallenged or unaddressed.

12:05 P.M.   Content Module 9.32—Documentation (chapter 9) (15 minutes)

Objective: To explore the most important aspects and need for a supervisor to document employee performance using a 5 W's model for documentation.

12:20 P.M.   LUNCH BREAK

1:20 P.M.   Content Module 9.36—A World Without Feedback (chapter 9) (15 minutes)

Objective: To explore the importance of feedback using a sports analogy in which participants are asked to envision participating in a sport without any feedback on their performance. Different levels of feedback are presented and discussed.

1:35 P.M.   Content Module 9.37—Formal and Informal Feedback (chapter 9) (10 minutes)

Objective: To discuss and explore formal and informal feedback with guidance provided on when each type of feedback may be most applicable and beneficial.

1:45 P.M.   Content Module 9.41—Recognition (chapter 9) (15 minutes)

Objective: To discuss and explore different types of recognition with a discussion concerning which ones are the most effective .

2:00 P.M.   Content Module 9.43—When Teams are Most Effective (chapter 9) (15 minutes)

Objective: To discuss the appropriate use of teams and when and when not to utilize them in the workplace.

2:15 P.M.   Content Module 9.47—Helping Teams Get Things Done (chapter 9) (15 minutes)

Objective: To provide tips and other practical advice so that participants are better able to help others work together as a team and accomplish their goals.

2:30 P.M.   Content Module 9.49—Characteristics of a Team Player (chapter 9) (15 minutes)

Objective: To discuss and explore a list of 10 characteristics of an engaged team player and find practical applications for team leaders and team members.

2:45 P.M.   Close

Step-by-Step Instructions

◆ Arrive at the facility early.

◆ Set up and test any technology (such as a laptop or digital project connections).

◆ Prepare the room and check on refreshments (if any).

◆ Welcome participants to the training program. It is best to keep your welcome and introductions simple and relatively brief. Although everyone should know what the subject matter of the program will be and why they are attending, it is still a good idea to restate this in the opening remarks and welcome. If possible, it is also a good idea to have the sponsor of the training program or some other member of the management of the organization greet participants and introduce the program to show support and add emphasis to its importance.

◆ Explain that in the half-day program you have planned, a wide range of material about coaching employee engagement will be presented, covering topics ranging from communication, listening, basic supervisory principles, basic coaching concepts, information about dealing with conflict, handling customer complaints, employee performance, giving feedback, to working effectively as a team member.

◆ As facilitator, you should encourage participants to ask questions, share their thoughts and experiences, and participate in the discussions you will lead on each of these various topics, as there has been time built into the agenda for these interactive activities.

◆ Conclude the program by again emphasizing the importance of some of the key principles covered during the 6-hour program (customize the topics to your particular needs).

◆ Encourage participants to utilize the principles and tools they learned during this program. Ask participants what they felt were the most important lessons they learned during the program in order to become better coaches and to engage their employees.

◆ Suggest that participants try to use at least one of the concepts reviewed during this program on a daily basis.

What to Do Next

◆ Identify the participants and assess the training most needed by the group.

◆ Identify the time available for training.

◆ Select appropriate training modules.

◆ Schedule the session and arrange a training room or other facility.

◆ Send training reminders to participants and include an agenda or any work to be done before the session.

◆ Prepare your training materials, including handouts, slide presentations, and supplies.

Slide 6-1

Employee
Engagement
Training

Slide 6-2

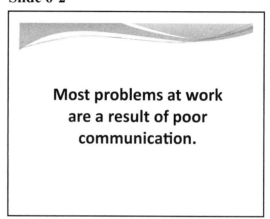

Most problems at work
are a result of poor
communication.

Slide 6-3

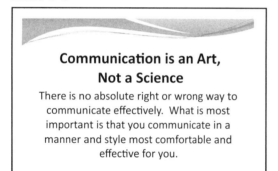

Communication is an Art,
Not a Science

There is no absolute right or wrong way to
communicate effectively. What is most
important is that you communicate in a
manner and style most comfortable and
effective for you.

Slide 6-4

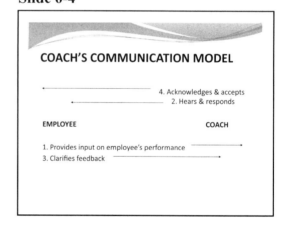

COACH'S COMMUNICATION MODEL

4. Acknowledges & accepts
2. Hears & responds

EMPLOYEE   COACH

1. Provides input on employee's performance
3. Clarifies feedback

Slide 6-5

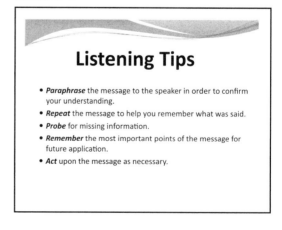

5 Levels of Listening

- Level 1—Tuned Out
- Level 2—Distracted
- Level 3—Selected
- Level 4—Focused
- Level 5—Engaged

Slide 6-6

Listening Tips

- *Paraphrase* the message to the speaker in order to confirm your understanding.
- *Repeat* the message to help you remember what was said.
- *Probe* for missing information.
- *Remember* the most important points of the message for future application.
- *Act* upon the message as necessary.

Slide 6-7

Basic Supervisory Principles

FIRM

- Adhering to company policies and procedures
- Meeting job requirements
- Insisting on job excellence
- Expecting the best at all times

Slide 6-8

Basic Supervisory Principles

FAIR

- In using discretion with employees
- In assigning work
- In providing training and growth opportunities
- In promoting employees

Slide 6-9

Basic Supervisory Principles

CONSISTENT

- In applying rules and policies
- In utilizing discipline
- In setting a personal example
- In your decision-making process

Slide 6-10

Basic Supervisory Principles

RESPECTFUL

- Treat everyone with dignity regardless of the situation.
- Listen, ask, explain.
- Follow up with answers to questions.

Slide 6-11

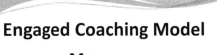

Engaged Coaching Model

More
- Trust
- Openness
- Ownership
- Versatility
- Influence
- Action

Slide 6-12

Engaged Coaching Model

Less
- Control
- Channels
- Routine
- Position power
- Analysis
- Bureaucracy

Slide 6-13

Helping Employees Contribute

- *Supervisor:* Ann, I really like the way you worked on that last project. You certainly showed a great deal of creativity and imagination in completing the job. I never realized that you are so creative!
- *Ann:* Thanks, I really do like doing something when I can use my imagination to come up with something different. I hope you can give me other assignments in which I can utilize my creativity.
- *Supervisor:* Now that I know how good you are at these kinds of things, I will certainly assign these types of jobs to you in the future.
- *Ann:* Great!

Slide 6-14

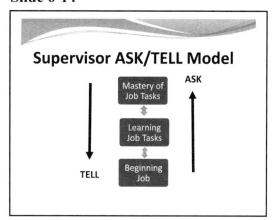

Slide 6-15

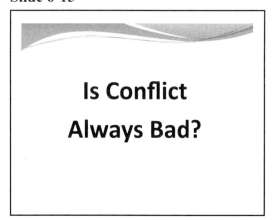

Slide 6-16

Causes of Conflict at Work

Miscommunication
- The employee either did not receive the message or received only part of a message, or the message was delivered in a way that may have been misinterpreted.

Different Interpretations
- The employee believes that adherence to rules, policies, or procedures should be carried out in one way, while the actual intent or the rule, policy, or procedure is something else entirely.

Different Values
- The employee has less regard than others for a specific task or duty and does not attach importance to its value.

Opposing Goals
- The goals of the company or supervisor are directly opposed to those of the employee.

Slide 6-17

Conflict Strategies

Win/Win—Collaboration
- Both parties achieve their goals
  - Example: Working together, an acceptable resolution is reached that helps everyone concerned regarding a conflict.

Win/Lose—Competition
- One person is defeated
- Example: Employee's request or complaint is denied without reason.

Slide 6-18

Conflict Strategies (Cont.)

Lose/Lose—Avoidance
- Neither parties achieves its goals.
  - Example: Employee quits because of perceived problems at work.

Lose/Win—Give in
- One person gives in.
  - Example: Supervisor not enforcing rules.

Slide 6-19

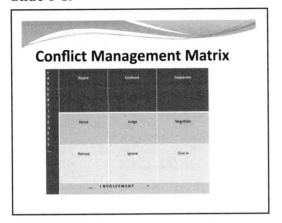

Conflict Management Matrix

Slide 6-20

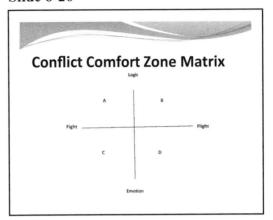

Conflict Comfort Zone Matrix

Slide 6-21

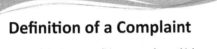

Definition of a Complaint

- *A complaint is any condition an employee thinks or feels is unjust or inequitable from her perspective. Even though a complaint may be seen from a very different perspective by other people (including yourself), this does not diminish the importance of it to the person who has the complaint.*

Slide 6-22

Complaint-Handling Steps

6. Follow up

5. Take action

4. Decide

3. Investigate

2. Get story straight

1. Listen

Slide 6-23

Reasons for Poor Performance

- Lack of communication
- Lack of conditions
- Lack of consequences

Slide 6-24

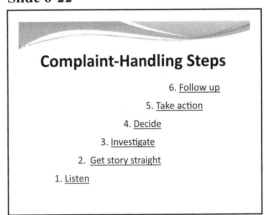

5-Step Performance Correction Process

- Step 1—Observe
- Step 2—Discuss
- Step 3—Correct
- Step 4—Advise
- Step 5—Confirm

Slide 6-25

2 Basic Rules About Managing Performance

1. Always expect excellent performance.
2. Never let poor work go unnoticed or performance issues go unchallenged.

Slide 6-26

The 5 Ws of Documentation

- **Who** is going to see this?
- **What** will I or someone else want to know about this event in the future?
- **Why** will I want to look at this again?
- **When** do I write or document this event?
- **Where** will I keep this document?

Slide 6-27

Levels of Feedback

- None at all
- Negative only
- Positive only
- Balanced

Slide 6-28

The Default Performance Feedback System

"If you don't hear anything, you are doing just fine but if you screw up we'll let you know!"

Slide 6-29

Types of Feedback

- **Formal**—documented annual/semiannual performance review
- **Informal**—day-to-day communication and feedback about performance

Slide 6-30

Deciding When Teams Can Be Most Effective

- When teamwork can unblock creativity
- When there is no obvious solution
- When team decision-making is most effective
- When there is a willingness to accept the team's recommendations

Slide 6-31

Definition of Consensus

"This decision was not my idea or even my first choice concerning the decision of the team, but I do agree to support and work toward the success of this decision just as if it were my own."

Slide 6-32

Team Leader's Responsibilities

- Train team members to work together
- Identify potential obstacles
- Suggest procedures or ideas for solving a problem
- Help get information
- Give input
- Help the team progress
- Monitor progress
- Recognize and reward results

Slide 6-33

Types of Difficult Team Members

- The reluctant team member
- The defiant team member
- The dominant team member
- The absentee team member
- The vacationer team member

Slide 6-34

Characteristics of an Engaged Team Player

1. Openly shares feelings, opinions, thoughts, and perceptions about problems and issues relating to the team.
2. When listening, attempts to hear and interpret communication from sender's point of view.
3. Utilizes resources, ideas, and suggestions of other team members.
4. Trusts and supports other team members, encouraging their growth and development.
5. Understands and is committed to team objectives.

Slide 6-35

Characteristics of an Engaged Team Player (Cont.)

6. Acknowledges and works through conflict openly, by respecting and being tolerant of individual differences.
7. Makes decisions based on information only, rather than being influenced by peer pressure.
8. Provides ideas and suggestions to the team leader that are helpful to the team.
9. Always strives for a win/win solution.
10. Strives for consensus on team decisions.

◆

1.5-Day Training

- ◆ Advice on how to choose content for a 1.5-day program
- ◆ Step-by-step preparation and training delivery instructions
- ◆ Sample agenda

Presenting Longer Programs

Having more than one day for training provides you with greater opportunity to have more in-depth presentations of the subject matter and to encourage greater discussion with participants. This format also allows participants to have time to reflect on many of the concepts presented the previous day and use this learning to build on the next day. This format is designed to be progressive in the complexity of the materials presented, making this multiple-day presentation work more effectively.

Training Objectives

Each of these module topics is important to teaching participants how to become more effective coaches of engaged employees. The lessons found in each module are designed to teach a specific skill or concept relating to the topic covered. This format also gives you the opportunity to supplement the training with materials or communication specific to the organization and participants.

It is important to keep in mind when presenting longer training programs that it is likely participants are not used to sitting for most of the day, as their jobs likely keep them active throughout their workday. Giving frequent breaks, including brief stand-up stretches, will help participants stay focused on the presentation. Also, keeping participants actively involved in the presentations by asking for their opinions, input, reactions, and so forth to subject matter and topics makes the learning experience more enjoyable and beneficial. Each of the lessons included in this program has been designed to stimulate this type of participant interaction to help you achieve this objective.

There are several key factors to keep in mind when designing a training program:

◆ Concepts presented should be kept simple and to the point.

◆ Don't try to accomplish more than the time allotted will allow.

◆ Your goal should be to have participants leave with an understanding of several key learning points they can use in the future at their jobs. Providing participants with a handout or some other written reference with these learning points can greatly enhance your ability to achieve this objective.

◆ You will find detailed instructions in this book for presenting each of the activities along with their corresponding slides, which can be shown and possibly provided to participants as "takeaway" references to reinforce the learning points presented. All of these materials are available on the website (www.astd.org/coachingemployeeengagementtraining) for easy accessibility, reference, and use in designing this program.

Choosing the Content

Each module in this format increases skill challenges for participants and becomes more interactive. For instance, content modules 9.1 through 9.8 cover more in-depth communication principles such as silent messages, phrases that kill ideas, levels of coaching communication, and rumors. Content modules 9.9 through 9.15 expand the concept of building trust and include a presentation that lists commitments for effective coaching, as well as a presentation titled "Spending Time With Employees" that asks participants to reflect on the amount of time they spend with the employees they supervise and decide if this is the right amount of time or not.

Content modules 9.16 through 9.21 challenge participants to become even more interactive in the program and more reflective in their coaching styles by introducing the conflict-management matrix and conflict comfort zones. Content module 9.21 introduces the first role play in the training program.

In the earlier shorter formats presented, the importance of dealing with employee complaints was introduced and highlighted. In this longer format, the modules introduce more in-depth material about handling complaints and includes a complaint-handling quiz as well as a session on resolving employee complaints. Each of these sessions challenges participants to examine their own skills and practices about how to deal with employee complaints and also to reflect on just how critical it is to deal with these employee issues effectively.

Another role play is offered at the beginning of the second day called the *Discipline Role Play.* In this session, participants are presented with a difficult situation about value judgments relating to a potential employee disciplinary situation. Later in the program, the importance of coaching time with employees is highlighted, and valuable coaching tips are provided.

The last section of the training includes two very important concepts relating to teamwork in the workplace, which are reaching consensus and synergy. Helping participants understand these concepts and share these concepts with their employees can have a big impact on teamwork initiatives. This program format concludes with an example template for creating a team project plan, something that is too often overlooked in leading teams but is critically important.

The appropriate content modules for this 1.5-day training are found in chapter 9.

You will find detailed instructions for presenting each of these activities along with their corresponding slides, which can be shown or possibly provided to participants as "takeaway" references to reinforce the learning points presented. All of these materials are available on the website (www.astd.org/coachingemployeeengagementtraining) for easy accessibility, reference, and use in designing this program.

TIME

◆ 1.5 Days

MATERIALS

For the instructor:

- ◆ Content Module 9.1—The Importance of Communication

- ◆ Content Module 9.2—Coaching Communication Model

- ◆ Content Module 9.3—Listening for Better Coaching

- ◆ Content Module 9.4—Silent Messages

- ◆ Content Module 9.5—Phrases That Kill Ideas

- ◆ Content Module 9.6—3 Levels of Coaching Communication

- ◆ Content Module 9.7—Communicating Assignments Quiz

- ◆ Content Module 9.8—Rumors

- ◆ Content Module 9.9—14 Commitments for Effective Coaching

- ◆ Content Module 9.10—Basic Coaching Principles

- ◆ Content Module 9.11—Engaged Coaching

- ◆ Content Module 9.12—The Real Experts

- ◆ Content Module 9.13—Helping Employees Contribute

- ◆ Content Module 9.14—Spending Time With Employees

- ◆ Content Module 9.15—Supervisor Ask/Tell Model

- ◆ Content Module 9.16—Positive Conflict

- ◆ Content Module 9.17—Causes of Conflict at Work

- ◆ Content Module 9.18—Conflict Strategies

- ◆ Content Module 9.19—Conflict Management Matrix

- ◆ Content Module 9.20—Conflict Comfort Zones

- ◆ Content Module 9.21—Conflict Role Play

- ◆ Content Module 9.22—Dealing With Upset Employees

- Content Module 9.23—Definition of a Complaint

- Content Module 9.24—No Complaints

- Content Module 9.25—Unsettled Complaints

- Content Module 9.26—Complaint-Handling Quiz

- Content Module 9.27—Resolving Employee Complaints

- Content Module 9.28—Causes of Poor Performance

- Content Module 9.29—5-Step Performance-Correction Process

- Content Module 9.30—Setting Performance Standards

- Content Module 9.31—Discipline Role Play

- Content Module 9.32—Documentation

- Content Module 9.36—A World Without Feedback

- Content Module 9.37—Formal and Informal Feedback

- Content Module 9.38—Coaching Time

- Content Module 9.39—Coaching Tips

- Content Module 9.41—Recognition

- Content Module 9.43—When Teams Are Most Effective

- Content Module 9.44—Reaching Consensus

- Content Module 9.45—Synergy

- Content Module 9.47—Helping Teams Get Things Done

- Content Module 9.49– Characteristics of a Team Player

- Content Module 9.50—Creating a Team Project Plan

- Structured Experience 11.9—Performance Appraisal Role Play

- Structured Experience 11.11—Creating a Team Project Plan

◆ PowerPoint presentation: Coaching Employee Engagement Training. To access slides for this program, open the file *1.5-Day Program.ppt* in the online materials. Copies of this training session are included at the end of this chapter (Slides 7.1 through 7.47).

For the participants:

◆ Assessment 10.1—Communicating Assignments Quiz

◆ Assessment 10.2—Conflict Comfort Zone Self-Assessment

◆ Assessment 10.3—Complaint-Handling Quiz

◆ Handout 11.1—Rumors

◆ Handout 11.2—Spending Time With Employees

◆ Handout 11.3—Conflict Strategies Role Play

◆ Handout 11.4—Supervisor Prompt

◆ Handout 11.5—Employee A Prompt

◆ Handout 11.6—Employee B Prompt

◆ Handout 11.7—Discipline Role Play Introduction Handout

◆ Handout 11.8—Supervisor's Role

◆ Handout 11.9—Employee's Role

◆ Handout 11.10—Synergy Trivia Quiz for participants

◆ Handout 11.17—Background Data Sheet—Supervisor's Role

◆ Handout 11.18—Background Data Sheet—Employee's Role

◆ Handout 11.19—Observer's Role Play Responsibilities

◆ Handout 11.21—Project Plan Example

◆ Handout 11.22—Completed Project Plan

◆ Writing instruments and paper for participants

Sample Agenda

8:00 A.M.   Introduction (5 minutes)

8:05 A.M.   Content Module 9.1—The Importance of Communication (chapter 9) (10 minutes)

Objective: Understand how important communication is in the supervisor/employee relationship to becoming an effective coach and creating an engaged workplace.

8:15 A.M.   Content Module 9.2—Coaching Communication Model (chapter 9) (15 minutes)

Objective: Presents a communication model for coaches to follow when communicating with employees.

8:30 A.M.   Content Module 9.3—Listening for Better Coaching (chapter 9) (15 minutes)

Objective: To help participants become better listeners.

8:45 A.M.   Content Module 9.4—Silent Messages (chapter 9) (10 minutes)

Objective: To understand the consequences of unintended messages delivered to employees.

8:55 A.M.   Content Module 9.5—Phrases That Kill Ideas (chapter 9) (15 minutes)

Objective: Describe the potential harm of common phrases often heard in most organizations on a regular basis and how these phrases essentially kill any new suggestions or ideas.

9:10 A.M.   Content Module 9.6—3 Levels of Coaching Communication (chapter 9) (15 minutes)

Objective: To understand the three levels of communication and how to use each for maximum impact.

9:25 A.M.   Content Module 9.7—Communicating Assignments Quiz (chapter 9) (10 minutes)

Objective: To assess each participant's own level of communication acumen using a 10-question communicating assignments quiz.

9:35 A.M.   Content Module 9.8—Rumors (chapter 9) (15 minutes)

Objective: To understand how rumors spread in organizations and their potential harmful consequences.

BREAK (10 minutes)

10:00 A.M.   Content Module 9.9—14 Commitments for Effective Coaching (chapter 9) (20 minutes)

Objective: To discuss the key elements of effective coaching and discover how to correctly apply them.

10:20 A.M.   Content Module 9.10—Basic Coaching Principles (chapter 9) (20 minutes)

Objective: To give participants basic principles they can use to engender greater trust and respect from those they supervise.

10:40 A.M.   Content Module 9.11—Engaged Coaching (chapter 9) (15 minutes)

Objective: To build understanding of the two leadership philosophies most people use and to explore the benefits of a more supportive supervisory model.

10:55 A.M.   Content Module 9.12—The Real Experts (chapter 9) (15 minutes)

Objective: To understand the undesirable consequences that occur when an employee does exactly what she is told to do by the supervisor.

11:10 A.M.   Content Module 9.13—Helping Employees Contribute (chapter 9) (10 minutes)

Objective: To explore the power of creating a work climate that supports employee contribution to the overall success of the organization.

11:20 A.M.   Content Module 9.14—Spending Time With Employees (chapter 9) (10 minutes)

Objective: To discover what the right amount of time is that a supervisor should spend with supervisees.

11:30 A.M.   Content Module 9.15—Supervisor Ask/Tell Model (chapter 9) (20 minutes)

Objective: To find applications for a Supervisor Ask/Tell model that measures the extent to which a supervisor engages in either asking or telling employees about the performance of their jobs, and based on each person's experience and skill level.

11:50 A.M.   LUNCH (1 hour)

12:50 P.M.   Content Module 9.16—Positive Conflict (chapter 9) (15 minutes)

Objective: To discover the positive outcomes possible as a result of conflict and to discuss direct applications to the workforce.

1:05 P.M.   Content Module 9.17—Causes of Conflict at Work (chapter 9) (20 minutes)

Objective: To explore the reasons that conflict may exist in the workplace and how to mitigate the impact.

1:25 P.M.   Content Module 9.18—Conflict Strategies (chapter 9) (20 minutes)

Objective: To discuss and explore commonly used strategies for dealing with conflict in the workplace and to evaluate their effectiveness.

1:45 P.M.   Content Module 9.19—Conflict Management Matrix (chapter 9) (30 minutes)

Objective: To explore the use of a conflict management matrix that offers nine different approaches to dealing with conflict: reject, confront, cooperate, resist, judge, bargain, retreat, give in, and ignore.

2:15 P.M.   Content Module 9.20—Conflict Comfort Zones (chapter 9) (20 minutes)

Objective: To help participants identify their own conflict comfort zone and how to learn to be more versatile when dealing with conflict in the future.

2:35 P.M.   Content Module 9.21—Conflict Role Play (chapter 9) (30 minutes)

Objective: To explore techniques of how participants can resolve difficulties while working together with other employees through the use of a role play involving two employees who are presently having difficulty getting along with each other at work.

3:05 P.M.   BREAK (10 minutes)

3:15 P.M.   Content Module 9.22—Dealing With Upset Employees (chapter 9) (20 minutes)

Objective: To understand the importance of acknowledging the feelings of an upset employee at that moment and how to demonstrate empathy for the employee.

3:35 P.M.   Content Module 9.23—Definition of a Complaint (chapter 9) (15 minutes)

Objective: To explore key aspects of an employee complaint and how to use a set of tips to deal with employee complaints more effectively.

3:50 P.M.   Content Module 9.24—No Complaints (chapter 9) (10 minutes)

Objective: To help participants understand the concept that the lack of complaints from those they supervise is not necessarily a good situation.

4:00 P.M.   Content Module 9.25—Unsettled Complaints (chapter 9) (15 minutes)

Objective: To explore the consequences of this dissatisfaction as well as why and when a complaint should be elevated to the next level.

4:15 P.M.   Content Module 9.26—Complaint-Handling Quiz (chapter 9) (20 minutes)

Objective: To assess competency at dealing with employee complaints through the use of a brief quiz provided for participants.

4:35 P.M.   Content Module 9.27—Resolving Employee Complaints (chapter 9) (10 minutes)

Objective: To discuss the bottom-line organizational goals of resolving employee complaints.

4:45 P.M.   END DAY 1

8:00 A.M.   Content Module 9.28—Causes of Poor Performance (chapter 9) (15 minutes)

Objective: To explore strategies for addressing the three major reasons for poor performance: lack of communication, lack of conditions, and lack of consequences.

8:15 A.M.   Content Module 9.29—5-Step Performance-Correction Process (chapter 9) (15 minutes)

Objective: To discuss and learn to apply a 5-step performance-correction process model that helps supervisors understand how to proceed when dealing with an employee's performance problem.

8:30 A.M.   Content Module 9.30—Setting Performance Standards (chapter 9) (10 minutes)

Objective: To explore the real organizational costs of allowing poor employee performance to go unchallenged or unaddressed.

8:40 A.M.   Content Module 9.31—Discipline Role Play (chapter 9) (30 minutes)

Objective: To discover and explore techniques for dealing with employee performance issues through the use of a role play where an employee is counseled by her supervisor concerning an absentee problem that has been occurring for the past eighteen months.

9:10 A.M.   Content Module 9.32—Documentation (chapter 9) (20 minutes)

Objective: To explore the most important aspects and need for a supervisor to document employee performance using a 5 Ws model for documentation.

9:30 A.M.   Content Module 9.36—A World Without Feedback (chapter 9) (15 minutes)

Objective: To explore the importance of feedback using a sports analogy in which participants are asked to envision participating in a sport without any feedback on their performance. Different levels of feedback are presented and discussed.

9:45 A.M.   Content Module 9.37—Formal and Informal Feedback (chapter 9) (10 minutes)

Objective: To discuss and explore formal and informal feedback with guidance provided on when each type of feedback may be most applicable and beneficial.

9:55 A.M.   Content Module 9.38—Coaching Time (chapter 9) (10 minutes)

Objective: The appropriate amount of time that a coach should spend coaching their employees is presented and discussed.

10:05 A.M.   Content Module 9.39—Coaching Tips (chapter 9) (10 minutes)

Objective: To understand how to most effectively correct poor performance when observed, as well as how to reinforce effective performance.

10:15 A.M.   Content Module 9.41—Recognition (chapter 9) (15 minutes)

Objective: To discuss and explore different types of recognition, with a discussion concerning which ones are the most effective.

10:30 A.M.   BREAK (10 minutes)

10:40 A.M.   Content Module 9.43—When Teams Are Most Effective (chapter 9) (15 minutes)

Objective: To discuss the appropriate use of teams and when and when not to utilize them in the workplace.

10:55 A.M.   Content Module 9.44—Reaching Consensus (chapter 9) (15 minutes)

Objective: To explore the meaning and importance of reaching consensus as a team.

11:10 A.M.   Content Module 9.45—Synergy (chapter 9) (10 minutes)

Objective: To explore the definition of synergy through the use of a brief quiz that demonstrates the power of working together.

11:20 A.M.   Content Module 9.47—Helping Teams Get Things Done (chapter 9) (15 minutes)

Objective: To provide tips and other practical advice so that participants are better able to help others work together as a team and accomplish their goals.

11:35 A.M.   Content Module 9.49—Characteristics of a Team Player (chapter 9) (20 minutes)

Objective: To discuss and explore a list of 10 characteristics of an engaged team player, and find practical applications for team leaders and team members.

11:55 A.M.   Content Module 9.50—Creating a Team Project Plan (chapter 9) (20 minutes)

Objective: To create a team project plan using an example plan and to discuss how the plan ensures that everyone on the team understands her role and responsibilities.

12:15 P.M.   END PROGRAM

Step-by-Step Instructions

◆ Arrive at the facility early.

◆ Set up and test any technology (such as a laptop or digital project connections).

◆ Prepare the room and check on refreshments (if any).

◆ Welcome participants to the training program. It is best to keep your welcome and introductions simple and relatively brief. Although everyone should know what the subject matter of the program will be and why they are attending, it still is a good idea to restate this in the opening remarks and welcome. If possible, it is also a good idea to have the sponsor of the training program or some other member of the management of the organization greet participants, and introduce the program to show support and add emphasis to its importance.

◆ Explain that in the 1.5-day program you have planned, a wide range of material about coaching employee engagement will be presented that covers topics ranging from communication, listening, basic supervisory principles, basic coaching concepts, information about dealing with conflict, handling customer complaints, employee performance, and giving feedback and recognition, to working effectively as a team member.

◆ As facilitator, you should encourage participants to ask questions, share their thoughts and experiences, and participate in the discussions you will lead on each of these various topics, as there has been time built into this agenda for interactive activities.

◆ Conclude the program by again emphasizing the importance of some of the key principles covered during the 1.5-day program (customize the topics to your particular needs).

◆ Encourage participants to utilize the principles and tools that they learned during this program. Ask participants what they felt were the most important lessons they learned during the program in order to become better coaches and to engage their employees.

◆ Suggest that participants try to use at least one of the concepts reviewed during this program on a daily basis.

What to Do Next

◆ Identify the participants and assess the training most needed by the group.

◆ Identify the time available for training.

◆ Select appropriate training modules.

◆ Schedule the session and arrange a training room or other facility.

◆ Send training reminders to participants and include an agenda or any work to be done before the session.

◆ Prepare your training materials, including handouts, slide presentations, and supplies.

Slide 7-1

**Employee
Engagement
Training**

Slide 7-2

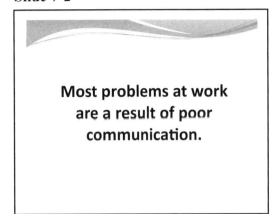

**Most problems at work
are a result of poor
communication.**

Slide 7-3

**Communication is an Art,
Not a Science**

There is no absolute right or wrong way to
communicate effectively. What is most
important is that you communicate in a
manner and style most comfortable and
effective for you.

Slide 7-4

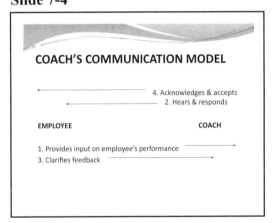

COACH'S COMMUNICATION MODEL

4. Acknowledges & accepts
2. Hears & responds

EMPLOYEE   COACH

1. Provides input on employee's performance
3. Clarifies feedback

Slide 7-5

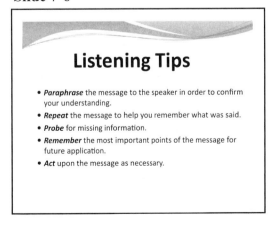

5 Levels of Listening

- Level 1—Tuned Out
- Level 2—Distracted
- Level 3—Selected
- Level 4—Focused
- Level 5—Engaged

Slide 7-6

Listening Tips

- *Paraphrase* the message to the speaker in order to confirm your understanding.
- *Repeat* the message to help you remember what was said.
- *Probe* for missing information.
- *Remember* the most important points of the message for future application.
- *Act* upon the message as necessary.

Slide 7-7

Silent Messages

Often when we say nothing, we are actually saying a great deal.

Slide 7-8

Phrases That Kill Ideas

- Don't be ridiculous
- It'll cost too much
- That's not my responsibility
- I don't have time to talk about it
- We've never done it before
- If it ain't broken don't fix it?
- We're not ready for that
- You can't teach an old dog new tricks
- We've tried that before
- It can't be done
- It's too big of a change

Slide 7-9

Phrases That Kill Ideas (Cont.)

- It's not our problem
- Let's get back to reality
- You're getting ahead of yourself
- It's not in our budget
- Let's wait to decide
- That doesn't really apply to us
- We have done alright without it
- It won't work in our business
- That's not the way we do things around here

Slide 7-10

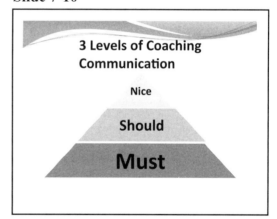

3 Levels of Coaching Communication

Nice

Should

Must

Slide 7-11

How True Are Rumors?

- Studies have shown that forms of informal communication such as the "grapevine" or "rumor mill" have been shown to be about 75% accurate at times. At first, this might seem to be more accurate than expected. But just imagine if all the information you received was only 75% accurate. What if information you needed for an important report to your boss was only 75% accurate? Would that be acceptable?

Slide 7-12

Effective Coaching Is About Trust

Slide 7-13

14 Commitments
of Effective Coaches

1. Provide orientation & training to new employees.
2. Maintain good working conditions.
3. Share business information.
4. Treat employees with respect.
5. Encourage employee involvement.
6. Establish written policies.
7. Promote cooperation throughout organization.

Slide 7-14

14 Commitments
of Effective Coaches (Cont.)

8. Resolve conflict in a positive manner.
9. Provide constructive discipline.
10. Ensure fair treatment for all employees.
11. Lead by example.
12. Address employee issues.
13. Provide performance feedback.
14. Help employees with personal problems.

Slide 7-15

Basic Supervisory Principles

FIRM

- Adhering to company policies and procedures
- Meeting job requirements
- Insisting on job excellence
- Expecting the best at all times

Slide 7-16

Basic Supervisory Principles

FAIR

- In using discretion with employees
- In assigning work
- In providing training and growth opportunities
- In promoting employees

Slide 7-17

Basic Supervisory Principles

CONSISTENT

- In applying rules and policies
- In utilizing discipline
- In setting a personal example
- In your decision-making process

Slide 7-18

Basic Supervisory Principles

RESPECTFUL

- Treat everyone with dignity regardless of the situation.
- Listen, ask, explain.
- Follow up with answers to questions.

Slide 7-19

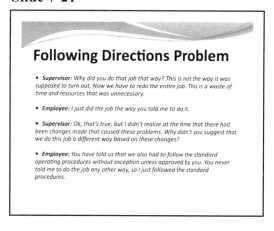

Engaged Coaching Model

More
- Trust
- Openness
- Ownership
- Versatility
- Influence
- Action

Slide 7-20

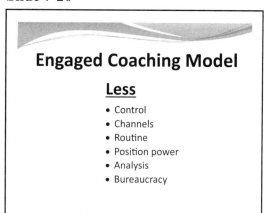

Engaged Coaching Model

Less
- Control
- Channels
- Routine
- Position power
- Analysis
- Bureaucracy

Slide 7-21

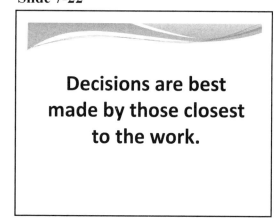

Following Directions Problem

- *Supervisor: Why did you do that job that way? This is not the way it was supposed to turn out. Now we have to redo the entire job. This is a waste of time and resources that was unnecessary.*

- *Employee: I just did the job the way you told me to do it.*

- *Supervisor: Ok, that's true, but I didn't realize at the time that there had been changes made that caused these problems. Why didn't you suggest that we do this job a different way based on these changes?*

- *Employee: You have told us that we also had to follow the standard operating procedures without exception unless approved by you. You never told me to do the job any other way, so I just followed the standard procedures.*

Slide 7-22

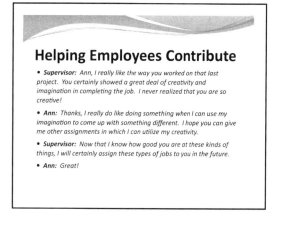

Decisions are best made by those closest to the work.

Slide 7-23

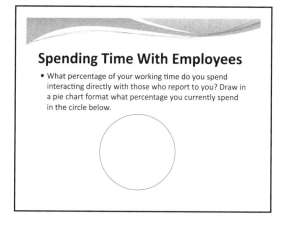

Helping Employees Contribute

- *Supervisor: Ann, I really like the way you worked on that last project. You certainly showed a great deal of creativity and imagination in completing the job. I never realized that you are so creative!*

- *Ann: Thanks, I really do like doing something when I can use my imagination to come up with something different. I hope you can give me other assignments in which I can utilize my creativity.*

- *Supervisor: Now that I know how good you are at these kinds of things, I will certainly assign these types of jobs to you in the future.*

- *Ann: Great!*

Slide 7-24

Spending Time With Employees

- What percentage of your working time do you spend interacting directly with those who report to you? Draw in a pie chart format what percentage you currently spend in the circle below.

Slide 7-25

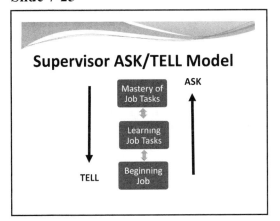

Slide 7-26

Slide 7-27

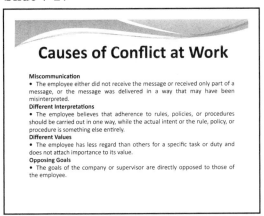

Slide 7-28

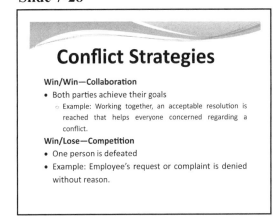

Slide 7-29

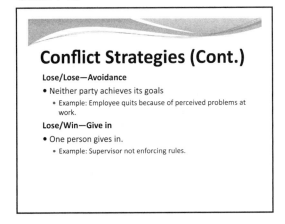

Slide 7-30

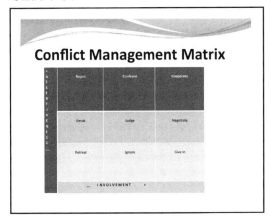

Slide 7-31

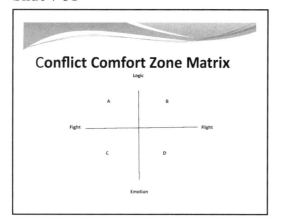

Slide 7-32

Definition of a Complaint

- *A complaint is any condition an employee thinks or feels is unjust or inequitable from her perspective. Even though a complaint may be seen from a very different perspective by other people (including yourself), this does not diminish the importance of it to the person who has the complaint.*

Slide 7-33

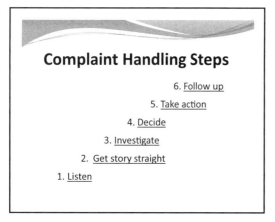

Slide 7-34

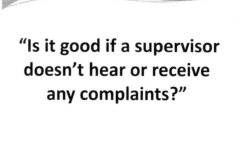

Slide 7-35

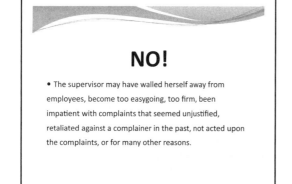

Slide 7-36

Employees' Reactions to Unsettled Complaints

What can the employee do?
- Adjust
- Complain
- Take action
- Worry or brood

- **Who can employees turn to?**
  - Help outside of company such as a government agency
  - Legal system
  - Within company

Slide 7-37

Passing a Complaint on UP

- Why might a supervisor hesitate to refer a complaint to the next level?

- Why should a complaint be referred to a higher level?

- Why do employees want a complaint to go higher?

Slide 7-38

A coach's goal in dealing with an employee's complaint should be to address the person's issue in the best and most appropriate manner possible—not "win" the complaint.

Slide 7-39

5-Step Performance–Correction Process

- Step 1—Observe
- Step 2—Discuss
- Step 3—Correct
- Step 4—Advise
- Step 5—Confirm

Slide 7-40

2 Basic Rules About Managing Performance

1. Always expect excellent performance.
2. Never let poor work go unnoticed or performance issues go unchallenged.

Slide 7-41

The 5 Ws of Documentation

- **Who** is going to see this?
- **What** will I or someone else want to know about this event in the future?
- **Why** will I want to look at this again?
- **When** do I write or document this event?
- **Where** will I keep this document?

Slide 7-42

Reasons for Performance Problems

- Job fit
- Motivation
- Ability
- Training
- Job itself
- Supervision

Slide 7-43

Levels of Feedback

- None at all
- Negative only
- Positive only
- Balanced

Slide 7-44

The Default Performance Feedback System

"If you don't hear anything, you are doing just fine but if you screw up we'll let you know!"

Slide 7-45

Types of Feedback

- **Formal**—documented annual/ semiannual performance review
- **Informal**—day-to-day communication and feedback about performance

Slide 7-46

Coaching Performance Tips

1. Observe and assess the specific job performance behavior(s) of an employee.
2. Decide if it is effective or ineffective job performance.
3. If it is effective behavior:
   - Point out what is effective about the behavior.
   - Explain why it should be continued and the benefits of doing the job right.
   - Praise or compliment the employee for this effective behavior as appropriate.
4. If it is ineffective behavior:
   - Tell the employee to stop the behavior and explain why it is ineffective.
   - Explain what an alternative behavior would be and why alternative behavior would be better.
5. Reinforce the correct behavior when observed in future.

Slide 7-47

Potential Reinforcers

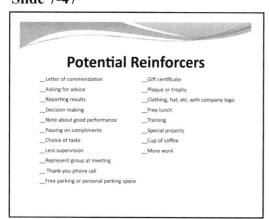

__Letter of commendation	__Gift certificate
__Asking for advice	__Plaque or trophy
__Reporting results	__Clothing, hat, etc. with company logo
__Decision making	__Free lunch
__Note about good performance	__Training
__Passing on compliments	__Special projects
__Choice of tasks	__Cup of coffee
__Less supervision	__More work
__Represent group at meeting	
__Thank-you phone call	
__Free parking or personal parking space	

Slide 7-48

Deciding When Teams Can Be Most Effective

- When teamwork can unblock creativity
- When there is no obvious solution
- When team decision-making is most effective
- When there is a willingness to accept the team's recommendations

Slide 7-49

Definition of Consensus

"This decision was not my idea or even my first choice concerning the decision of the team, but I do agree to support and work toward the success of this decision just as if it were my own."

Slide 7-50

Synergy

Synergy is the blending of different human skills, talents, and experience to produce a total effect greater than the sum of the individual team members' skills, talents, and experiences alone.

- With synergy 5 + 5 = > 10.

Slide 7-51

Team Leader's Responsibilities

- Train team members to work together
- Identify potential obstacles
- Suggest procedures or ideas for solving a problem
- Help get information
- Give input
- Help the team progress
- Monitor progress
- Recognize and reward results

Slide 7-52

Types of Difficult Team Members

- The reluctant team member
- The defiant team member
- The dominant team member
- The absentee team member
- The vacationer team member

Slide 7-53

Characteristics of an Engaged Team Player

1. Openly shares feelings, opinions, thoughts, and perceptions about problems and issues relating to the team.
2. When listening, attempts to hear and interpret communication from sender's point of view.
3. Utilizes resources, ideas, and suggestions of other team members.
4. Trusts and supports other team members, encouraging their growth and development.
5. Understands and is committed to team objectives.

Slide 7-54

Characteristics of an Engaged Team Player (Cont.)

6. Acknowledges and works through conflict openly, by respecting and being tolerant of individual differences.
7. Makes decisions based on information only, rather than being influenced by peer pressure.
8. Provides ideas and suggestions to the team leader that are helpful to the team.
9. Always strives for a win/win solution.
10. Strives for consensus on team decisions.

Slide 7-55

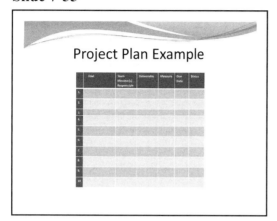

Slide 7-56

◆

2-Day Training

- ◆ Advice on how to choose content for a 2-day program
- ◆ Step-by-step preparation and training delivery instructions
- ◆ Sample agenda

Presenting Longer Programs

In this full 2-day format, participants are introduced to an array of training experiences covering all 50 content modules included in this workbook. This longest program allows each module topic to be fully developed as well as allows more opportunity to encourage greater discussion with participants. Like the 1.5-day format, the 2-day format also allows participants time to reflect on many of the concepts presented the previous day and use this learning to build on the next day. This format is designed to be progressive in the complexity of the materials presented, making this multiple-day presentation work more effectively.

Training Objectives

One of the differences between this 2-day format and the 1.5-day format is that this program includes more in-depth role plays during the sessions on feedback and recognition, as well as the inclusion of more challenging material. This material includes sessions on documentation, performance-improvement process, PIPP role play, performance appraisal role play, recognition role play, designing engagement into your organization, dealing with difficult team members, and creating a team project plan.

Each of these additional lessons helps participants practice and learn how to deal with some of the most challenging situations they may face at their jobs.

As noted in the discussion of the 1.5-day program, it is important to keep in mind when presenting longer training programs that it is likely participants are not used to sitting for most of the day, as their jobs likely keep them active throughout their workday. Giving frequent breaks, including brief stand-up stretches, will help participants stay focused on the presentation.

Also, keeping participants actively involved in the presentation by asking for their opinions, input, and reactions to subject matter and topics makes the learning experience more enjoyable and beneficial. Each of the lessons included in this program has been designed to stimulate this type of participant interaction to help you achieve this objective.

There are several key factors to keep in mind when designing a training program:

◆ Concepts presented should be kept simple and to the point.

◆ Don't try to accomplish more than the alloted time will allow.

◆ Your goal should be to have participants leave with an understanding of several key learning points that they can use in the future at their jobs. Providing participants with a handout or some other written reference with these learning points can greatly enhance your ability to achieve this objective.

You will find detailed instructions in this book for presenting each of the activities, along with their corresponding slides, which can be shown or possibly provided to participants as "takeaway" references to reinforce the learning points presented. All of these materials are available on the website (www.astd.org/coachingemployeeengagementtraining) for easy accessibility, reference, and use in designing a training program.

Choosing the Content

This program uses all 50 content modules included in this book and presents a slightly greater skill challenge for participants than the 1.5-day program. Content modules 9.1 through 9.50 cover the following content areas:

◆ Communication

◆ Building trust

◆ Managing conflict

◆ Complaint handling

◆ Managing performance problems

◆ Recognition and feedback

◆ Leading engaged teams

Each of these broad content areas challenges participants to examine their own skills and practices, and reflect on them to make necessary changes or improvements.

The last section of the training includes two very important concepts relating to teamwork in the workplace, which are reaching consensus and synergy. Helping participants understand these concepts and sharing these concepts with their employees can have a big impact on teamwork initiatives. This program format concludes with an example template for creating a team project plan, something that is too often overlooked in leading teams but is critically important. The appropriate content modules for this 2-day training are found in chapter 9.

TIME

◆ 2 Days

MATERIALS

For the instructor:

◆ Content Module 9.1—The Importance of Communication

◆ Content Module 9—Coaching Communication Model

◆ Content Module 9.3—Listening for Better Coaching

◆ Content Module 9.4—Silent Messages

◆ Content Module 9.5—Phrases That Kill Ideas

◆ Content Module 9.6—3 Levels of Coaching Communication

◆ Content Module 9.7—Communicating Assignments Quiz

- Content Module 9.8—Rumors

- Content Module 9.9—14 Commitments for Effective Coaching

- Content Module 9.10—Basic Coaching Principles

- Content Module 9.11—Engaged Coaching

- Content Module 9.12—The Real Experts

- Content Module 9.13—Helping Employees Contribute

- Content Module 9.14—Spending Time With Employees

- Content Module 9.15—Supervisor Ask/Tell Model

- Content Module 9.16—Positive Conflict

- Content Module 9.17—Causes of Conflict at Work

- Content Module 9.18—Conflict Strategies

- Content Module 9.19—Conflict Management Matrix

- Content Module 9.20—Conflict Comfort Zones

- Content Module 9.21—Conflict Role Play

- Content Module 9.22—Dealing With Upset Employees

- Content Module 9.23—Definition of a Complaint

- Content Module 9.24—No Complaints

- Content Module 9.25—Unsettled Complaints

- Content Module 9.26—Complaint-Handling Quiz

- Content Module 9.27—Resolving Employee Complaints

- Content Module 9.28—Causes of Poor Performance

- Content Module 9.29—5-Step Performance-Correction Process

- Content Module 9.30—Setting Performance Standards

- ◆ Content Module 9.31—Discipline Role Play

- ◆ Content Module 9.32—Documentation

- ◆ Content Module 9.33—Documentation Role Play

- ◆ Content Module 9.34—Performance-Improvement Process Plan

- ◆ Content Module 9.35—Performance-Improvement Process Plan Role Play

- ◆ Content Module 9.36—A World Without Feedback

- ◆ Content Module 9.37—Formal and Informal Feedback

- ◆ Content Module 9.38—Coaching Time

- ◆ Content Module 9.39—Coaching Tips

- ◆ Content Module 9.40—Performance-Appraisal Role Play

- ◆ Content Module 9.41—Recognition

- ◆ Content Module 9.42—Recognition Role Play

- ◆ Content Module 9.43—When Teams Are Most Effective

- ◆ Content Module 9.44—Reaching Consensus

- ◆ Content Module 9.45—Synergy

- ◆ Content Module 9.46—Designing Engagement Into Your Organization

- ◆ Content Module 9.47—Helping Teams Get Things Done

- ◆ Content Module 9.48—Dealing With Difficult Team Members

- ◆ Content Module 9.49—Characteristics of a Team Player

- ◆ Content Module 9.50—Creating a Team Project Plan

- ◆ Structured Experience 11.1—The Rumor

- ◆ Structured Experience 11.2—Spending Time With Employees

- ◆ Structured Experience 11.3—Conflict Strategies

- ◆ Structured Experience 11.4—Conflict Role Play

- Structured Experience 11.5—Discipline Role Play

- Structured Experience 11.6—Documentation Role Play

- Structured Experience 11.7—Performance-Improvement Process Plan

- Structured Experience 11.8—Performance-Improvement Process Plan Role Play

- Structured Experience 11.9—Performance Appraisal Role Play

- Structured Experience 11.10—Synergy

- Structured Experience 11.11—Creating a Team Project Plan

- PowerPoint presentation: Coaching Employee Engagement Training. To access slides for this program, open the file *2 Day Program.ppt* in the online materials. Copies of this training session are included at the end of this chapter (Slides 8.1 through 8.51).

For the participants:

- Handout 11.1—Rumors (chapter 11)

- Handout 11.2—Spending Time With Employees (chapter 11)

- Handout 11.3—Conflict Strategies Role Play (chapter 11)

- Handout 11.4—Supervisor Prompt (chapter 11)

- Handout 11.5—Employee A Prompt (chapter 11)

- Handout 11.6—Employee B Prompt (chapter 11)

- Handout 11.7—Discipline Role Play Introduction Handout (chapter 11)

- Handout 11.8—Supervisor's Role (chapter 11)

- Handout 11.9—Employee's Role (chapter 11)

- Handout 11.10—Synergy Trivia Quiz for Participants (chapter 11)

- Handout 11.11—Role Play Script—Supervisor's Part (chapter 11)

- Handout 11.12—Role Play Script—Employee's Part (chapter 11)

- Handout 11.13—Role Play Documentation Example (chapter 11)

◆ Handout 11.14—Performance-Improvement Process Plan (chapter 11)

◆ Handout 11.15—PIPP Role Play Background—Supervisor (chapter 11)

◆ Handout 11.16—PIPP Role Play Background—Employee (chapter 11)

◆ Handout 11.17—Background Data Sheet—Supervisor's Role (chapter 11)

◆ Handout 11.18—Background Data Sheet—Employee's Role (chapter 11)

◆ Handout 11.19—Observer's Role Play Responsibilities (chapter 11)

◆ Handout 11.20—Team Award Presentation (chapter 11)

◆ Handout 11.21—Individual Recognition (chapter 11)

◆ Handout 11.22—Project Plan Example (chapter 11)

◆ Handout 11.23—Completed Project Plan (chapter 11)

◆ Assessment 10.1—Communicating Assignments Quiz (chapter 10)

◆ Assessment 10.2—Conflict Comfort Zone Self-Assessment (chapter 10)

◆ Assessment 10.3—Complaint-Handling Quiz (chapter 10)

◆ Writing instruments and paper for participants

Sample Agenda

8:00 A.M. Introduction

8:05 A.M. Content Module 9.1—The Importance of Communication (chapter 9) (10 minutes)

Objective: Understand how important communication is in the supervisor/employee relationship to becoming an effective coach and creating an engaged workplace.

8:15 A.M. Content Module 9.2—Coaching Communication Model (chapter 9) (15 minutes)

Objective: Presents a communication model for coaches to follow when communicating with employees.

8:30 A.M.   Content Module 9.3—Listening for Better Coaching (chapter 9) (15 minutes)

Objective: To help participants become better listeners.

8:45 A.M.   Content Module 9.4—Silent Messages (chapter 9) (10 minutes)

Objective: To understand the consequences of unintended messages delivered to employees.

8:55 A.M.   Content Module 9.5—Phrases That Kill Ideas (chapter 9) (15 minutes)

Objective: Describe the potential harm of common phrases often heard in most organizations on a regular basis and how these phrases essentially kill any new suggestions or ideas.

9:10 A.M.   Content Module 9.6—3 Levels of Coaching Communication (chapter 9) (15 minutes)

Objective: To understand the three levels of communication and how to use each for maximum impact.

9:25 A.M.   Content Module 9.7—Communicating Assignments Quiz (chapter 9) (10 minutes)

Objective: To assess each participant's own level of communication acumen using a 10-question communicating assignments quiz.

9:35 A.M.   Content Module 9.8—Rumors (chapter 9) (15 minutes)

Objective: To understand how rumors spread in organizations and understand their potential harmful consequences.

9:50 A.M.   BREAK (10 minutes)

10:00 A.M.   Content Module 9.9—14 Commitments for Effective Coaching (chapter 9) (20 minutes)

Objective: To discuss the key elements of effective coaching and to discover how to effectively apply them.

10:20 A.M. Content Module 9.10—Basic Coaching Principles (chapter 9) (20 minutes)

Objective: To give participants basic principles they can use to engender greater trust and respect from those they supervise.

10:40 A.M. Content Module 9.11—Engaged Coaching (chapter 9) (15 minutes)

Objective: To build understanding of the two leadership philosophies most people use and to explore the benefits of a more supportive supervisory model.

10:55 A.M. Content Module 9.12—The Real Experts (chapter 9) (15 minutes)

Objective: To understand the undesirable consequences that can occur when an employee does exactly what she is told to do by the supervisor.

11:10 A.M. Content Module 9.13—Helping Employees Contribute (chapter 9) (10 minutes)

Objective: To explore the power of creating a work climate that supports employee contribution to the overall success of the organization.

11:20 A.M. Content Module 9.14—Spending Time With Employees (chapter 9) (10 minutes)

Objective: To discover what the right amount of time is that a supervisor should spend supervisees.

11:30 A.M. Content Module 9.15—Supervisor Ask/Tell Model (chapter 9) (20 minutes)

Objective: To find applications for a Supervisor Ask/Tell model that measures the extent to which a supervisor engages in either asking or telling employees about the performance of their jobs, and based on each person's experience and skill level.

11:50 A.M. LUNCH (1 hour)

12:50 P.M.   Content Module 9.16—Positive Conflict (chapter 9) (15 minutes)

Objective: To discover the positive outcomes possible as a result of conflict and to discuss direct applications to the workforce.

1:05 P.M.   Content Module 9.17—Causes of Conflict at Work (chapter 9) (20 minutes)

Objective: To explore the reasons that conflict may exist in the workplace and how to mitigate the impact.

1:25 P.M.   Content Module 9.18—Conflict Strategies (chapter 9) (20 minutes)

Objective: To discuss and explore commonly used strategies for dealing with conflict in the workplace and evaluate their effectiveness.

1:45 P.M.   Content Module 9.19—Conflict Management Matrix (chapter 9) (30 minutes)

Objective: To explore the use of a conflict management matrix that offers nine different approaches to dealing with conflict: reject, confront, cooperate, resist, judge, bargain, retreat, give in, and ignore.

2:15 P.M.   Content Module 9.20—Conflict Comfort Zones (chapter 9) (20 minutes)

Objective: To help participants identify their own conflict comfort zone and how to learn to be more versatile when dealing with conflict in the future.

2:35 P.M.   Content Module 9.21—Conflict Role Play (chapter 9) (30 minutes)

Objective: To explore techniques of how participants can resolve difficulties working together through role play with two employees who are presently having difficulty getting along with each other at work.

3:05 P.M.   BREAK (10 minutes)

3:15 P.M.   Content Module 9.22—Dealing With Upset Employees (chapter 9) (20 minutes)

Objective: To understand the importance of acknowledging the feelings of an upset employee at that moment and how to demonstrate empathy for the employee.

3:35 P.M.   Content Module 9.23—Definition of a Complaint (chapter 9) (15 minutes)

Objective: To explore key aspects of an employee complaint and how to use a set of tips to deal with employee complaints more effectively.

3:50 P.M.   Content Module 9.24—No Complaints (chapter 9) (10 minutes)

Objective: To help participants understand the concept that the lack of complaints from those they supervise is not necessarily a good situation.

4:00 P.M.   Content Module 9.25—Unsettled Complaints (chapter 9) (15 minutes)

Objective: To explore the consequences of this dissatisfaction as well as why and when a complaint should be elevated to the next level.

4:15 P.M.   Content Module 9.26—Complaint-Handling Quiz (chapter 9) (20 minutes)

Objective: To assess competency at dealing with employee complaints through the use of a brief quiz provided for participants.

4:35 P.M.   Content Module 9.27—Resolving Employee Complaints (chapter 9) (10 minutes)

Objective: To discuss the bottom-line organizational goals of resolving employee complaints.

4:45 P.M.   END DAY 1

8:00 A.M.   Content Module 9.28—Causes of Poor Performance (chapter 9) (15 minutes)

Objective: To explore strategies for addressing the three major reasons for poor performance: lack of communication, lack of conditions, and lack of consequences.

8:15 A.M.   Content Module 9.29—5-Step Performance-Correction Process (chapter 9) (15 minutes)

Objective: To discuss and learn to apply a 5-step performance-correction process model that helps supervisors understand how to proceed when dealing with an employee's performance problem.

8:30 A.M.   Content Module 9.30—Setting Performance Standards (chapter 9) (10 minutes)

Objective: To explore the real organizational costs of allowing poor employee performance to go unchallenged or unaddressed.

8:40 A.M.   Content Module 9.31—Discipline Role Play (chapter 9) (30 minutes)

Objective: To discover and explore techniques for dealing with employee performance issues through role play with an employee being counseled by her supervisor concerning an absentee problem that has been occurring for the past eighteen months.

9:10 A.M.   Content Module 9.32—Documentation (chapter 9) (20 minutes)

Objective: To explore the most important aspects and need for a supervisor to document employee performance using a 5 Ws model for documentation.

9:30 A.M.   Content Module 9.33—Documentation Role Play (chapter 9) (30 minutes)

Objective: Through the use of a role play involving a supervisor and an employee experiencing attendance problems, the group gains practical experience in documenting performance meetings.

10:00 A.M.   Content Module 9.34—Performance-Improvement Process (chapter 9) (10 minutes)

Objective: To explore the design and implementation of a performance-improvement process plan in an organization.

10:10 A.M.   Content Module 9.35—Performance-Improvement Process Role Play (chapter 9) (10 minutes)

Objective: Through the use of a role play, participants gain practical experience in the set up and use of a performance-improvement process plan using templates and other provided material.

10:20 A.M.   Content Module 9.36—A World Without Feedback (chapter 9) (15 minutes)

Objective: To explore the importance of feedback using a sports analogy where participants are asked to envision participating in a sport without any feedback on their performance. Different levels of feedback are presented and discussed.

10:35 A.M.   Content Module 9.37—Formal and Informal Feedback (chapter 9) (10 minutes)

Objective: To discuss and explore formal and informal feedback with guidance provided on when each type of feedback may be most applicable and beneficial.

10:45 A.M.   Content Module 9.38—Coaching Time (chapter 9) (10 minutes)

Objective: The appropriate amount of time that a coach should spend coaching their employees is presented and discussed.

10:55 A.M. Content Module 9.39—Coaching Tips (chapter 9) (10 minutes)

Objective: To understand how to most effectively correct ineffective performance when observed, as well as how to reinforce effective performance.

11:05 A.M. Content Module 9.40—Performance Appraisal Role Play (chapter 9) (10 minutes)

Objective: Through the use of a role play, participants gain practical experience from both the supervisor and employee perspective on giving and receiving feedback during a performance review.

11:15 A.M. Content Module 9.41—Recognition (chapter 9) (15 minutes)

Objective: To discuss and explore different types of recognition, with a discussion concerning which ones are the most effective.

11:30 A.M. BREAK (10 minutes)

11:40 A.M. Content Module 9.42—Recognition Role Play (chapter 9) (10 minutes)

Objective: To use a role play to explore the impact and benefits of giving both formal and informal recognition to employees.

11:50 A.M. Content Module 9.43—When Teams Are Most Effective (chapter 9) (15 minutes)

Objective: To discuss the appropriate use of teams and when and when not to utilize them in the workplace.

12:05 P.M. Content Module 9.44—Reaching Consensus (chapter 9) (15 minutes)

Objective: To explore the meaning and importance of reaching consensus as a team.

12:20 P.M.   Content Module 9.45—Synergy (chapter 9) (10 minutes)

Objective: To explore the definition of synergy through the use of a brief quiz that demonstrates the power of working together.

12:30 P.M.   Content Module 9.46—Designing Engagement Into Your Organization (chapter 9) (10 minutes)

Objective: To explore working together toward a common goal and how not to unintentionally discourage employees using an example of a production measurement system.

12:40 P.M.   Content Module 9.47—Helping Teams Get Things Done (chapter 9) (15 minutes)

Objective: To provide tips and other practical advice to help participants be better able to help others work together as a team and accomplish their goals.

12:55 P.M.   Content Module 9.48—Dealing With Difficult Team Members (chapter 9) (10 minutes)

Objective: To explore strategies for dealing with various descriptions of challenging and difficult types of personalities found among team members that can be disruptive to the team's work and progress.

1:05 P.M.   Content Module 9.49—Characteristics of a Team Player (chapter 9) (20 minutes)

Objective: To discuss and explore a list of 10 characteristics of an engaged team player and find practical applications for team leaders and team members.

1:25 P.M.   Content Module 9.50—Creating a Team Project Plan (chapter 9) (20 minutes)

Objective: To create a team project plan using an example plan and to discuss how the plan ensures that everyone on the team understands her role and responsibilities.

1:45 P.M.   END PROGRAM

Step-by-Step Instructions

- ◆ Arrive at the facility early.

- ◆ Set up and test any technology (such as a laptop or digital project connections).

- ◆ Prepare the room and check on refreshments (if any).

- ◆ Welcome participants to the training program. It is best to keep your welcome and introductions simple and relatively brief. Although everyone should know what the subject matter of the program will be and why they are attending, it is still a good idea to restate this in the opening remarks and welcome. If possible, it is also a good idea to have the sponsor of the training program or some other member of the management of the organization greet participants and introduce the program to show support and add emphasis to its importance.

- ◆ Explain that in the 2-day program you have planned, a wide range of material about coaching employee engagement will be presented, with topics ranging from communications, listening, basic supervisory principles, basic coaching concepts, information about dealing with conflict, handling customer complaints, employee performance, and giving feedback and recognition, to working effectively as a team member.

- ◆ As facilitator, you should encourage participants to ask questions, share their thoughts and experiences, and participate in the discussions you will lead on each of these various topics, as there has been time built into the agenda for interactive activities.

- ◆ Conclude the program by again emphasizing the importance of some of the key principles covered during the 2-day program (customize the topics to your particular needs).

- ◆ Encourage participants to utilize the principles and tools they learned during this program. Ask participants what they felt were the most important lessons they learned during the program in order to become better coaches and to engage their employees.

- ◆ Suggest that participants try to use at least one of the concepts reviewed during this program on a daily basis.

What to Do Next

- Identify the participants and assess the training most needed by the group.

- Identify the time available for training.

- Select appropriate training modules.

- Schedule the session and arrange a training room or other facility.

- Send training reminders to participants and include an agenda or any work to be done before the session.

- Prepare your training materials, including handouts, slide presentations, and supplies.

- Order food and beverages.

Slide 8-1

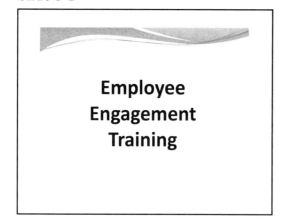

Employee
Engagement
Training

Slide 8-2

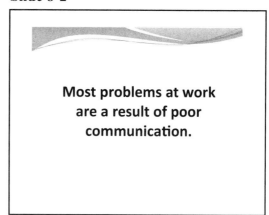

Most problems at work
are a result of poor
communication.

Slide 8-3

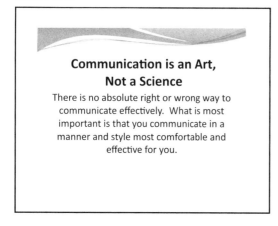

Communication is an Art,
Not a Science

There is no absolute right or wrong way to communicate effectively. What is most important is that you communicate in a manner and style most comfortable and effective for you.

Slide 8-4

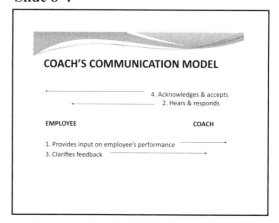

COACH'S COMMUNICATION MODEL

4. Acknowledges & accepts
2. Hears & responds

EMPLOYEE   COACH

1. Provides input on employee's performance
3. Clarifies feedback

Slide 8-5

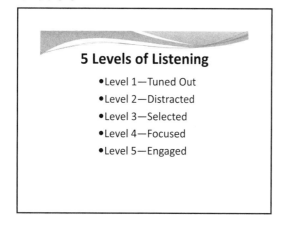

5 Levels of Listening

- Level 1—Tuned Out
- Level 2—Distracted
- Level 3—Selected
- Level 4—Focused
- Level 5—Engaged

Slide 8-6

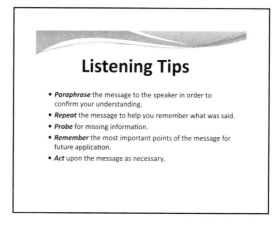

Listening Tips

- *Paraphrase* the message to the speaker in order to confirm your understanding.
- *Repeat* the message to help you remember what was said.
- *Probe* for missing information.
- *Remember* the most important points of the message for future application.
- *Act* upon the message as necessary.

Slide 8-7

Silent Messages

Often when we say nothing
we are actually saying a
great deal.

Slide 8-8

Phrases That Kill Ideas

- Don't be ridiculous
- It'll cost too much
- That's not my responsibility
- I don't have time to talk about it
- We've never done it before
- If it ain't broken don't fix it?
- We're not ready for that
- You can't teach an old dog new tricks
- We've tried that before
- It can't be done
- It's too big of a change

Slide 8-9

Phrases That Kill Ideas (Cont.)

- It's not our problem
- Let's get back to reality
- You're getting ahead of yourself
- It's not in our budget
- Let's wait to decide
- That doesn't really apply to us
- We have done alright without it
- It won't work in our business
- That's not the way we do things around here

Slide 8-10

3 Levels of Coaching
Communication

Nice

Should

Must

Slide 8-11

How True Are Rumors?

- Studies have shown that forms of informal
communication such as the "grapevine" or "rumor mill"
are about 75% accurate at times. At first, this might
seem to be more accurate than expected. But just
imagine if all the information you received was only 75%
accurate. What if information you needed for an
important report to your boss was only 75% accurate?
Would that be acceptable?

Slide 8-12

Effective Coaching
Is About Trust

Slide 8-13

14 Commitments
of Effective Coaches

1. Provide orientation & training to new employees.
2. Maintain good working conditions.
3. Share business information.
4. Treat employees with respect.
5. Encourage employee involvement.
6. Establish written policies.
7. Promote cooperation throughout organization.

Slide 8-14

14 Commitments
of Effective Coaches (Cont.)

8. Resolve conflict in a positive manner.
9. Provide constructive discipline.
10. Ensure fair treatment for all employees.
11. Lead by example.
12. Address employee issues.
13. Provide performance feedback.
14. Help employees with personal problems.

Slide 8-15

Basic Supervisory Principles

FIRM

- Adhering to company policies and procedures
- Meeting job requirements
- Insisting on job excellence
- Expecting the best at all times

Slide 8-16

Basic Supervisory Principles

FAIR

- In using discretion with employees
- In assigning work
- In providing training and growth opportunities
- In promoting employees

Slide 8-17

Basic Supervisory Principles

CONSISTENT

- In applying rules and policies
- In utilizing discipline
- In setting a personal example
- In your decision-making process

Slide 8-18

Basic Supervisory Principles

RESPECTFUL

- Treat everyone with dignity regardless of the situation.
- Listen, ask, explain.
- Follow up with answers to questions.

Slide 8-19

Engaged Coaching Model

More
- Trust
- Openness
- Ownership
- Versatility
- Influence
- Action

Slide 8-20

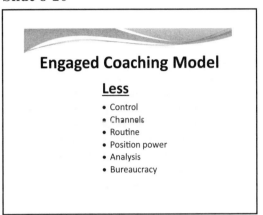

Engaged Coaching Model

Less
- Control
- Channels
- Routine
- Position power
- Analysis
- Bureaucracy

Slide 8-21

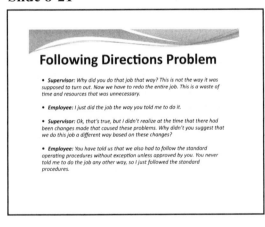

Following Directions Problem

- *Supervisor: Why did you do that job that way? This is not the way it was supposed to turn out. Now we have to redo the entire job. This is a waste of time and resources that was unnecessary.*

- *Employee: I just did the job the way you told me to do it.*

- *Supervisor: Ok, that's true, but I didn't realize at the time that there had been changes made that caused these problems. Why didn't you suggest that we do this job a different way based on these changes?*

- *Employee: You have told us that we also had to follow the standard operating procedures without exception unless approved by you. You never told me to do the job any other way, so I just followed the standard procedures.*

Slide 8-22

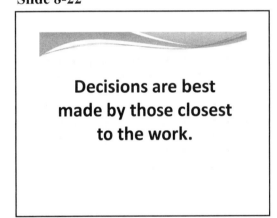

Decisions are best made by those closest to the work.

Slide 8-23

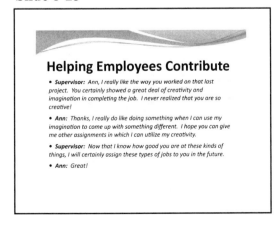

Helping Employees Contribute

- *Supervisor: Ann, I really like the way you worked on that last project. You certainly showed a great deal of creativity and imagination in completing the job. I never realized that you are so creative!*

- *Ann: Thanks, I really do like doing something when I can use my imagination to come up with something different. I hope you can give me other assignments in which I can utilize my creativity.*

- *Supervisor: Now that I know how good you are at these kinds of things, I will certainly assign these types of jobs to you in the future.*

- *Ann: Great!*

Slide 8-24

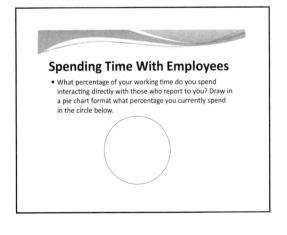

Spending Time With Employees

- What percentage of your working time do you spend interacting directly with those who report to you? Draw in a pie chart format what percentage you currently spend in the circle below.

Slide 8-25

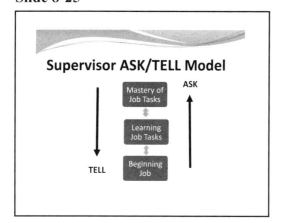

Slide 8-26

Slide 8-27

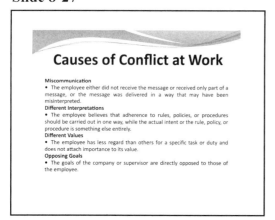

Slide 8-28

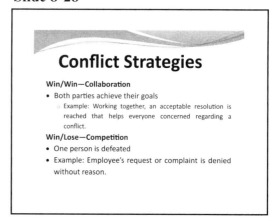

Slide 8-29

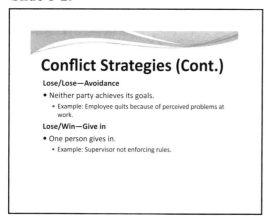

Slide 8-30

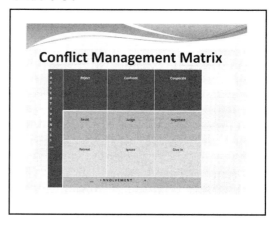

Slide 8-31

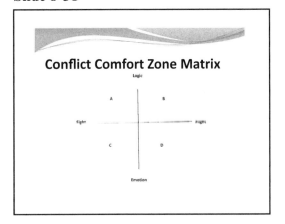

Slide 8-32

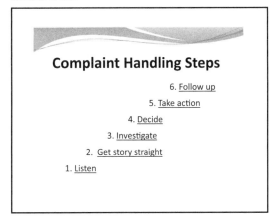

Slide 8-33

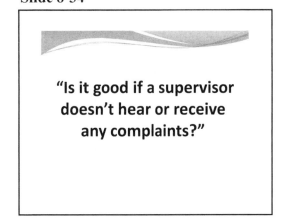

Slide 8-34

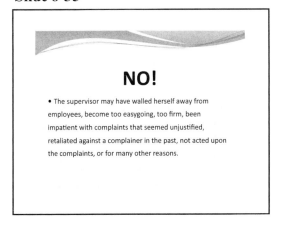

Slide 8-35

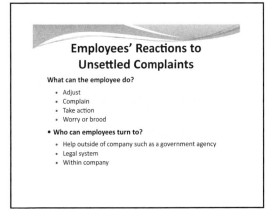

Slide 8-36

Slide 8-37

Passing a Complaint on UP

- Why might a supervisor hesitate to refer a complaint to the next level?

- Why should a complaint be referred to a higher level?

- Why do employees want a complaint to go higher?

Slide 8-38

A coach's goal in dealing with an employee's complaint should be to address the person's issue in the best and most appropriate manner possible—not "win" the complaint.

Slide 8-39

Reasons for Poor Performance

- Lack of communication
- Lack of conditions
- Lack of consequences

Slide 8-40

5-Step Performance– Correction Process

- Step 1—Observe
- Step 2—Discuss
- Step 3—Correct
- Step 4—Advise
- Step 5—Confirm

Slide 8-41

2 Basic Rules About Managing Performance

1. Always expect excellent performance.
2. Never let poor work go unnoticed or performance issues go unchallenged.

Slide 8-42

The 5 Ws of Documentation

- **Who** is going to see this?
- **What** will I or someone else want to know about this event in the future?
- **Why** will I want to look at this again?
- **When** do I write or document this event?
- **Where** will I keep this document?

Slide 8-43

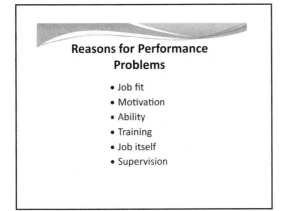

Reasons for Performance Problems

- Job fit
- Motivation
- Ability
- Training
- Job itself
- Supervision

Slide 8-44

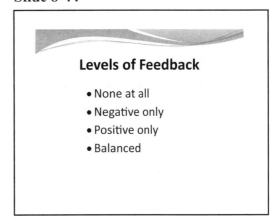

Levels of Feedback

- None at all
- Negative only
- Positive only
- Balanced

Slide 8-45

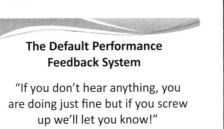

The Default Performance Feedback System

"If you don't hear anything, you are doing just fine but if you screw up we'll let you know!"

Slide 8-46

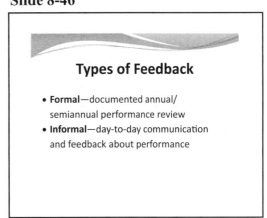

Types of Feedback

- **Formal**—documented annual/ semiannual performance review
- **Informal**—day-to-day communication and feedback about performance

Slide 8-47

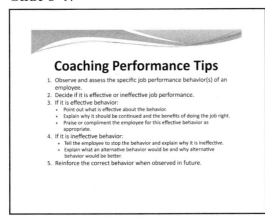

Coaching Performance Tips

1. Observe and assess the specific job performance behavior(s) of an employee.
2. Decide if it is effective or ineffective job performance.
3. If it is effective behavior:
   - Point out what is effective about the behavior.
   - Explain why it should be continued and the benefits of doing the job right.
   - Praise or compliment the employee for this effective behavior as appropriate.
4. If it is ineffective behavior:
   - Tell the employee to stop the behavior and explain why it is ineffective.
   - Explain what an alternative behavior would be and why alternative behavior would be better.
5. Reinforce the correct behavior when observed in future.

Slide 8-48

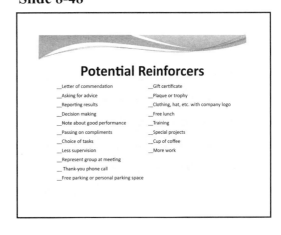

Potential Reinforcers

__Letter of commendation	__Gift certificate
__Asking for advice	__Plaque or trophy
__Reporting results	__Clothing, hat, etc. with company logo
__Decision making	__Free lunch
__Note about good performance	__Training
__Passing on compliments	__Special projects
__Choice of tasks	__Cup of coffee
__Less supervision	__More work
__Represent group at meeting	
__ Thank-you phone call	
__Free parking or personal parking space	

Slide 8-49

Deciding When Teams Can Be Most Effective

- When teamwork can unblock creativity
- When there is no obvious solution
- When team decision-making is most effective
- When there is a willingness to accept the team's recommendations

Slide 8-50

Definition of Consensus

"This decision was not my idea or even my first choice concerning the decision of the team, but I do agree to support and work toward the success of this decision just as if it were my own."

Slide 8-51

Synergy

Synergy is the blending of different human skills, talents, and experience to produce a total effect greater than the sum of the individual team members' skills, talents, and experiences alone.

- With synergy 5 + 5 = > 10.

Slide 8-52

Team Leader's Responsibilities

- Train team members to work together
- Identify potential obstacles
- Suggest procedures or ideas for solving a problem
- Help get information
- Give input
- Help the team progress
- Monitor progress
- Recognize and reward results

Slide 8-53

Types of Difficult Team Members

- The reluctant team member
- The defiant team member
- The dominant team member
- The absentee team member
- The vacationer team member

Slide 8-54

Characteristics of an Engaged Team Player

1. Openly shares feelings, opinions, thoughts, and perceptions about problems and issues relating to the team.
2. When listening, attempts to hear and interpret communication from sender's point of view.
3. Utilizes resources, ideas and suggestions of other team members.
4. Trusts and supports other team members, encouraging their growth and development.
5. Understands and is committed to team objectives.

Slide 8-55

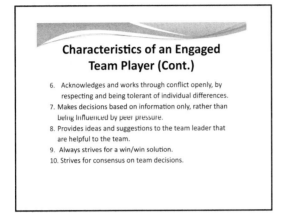

Characteristics of an Engaged Team Player (Cont.)

6. Acknowledges and works through conflict openly, by respecting and being tolerant of individual differences.
7. Makes decisions based on information only, rather than being influenced by peer pressure.
8. Provides ideas and suggestions to the team leader that are helpful to the team.
9. Always strives for a win/win solution.
10. Strives for consensus on team decisions.

Slide 8-56

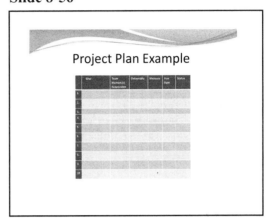

Project Plan Example

Slide 8-57

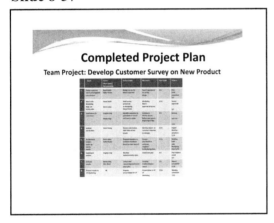

Completed Project Plan

Team Project: Develop Customer Survey on New Product

Content Modules

What's in This Chapter

- Detailed instructions on how to use the content modules

- Content modules 9.1 through 9.50

This chapter contains the content modules that were referenced in the Sample Agendas offered in chapters 5, 6, 7, and 8. Each module is a stand-alone unit that can be part of a single program or used in a larger program. Each of these 50 content modules is presented in a simple step-by-step manner.

Using the Content Modules

Content modules offered in this chapter include the following material:

- Step-by-step instructions: detailed descriptions and timing suggestions.

- Key learning points

- A list of the materials to use in each module: training instruments, PowerPoint presentations, structured experiences, and content module descriptions of what is included in the lesson.

The material presented here can be shortened or expanded to meet your training objectives. The most effective facilitators pay attention to the reaction and response of participants in determining the actual length of the lesson being presented. You should customize or adapt each facilitation guide to fit your own particular needs and presentation style if you wish, or you may choose to follow these plans step-by-step.

The best measure of the level of interest is the response to and participation in the subject that is currently being discussed. No training plan should be so inflexible that something of great interest to participants should be rushed or not allowed to be fully discussed in order to simply complete a planned training agenda.

These lessons generally do not require any resources to present other than the materials included in this workbook or on the website, with the exception of basic training materials such as pencils/pens and physical training facilities that include room enough for role plays to be conducted.

Perhaps the most important part of each lesson is the debrief or summarization of the learning points covered. Often the debrief included in these lessons focuses on the practical application of the information just presented and usually asks for participants' input about how they will apply the lesson just learned when they return to the job.

The Modules

The modules in this chapter emphasize learning through participation. It is recommended that you use the needs assessment methods described in chapter 2 before you decide which modules to use and how they will be modified. This chapter includes the following modules:

◆ **Content Module 9.1—The Importance of Communication.** This module emphasizes just how important communication is in the supervisor/employee relationship to becoming an effective coach and creating an engaged workplace.

◆ **Content Module 9.2—Coaching Communication Model.** This module presents a communication model for coaches to follow when communicating with employees.

◆ **Content Module 9.3—Listening for Better Coaching.** The activity includes two listening models: five levels of listening and five listening tips, which are presented to help participants become better listeners.

◆ **Content Module 9.4—Silent Messages.** An example of a supervisor taking no action or not addressing a problem is described, as well as the unintended message that this could deliver to employees.

◆ **Content Module 9.5—Phrases That Kill Ideas.** A list of phrases is presented that are often heard in most organizations on a regular basis and that have the potential to essentially kill any new suggestions or ideas.

◆ **Content Module 9.6—3 Levels of Coaching Communication.** This model describes three levels of communication: information that employees **must** know to perform their jobs; information that employees **should** know to perform their jobs; and information that is just simply **nice** for employees to know.

◆ **Content Module 9.7—Communicating Assignments Quiz.** A 10-question communicating assignments quiz is presented to participants to complete and score results.

◆ **Content Module 9.8—Rumors.** A rumor is simulated as being spread among participants in the session. The rumor will begin as a written message, which is then communicated verbally to each participant one by one until everyone in the session has had the opportunity to hear the message. Once the rumor has been spread to everyone, its final version will be compared to the original written message.

◆ **Content Module 9.9—14 Commitments for Effective Coaching.** The 14 commitments for effective coaching are presented and explained in this lesson.

◆ **Content Module 9.10—Basic Coaching Principles.** The four basic coaching principles are presented and discussed. Following these basic principles can help guide participants in most if not all situations they may face in their leadership roles. Following these basic principles can help participants build greater trust and respect from those they supervise.

◆ **Content Module 9.11—Engaged Coaching.** Two lists of leadership philosophies and approaches are presented about leading others. One is a traditional supervisory philosophy and the second is more supportive of coaching and employee engagement in the workplace.

◆ **Content Module 9.12—The Real Experts.** A dialog between a supervisor and an employee is presented in which the employee did exactly what she was told to do by the supervisor, which resulted in an undesirable consequence.

◆ **Content Module 9.13—Helping Employees Contribute.** Basic principles are presented in this lesson about how to create a work climate that supports employees' feeling that they want to contribute to the overall success of the organization.

◆ **Content Module 9.14—Spending Time With Employees.** The question of what the right amount of time is that a supervisor should spend with supervisees is discussed.

◆ **Content Module 9.15—Supervisor Ask/Tell Model.** A model is presented which shows the Supervisor Ask/Tell model and the relationship between the extent to which a supervisor engages in either asking or telling employees concerning the performance of their jobs, and based on each person's experience and skill level.

◆ **Content Module 9.16—Positive Conflict.** Participants are asked about their feelings regarding conflict and if it can ever be a positive thing to exist in the workplace. The facilitator should discuss how conflict can lead to a positive outcome if managed in a positive manner.

◆ **Content Module 9.17—Causes of Conflict at Work.** A model showing causes of conflict is presented, illustrating some of the reasons that conflict may exist in the workplace.

◆ **Content Module 9.18—Conflict Strategies.** This module presents four conflict strategies that are commonly utilized. They are discussed and evaluated for their effectiveness, some of which are more productive than others but nevertheless still used when dealing with conflict in the workplace.

◆ **Content Module 9.19—Conflict Management Matrix.** A matrix with continuums of assertiveness and involvement is presented, showing nine different approaches to dealing with conflict. These nine strategies include: reject, confront, cooperate, resist, judge, bargain, retreat, give in, and ignore.

◆ **Content Module 9.20—Conflict Comfort Zones.** Each person has a natural way of dealing with conflict and has her own conflict comfort zones. These are similar to back-up styles that people revert to when faced with a conflict situation. The lesson helps participants identify their own conflict comfort zone and helps them learn to be more versatile when dealing with conflict in the future.

◆ **Content Module 9.21—Conflict Role Play.** A role play is conducted involving two employees who are presently having difficulty getting along with each other at work. In the role play, the participant playing the part of the supervisor intervenes to help these employees resolve their difficulty.

◆ **Content Module 9.22—Dealing With Upset Employees.** Dealing with an upset employee can be a critical moment in the supervisor/employee working relationship. The importance of acknowledging the upset employee's emotions at that moment and demonstrating empathy for the employee is reviewed.

◆ **Content Module 9.23—Definition of a Complaint.** Participants are presented with a definition of a complaint and are provided tips on dealing with employee complaints more effectively.

◆ **Content Module 9.24—No Complaints.** Participants are asked if they believe it is a good situation if a supervisor doesn't receive any complaints from employees.

◆ **Content Module 9.25—Unsettled Complaints.** The lesson describes how employees might react if their complaints are not adequately addressed and the consequences of this dissatisfaction, as well as why and when a complaint should be elevated to the next level.

◆ **Content Module 9.26—Complaint-Handling Quiz.** A brief quiz is provided for participants to test their understanding of how to deal more effectively with employee complaints.

◆ **Content Module 9.27—Resolving Employee Complaints.** The ultimate goal of dealing effectively with an employee complaint is discussed in this lesson.

- **Content Module 9.28—Causes of Poor Performance.** Three major reasons for poor performance are presented: lack of communication, lack of conditions, and lack of consequences. Strategies for addressing each of these causes of poor performance are discussed during the lesson.

- **Content Module 9.29—5-Step Performance-Correction Process.** A 5-step performance-correction process is introduced that helps supervisors understand how to proceed when dealing with an employee's performance problem.

- **Content Module 9.30—Setting Performance Standards.** Participants are asked what message they are really sending to employees if they allow poor performance to go unchallenged or unaddressed.

- **Content Module 9.31—Discipline Role Play.** In this role play, an employee is being counseled by her supervisor concerning an absentee problem that has been occurring for the past eighteen months.

- **Content Module 9.32—Documentation.** A 5 Ws model for documentation is presented to help participants think about the most important aspects of documentation each time they need to create this type of written record as part of their responsibilities as a supervisor or coach.

- **Content Module 9.33—Documentation Role Play.** A role play involving a supervisor and an employee experiencing attendance problems is observed by groups and then each participant is asked to create documentation about this meeting.

- **Content Module 9.34—Performance-Improvement Process Plan.** An example of a performance-improvement process plan is presented. During the lesson, the objectives, design, and implementation of the performance-improvement process are reviewed.

- **Content Module 9.35—Performance-Improvement Process Plan Role Play**. The same performance-improvement process plan templates are utilized in this lesson as in the previous one (lesson 34). In this lesson, teams of two participants are assigned the role of either supervisor or employee. Each participant is provided background information for her role to review before this exercise begins. The participant playing the role of supervisor will present and review the performance-improvement process plan to the participant playing the role of the employee.

◆ **Content Module 9.36—A World Without Feedback.** The importance of feedback is emphasized using a sports analogy where participants are asked to envision participating in a sport without any feedback on their performance. Different levels of feedback are presented and discussed.

◆ **Content Module 9.37—Formal and Informal Feedback.** Formal and informal feedback are defined and discussed with guidance provided on when each type of feedback may be most applicable and beneficial.

◆ **Content Module 9.38—Coaching Time.** The question of how much time participants in the lesson should spend coaching their employees is presented and discussed during the lesson.

◆ **Content Module 9.39—Coaching Tips.** This lesson provides advice on how to most effectively correct poor performance when observed, as well as how to reinforce effective performance.

◆ **Content Module 9.40—Performance Appraisal Role Play.** Groups of three participants act in a role play where each is assigned one of the following roles: supervisor, employee, or observer. Each role is given specific instructions and background information concerning their responsibilities during the lesson. After each role play is completed, the observer should provide feedback to the person playing the role of the supervisor as well as those playing the employees. Participants could also take turns playing each role as time permits.

◆ **Content Module 9.41—Recognition.** Different types of recognition are reviewed in the lesson with a discussion concerning which ones are the most effective.

◆ **Content Module 9.42—Recognition Role Play.** This role play lesson actually consists of two different exercises about providing recognition for employees. In the first role play, a supervisor presents a group of employees with a formal award for a special project they recently completed. In the second role play, the supervisor presents informal recognition to an employee for excellent job performance.

- ◆ **Content Module 9.43—When Teams Are Most Effective.** This lesson involves a discussion concerning the appropriate use of teams and when and when not to utilize them in the workplace.

- ◆ **Content Module 9.44—Reaching Consensus.** The meaning and importance of reaching consensus as a team is reviewed during this lesson.

- ◆ **Content Module 9.45—Synergy.** To explore the definition of synergy through the use of a brief quiz that demonstrates the power of working together.

- ◆ **Content Module 9.46—Designing Engagement Into Your Organization.** An example of a production measurement system which was actually unintentionally discouraging employees from working together toward a common goal is presented with a discussion about how to prevent this from occurring in participants' workplaces.

- ◆ **Content Module 9.47—Helping Teams Get Things Done.** This lesson provides tips and advice so that participants are better able to help others work together and accomplish their goals as a team.

- ◆ **Content Module 9.48—Dealing With Difficult Team Members.** Various descriptions of challenging and difficult types of personalities of team members that can be disruptive to the team's work and progress are presented, along with strategies suggested for dealing with each of these problem team members.

- ◆ **Content Module 9.49—Characteristics of a Team Player.** A list of 10 characteristics of an engaged team player is presented and discussed during the lesson.

- ◆ **Content Module 9.50—Creating a Team Project Plan.** An example of a team project plan is presented to show how such a plan can help everyone on the team understand her role and responsibilities.

Content Module 9.1—The Importance of Communication

This module emphasizes just how important communication is in the supervisor/employee relationship to becoming an effective coach and creating an engaged workplace.

TIME

◆ 10 minutes

MATERIALS

◆ PowerPoint presentation *The Importance of Communication.ppt* (in the online materials)

AGENDA

◆ Begin by displaying *The Importance of Communication.ppt*

◆ Ask participants if they can think of a situation at work in which communication on some level was not the root cause of the problem. It is unlikely that anyone will be able to give such an example. Based on this, emphasize just how important establishing better communication can be in the supervisor/employee working relationships and why focusing on this important factor is a worthwhile endeavor. Explain how important communication is in any working relationship. Ask participants for their thoughts on the importance of communication in their roles in their organizations. (5 minutes)

◆ Review PowerPoint presentation *The Importance of Communication.ppt* (5 minutes)

◆ Emphasize again that communication affects virtually everything that happens in organizations. Communication can be one of the greatest strengths of an organization or one of its weaknesses. This is also true for supervisors and coaches. A coach or supervisor's communication skills and abilities can make a big difference in how effectively she performs the job. The good news is that anyone can improve her communication skills and abilities. You don't have to be a great orator or public speaker, but you simply need to try to be a better communicator. (5 minutes)

KEY POINTS

- ◆ Communication in the supervisor/employee relationship is key to becoming an effective coach and creating an engaged workplace.

DEBRIEF

- ◆ Conclude the lesson by pointing out that communication is an art, not a science. There is no absolute right or wrong way to communicate effectively.

- ◆ Tell the participants that what is most important is that they communicate in a manner and style most comfortable and effective for them.

- ◆ Ask participants to specifically discuss how communication is important in their jobs.

Content Module 9.2—Coaching Communication Model

This module presents a communication model for coaches to follow when communicating with employees.

TIME

◆ 15 minutes

MATERIALS

◆ PowerPoint presentation *Coaches Communication Model.ppt* (in the online materials)

AGENDA

◆ Display *Coaches Communication Model.ppt*

◆ Begin by explaining that this model illustrates how effective communication can be achieved. Although this may seem like a cumbersome process to go through at first, there are people who practice this model in some manner in all of their communication, although perhaps not so formally, and instead follow the basic principles presented in the model.

◆ Go through the four steps as depicted in the model.

◆ Start with step 1, in which the supervisor coach provides input about an employee's performance. Explain that even at this early step in the process, many problems can occur. For instance, the message may not be clearly communicated by the supervisor. This could be a function of the supervisor's communication skills or even the effort that this person puts forth to communicate clearly.

◆ The second step involves the employee receiving the message and both hearing and responding to the message. There can be problems with both. The employee may not be able to clearly hear the message for any number of reasons, including other distracting sounds or competition for her attention by others. The other part of this step is the employee responding to the message. Of course, this can't be done if she doesn't hear the message or chooses not to respond. In either case, the message would end at this point in the communication process, as is often the case.

◆ The third step (#3) goes back to the supervisor or coach to clarify anything that the employee may have misinterpreted in the message or feedback delivered. This may give the supervisor or coach another chance to make sure her message was heard correctly and to clarify anything that may have been misinterpreted.

◆ The fourth step (#4) involves the employee acknowledging and confirming that she now understands the message and accepts the suggestions of the coach.

KEY POINTS

◆ Communication in the supervisor/employee relationship is key to becoming an effective coach and creating an engaged workplace.

◆ A model is presented which shows the dynamics that need to take place for effective communication to exist between a coach and those people she supervises.

DEBRIEF

Repeat the story about the supervisor who, when giving instructions to employees, would ask them afterward to repeat what she just said back to her. By doing this, she taught them to become better listeners. They listened carefully to everything she instructed or told them because they knew that they would be asked to repeat this back to her. Emphasize to participants that each person needs to utilize this model in a manner and style that they are most comfortable, but the most important point of the lesson to remember is that effective communication involves staying in the communication longer to ensure that this calcification/confirmation process is completed.

Content Module 9.3—Listening for Better Coaching

The activity includes two listening models: five levels of listening and five listening tips.

TIME

◆ 15 minutes

MATERIALS

◆ PowerPoint presentation *5 Levels of Listening.ppt* (in the online materials)

AGENDA

1. Begin lesson by reminding participants just how important listening is in any job, especially that of a supervisor.

2. Display *5 Levels of Listening.ppt* introducing the **5 Levels of Listening.** Explain that each level is at a higher or more attentive level of listening.

3. The first level of listening is **Tuned Out.** This lowest level of listening actually describes a situation in which an individual is not listening at all. Someone who is tuned out is not receiving any messages being sent to her. The person at this level of listening is not making any attempt to listen or pay any attention to the sender of the message, for reasons perhaps known only to that person.

4. The next level is **Distracted.** At this level of listening, there is at least some interest on the part of the individual to listen, but the person is distracted and not receiving all or even any part of the message. The listener could in some situations do something to remedy this situation by eliminating the distractions, but either chooses not to or isn't in control of these distractions. The listener might also be distracted by her own inability at the moment to concentrate on the message being delivered, due to being focused on other things.

5. The next level is **Selected** listening. This is when a person only hears the part or parts of a message that she wants to or is interested in hearing. Sometimes this selective listening happens automatically

when there are multiple messages being sent to someone and the person is able to selectively hear only those that pertain to her. For example, a supervisor may only hear her name over a paging system and actually tune out the other pages not pertaining to her.

6. **Focused** listening is the next to the last level. Focused listening is when a person does give the other person her undivided attention and is fully listening. This is simply hearing the message but this doesn't necessarily mean that the listener has fully understood or interpreted the message, which occurs at the next and last level of listening.

7. **Engaged** listening means that the listener is not only fully listening to the message being received, but is also processing and interpreting the meaning of the message and responding to the sender. The listener compares the message to her own emotions, experiences, beliefs, values, priorities, and so forth, and shares this information in some way back to the other person in the communication. This could be done in any number of ways, not only by the actual words the listener uses in responding but also by including the voice inflections and body language back to the other person, either consciously or unconsciously.

8. Next, present or distribute Handout 3.2 to participants.

9. Display *Listening Tips.ppt*

10. Review each of the five tips:

Paraphrase the message to the speaker in order to confirm your understanding.

Explain that repeating what you believe to be the meaning of the message to the sender can help clarify the actual intended meaning of the message if misunderstood.

Repeat the message to help you remember what was said.

Point out that a common memorization technique is to repeat out loud what you just heard to retain the information longer.

Probe for missing information.

Explain that probing for information allows you to ensure that you receive all information you need to act upon the information as well to keep you actively involved in the communication process.

Remember the important points of the message for future application.

Focusing on those most important points of the communication can help you focus on precisely the parts of the message you need the most.

Act upon the message as necessary.

The best time to respond to the message is instantly if possible, before you get distracted with other competing tasks. Do it now before you forget!

11. Tying these two models together, explain that utilizing these tips means that you are most likely listening at an engaged level.

KEY POINTS

- ◆ Following the two listening models—5 levels of listening and 5 listening tips—will help participants become better listeners.

- ◆ Using these techniques leads to more engaged listening.

DEBRIEF

Conclude the lesson by emphasizing just how important listening is to becoming a more effective communicator and a better coach. Improving your listening skills can help you in your relationships, not only with people that participants supervise, but also with others in the organization that they work with.

Content Module 9.4—Silent Messages

An example of a supervisor taking no action or not addressing a problem is described, as well as the unintended message this could deliver to employees.

TIME

- ◆ 10 minutes

MATERIALS

- ◆ None

AGENDA

1. Begin the lesson by explaining that many times when we think we are not communicating, we are actually sending a very strong message. Ask participants what they believe the following statement means, particularly concerning supervisor to employee communication: *Often when we say nothing, we are actually saying a great deal.*

2. Explain that being silent and not saying anything may be actually sending a strong message to others. This is particularly true for supervisors.

3. For instance, if a supervisor sees inappropriate or unproductive behavior being displayed by an employee and says or does nothing to correct the situation, a great deal has just been communicated.

4. Ask participants what they think the message would be that the employee in this circumstance might have received. Expect to hear comments that by saying nothing, the supervisor might have been perceived by the employee as condoning or permitting this type of inappropriate behavior or just not caring. This would be obviously the wrong message and the opposite of what the supervisor wanted or expected from this employee.

KEY POINTS

- ◆ Taking no action or not addressing a problem has the potential to send unintended messages to employees.

DEBRIEF

Ask participants to share other examples of these types of silent messages the supervisor may receive from them or others in the organization. Ask the group how these misconceptions can be addressed and how they as supervisors can prevent these incorrect "silent messages" from occurring in the future.

Content Module 9.5—Phrases That Kill Ideas

A list of phrases that are often heard in most organizations on a regular basis is presented that has the potential to essentially kill any new suggestions or ideas that might come up.

TIME

◆ 15 minutes

MATERIALS

◆ PowerPoint presentation *Phrases That Kill Ideas.ppt* (in the online materials)

AGENDA

1. Begin the lesson by discussing the importance of creating an engaging work climate in which all employees feel encouraged and supported when making suggestions about new and innovative ways to improve the work process and/or organization. Also relate the benefits which could potentially be realized by such a work culture.

2. Turn discussion toward why such a work culture or climate may not always exist in organizations today. Ask participants what "obstacles" they may see or envision that might prevent such a climate from existing.

3. Display *Phrases That Kill Ideas.ppt* and review the list.

4. Ask participants if they ever hear any of these phrases at work and ask if they can offer other *killer phrases* they have heard that were not included on this list.

5. Ask participants what impact these types of phrases have on creativity, teamwork and employee engagement at work.

6. Emphasize how important it is for participants to be open to new or different ideas that employees may have concerning how their jobs and the workplace can be improved.

7. Discuss how important this is when desiring to create a workplace supportive of employee engagement, as it allows employees to really feel as if their opinions are respected and their good suggestions will be acted upon.

KEY POINTS

- ◆ Organizations often kill any new suggestions or ideas that might be presented through the unintentional use of standard catch phrases.

- ◆ These negative words and phrases defeat creativity and the airing of new ideas.

DEBRIEF

Ask participants if they have any real-life examples of how these or other similar types of statements have prevented new ideas from being introduced at work, and tell what the consequences were. Summarize by again emphasizing the detrimental effect this type of negativity can have in any organization. Ask participants to commit to avoiding using these or other similar phrases, and commit to not killing the good ideas and suggestions of employees. The result will be a much more engaged workplace.

Content Module 9.6—3 Levels of Coaching Communication

This model describes three levels of communication: information that employees **must** know to perform their jobs; information that employees **should** know to perform their jobs; and information that is just simply **nice** for employees to know.

TIME

◆ 15 minutes

MATERIALS

◆ PowerPoint presentation *3 Levels of Coaching Communication.ppt* (in the online materials)

AGENDA

1. Display *3 Levels of Coaching Communication.ppt*

2. Introduce the lesson as a communication model that describes three levels of communication a supervisor might share with those who report to her.

3. Start with the level shown at the bottom of the model as *must*. Explain that this is the information that an employee has to have to be able to perform her job. In most circumstances, this level of communication between a supervisor and an employee is met. If not, obviously the employee wouldn't be able to perform her job, which sometimes is the problem. This information would include things like what the employee is supposed to work on, where the job is to be performed, where to get essential resources to be able to perform the work, and so on.

4. Explain the next level of communication is *should*. This type of information is that which an employee could actually perform the job without, but she would be much better equipped to do the job with this information. This type of information could be feedback on how she is performing the job, upcoming events that could impact the work, changes that are expected that could directly impact the job, tips and advice on how to perform the job better, and more.

5. The last level of communication is information that is simply *nice* to know but really doesn't have any direct impact on the work. These are things that make someone feel "in" on things and an important member of the team. Examples are events or news about other parts of the organization, plans for the future of the organization, business updates, and so forth.

6. Ask participants what they perceive the value to be in communicating at least at the should level of this model and even at the nice level. Ask participants if they believe employees really appreciate hearing things that are nice to know, even though they may not directly impact their jobs or careers. Is communication at this highest level necessary to create an engaged workplace? The answer to these questions is undoubtedly "yes."

KEY POINTS

◆ Information in organizations has a hierarchy that ranges from information that employees **must** know to perform their jobs to information that employees **should** know to perform their jobs to information that is simply **nice** for employees to know.

◆ It is important that a supervisor understands these levels to effectively communicate with employees, since this ability impacts employee engagement.

DEBRIEF

There is a story about an employee who, when asked about something relating to his job that wasn't going to happen until later in the future responded, "Every day when I come to work, I only receive just enough information to be able to perform my job for the day, nothing more. I never know what I am going to be doing the next day or anytime in the future until that time comes and I get my job instructions for that day."

Ask the group at what level on this communication model they believe this employee was being communicated to by his supervisor. Obviously, he was only receiving *must* level communication, if that. Ask the group how engaged they believe this employee was and how much he felt his supervisor trusted him. The point is that employees do want to receive information about their jobs and the organization in general, even if it doesn't directly affect them. Emphasize that part of creating an engaged workplace is sharing this type of information with employees. This makes them feel more a part of the entire team and that you care enough to ensure that they receive this nice-to-know level of information with them. Besides, you never know when *nice-to-know* actually becomes *should* know or even *must* know information for the employee to receive.

Finally, ask the group what they think about information that employees *shouldn't* know as it relates to this communication model. Ask the group if they communicated consistently on the *nice* level, would employees be more accepting of the fact that a supervisor may have information she can't share? The point is, if you have created this highest level of trust in your communication with employees, they will be more accepting when you have to acknowledge that you do know something they may have asked about, but you are unable to discuss it at this time.

Content Module 9.7—Communicating Assignments Quiz

A 10-question communicating assignments quiz is presented to participants to complete and score results.

TIME

- ◆ 20 minutes

MATERIALS

- ◆ Assessment 10.1—Communicating Assignments Quiz (chapter 10)

AGENDA

1. Begin the lesson by discussing the importance of effective communication when assigning a task or job.

2. Elaborate that the successful completion of the assignment may be largely dependent on how well it was communicated to the employee who is to perform the task or job.

3. Facilitate Communicating Assignments Quiz 10.1 (10 minutes)

4. Solicit feedback from participants concerning which areas in general they felt they were the strongest and the weakest.

5. Ask participants for their feedback on the importance of these 10 assignment communication factors in the quiz. Ask which they feel are most important and why.

KEY POINTS

- ◆ Successful completion of assignments is directly related to how well you communicate with employees when assigning a task.

DEBRIEF

Point out that the questions in the quiz are instructive by themselves. In other words, the questions give direction concerning what type of communication is most needed when giving employees assignments. Suggest they keep these questions in mind when giving future assignments to employees.

Content Module 9.8—Rumors

A rumor is simulated as being spread among participants in the session. The rumor will begin as a written message, which is then communicated verbally to each participant one by one until everyone in the session has had the opportunity to hear the message. Once the rumor has been spread to everyone, its final version will be compared to the original written message.

TIME

◆ 15 minutes (depending on number of participants)

MATERIALS

◆ Handout 11.1—Rumors (chapter 11)

◆ Paper

◆ Writing instruments for participants

AGENDA

1. Facilitate Structured Experience 11.1—Rumors (15 minutes)

2. Lead group through the rumors exercise

KEY POINTS

◆ The accuracy of rumors degrades as they spread throughout an organization.

◆ The impact of these rumors is difficult to control or quantify.

DEBRIEF

Allow participants to have some fun and laugh about what just happened in this lesson, as it will be very likely that what the last person heard was very different than the original written message. The larger the group, the more the original message will change as the rumor spreads during this lesson. As facilitator, you might joke that the last sentence of the rumor said that this information should be kept confidential at this time, which only makes it more tempting for some to tell others about it!

Content Module 9.9—14 Commitments for Effective Coaching

The 14 commitments for effective coaching are presented and explained in this lesson.

TIME

◆ 20 minutes

MATERIALS

◆ PowerPoint presentation *14 Commitments of Effective Coaches.ppt*

AGENDA

1. Display title slide *Effective Coaching Is About Trust* as you begin your presentation.

2. Say that the 14 commitments represent the basic fundamentals of effective supervision. Employee engagement is actually based on creating a solid basis of trust between a supervisor or coach and those who report to her. **NOTE**—Facilitator should prepare for presenting this lesson by reviewing the information below to become thoroughly familiar with the concepts and basis of these 14 commitments.

3. Display *14 Commitments of Effective Coaches.ppt*

4. Explain that these 14 commitments are basic building blocks for effective supervision and ultimately coaching. Consider these to be employees' "rights" to being supervised or coached effectively.

5. After reviewing each of these commitments, ask participants which of these are presently in place in their organization or workplace and which ones need more focus.

6. Ask participants how they believe any deficiencies identified in this discussion could be addressed.

7. Ask for feedback from participants concerning how important they feel these 14 commitments are to their employees and how they could help create or support a more engaged workplace. Ask if there

are there certain commitments they feel are more important than others. For instance, certain commitments such as communication or trust and respect may have greater influence on employee engagement in some circumstances. Ask if participants agree or disagree or if there are other commitments that they feel are more important to employee engagement.

14 Commitments of Effective Coaches

1. Provide Orientation and Training for New Employees

Explain the importance of providing a thorough orientation and training for new employees so they can make a smooth transition to the organization and the job.

2. Maintain Good Working Conditions

This involves creating safety and health awareness in every employee and educating employees concerning any protective equipment that may be required for the job, ensuring that safe work practices are followed, and providing a work environment which meets established standards for the industry. In an office or professional environment, this can involve the actual physical setup and locations of offices, ergonomics or comfort of desks and chairs, accessibility of equipment, meeting facilities, privacy, and other factors that may be important to employees.

3. Share Business Information

Explain the importance of ensuring that employees understand the organization's business decisions, the economic considerations, the status of the business, and other important matters that affect employees and their jobs.

4. Treat Employees With Respect

Explain how important it is to develop a style of management and supervision that fosters a climate of respect and trust among all employees. Employees should be treated in a respectful manner at all times and should be expected to treat others, including their supervisor, in the same way.

5. Encourage Employee Involvement

Emphasize that participants should seek and acknowledge employees' ideas and suggestions and give them credit for those that are implemented. They should consider all employees as members of a team who have something of importance to contribute. This can be the basis for creating greater employee engagement in their workplace.

6. Maintain Written Policies

Review the importance of maintaining policies in some written form such as in an employee handbook or electronically on a company intranet website so that everyone will have a clear understanding of the organization's policies and procedures. It is also critically important that these policies are administered in a fair and consistent manner.

7. Promote Cooperation Throughout Organization

Explain the importance and advantage of fostering an atmosphere of cooperation between different parts of the organization working toward what is best for the entire operation or enterprise. When different parts of the organization compete with one another, it only serves to distract from the company's success and ability to achieve its overall goals for success in the marketplace.

8. Resolve Conflict in a Positive Manner

Emphasize that as supervisors, they need to accept complaints in a positive manner and address them fairly and objectively, often putting their own personal feelings or emotions aside. If an employee is not satisfied with the response to her complaint, she should be allowed to take the complaint to the next level of management. Conflict between employees should also be addressed in a positive problem-solving manner that seeks an acceptable resolution.

9. Provide Constructive Discipline

Explain that any discipline issued should be used as a tool to correct problems up to the point an employee proves through her conduct or performance that she will not respond to corrective efforts. Discipline should be progressive; a series of progressive steps should be established and employees should be provided the opportunity to clear their disciplinary records by correcting the problem(s) and not repeating them in the future.

10. Ensure Fair Treatment for all Employees

Emphasize the importance of promoting employees, making job assignments and decisions for other personnel actions on the basis of objective criteria and qualification, and taking every precaution to avoid favoritism or bias of any kind against an employee.

11. Lead by Example

Explain the importance of setting a positive example by your own good attendance, work habits, personal use of time, and commitment and attention to the job. You can't supervise effectively with a "do as I say, not as I do" model of behavior.

12. Address Employee Issues

Emphasize the importance of staying in tune with employee needs and monitoring the impact of any policies and decisions made as they affect employees. Watch their response and reaction to these changes and respond when appropriate and possible to do so. If not possible to address these concerns, it is still very important that supervisors listen to how employees feel about the changes or issues at hand, and keep an active dialog open concerning their feelings.

13. Provide Performance Feedback

Reaffirm the importance of appraising and counseling employees at least annually so that each employee is provided with formal feedback on their performance and other related matters, and is given the opportunity to have a dialog with the supervisor concerning the job and future with the organization.

14. Help Employees With Personal Problems

Remind participants that problems outside the workplace can have a major impact on employee productivity, morale, and motivation. Supervisors should attempt to help employees whenever possible by showing interest and making referrals to outside professional assistance if needed.

KEY POINTS

◆ Understanding commitments serves as a good basis for establishing a workplace climate of employee engagement.

DEBRIEF

Ask participants how they feel about the last commitment, which is helping employees with personal problems. Probe just how important participants feel this commitment is to employees.

Explain that employee surveys often show this is actually a very important commitment to employees. Be prepared to hear participants cite examples of employees who seem to constantly have personal problems they bring into the workplace and that it would occupy all of their time to deal with these problems. Emphasize that this commitment is addressing the employee who doesn't usually, if ever, bring these kinds of problems to work but has some sort of life crisis (at least to her) in which she does legitimately need some additional consideration.

Ask participants what they feel could happen if they as supervisors miss this opportunity and how it might affect their future working relations with the employee, possibly for the rest of that employee's career.

Content Module 9.10—Basic Coaching Principles

The four basic coaching principles are presented and discussed. Following these basic principles can help guide participants in most if not all situations they may face in their leadership roles. These basic principles can help participants build greater trust and respect from those they supervise.

TIME

- 20 minutes

MATERIALS

- PowerPoint presentation *Basic Supervisory Principles.ppt* (in the online materials)

AGENDA

1. Display *Basic Supervisory Principles.ppt*

2. Introduce the lesson by explaining that these basic supervisory principles are the foundation for building trust with those you supervise. These basic principles are: firm, fair, consistent, and respectful. Review and explain the descriptions and lead a discussion on how these concepts can be utilized by a supervisor in the workplace, as well as how these principles lead to effective coaching. Ask participants how effective coaches they have known in their lives used these basic principles.

3. Emphasize that being an effective coach doesn't mean you never do things that may be perceived as potentially negative by employees. You must enforce the rules. Explain that this is not always a popular thing to do. However, how you do this is what is most important. You must apply the rules in a firm, fair, and consistent manner to everyone. This means that sometimes you may need to do things that you might prefer not to do. But you must be consistent in the way that you apply policies and rules. You must also set a good example by your own behavior.

4. Remind participants that those who obey the rules will get upset if they see others who are allowed to get away with this kind of behavior without consequences. Not enforcing the rules doesn't make you

more popular, well-liked, or more respected and trusted as a coach or supervisor. In fact, it would have the opposite effect.

KEY POINTS

◆ Following the four basic supervisory principles presented can help participants build greater trust and respect from those they supervise or lead.

DEBRIEF

Discuss that the first three principles are well-known, but added to this list is the last principle of being respectful. Emphasize the need to treat every employee, regardless of the circumstance or situation, with dignity and respect, even if an employee is not treating you the same way. Setting such an example is important for any supervisor and helps create the type of work climate and culture that encourages and supports employee engagement in the workplace.

Content Module 9.11—Engaged Coaching

Two lists of leadership philosophies and approaches are presented that describe different philosophies about how to lead others. The first is a more traditional supervisory philosophy and the second is more supportive of the concepts of coaching and employee engagement in the workplace.

TIME

◆ 15 minutes

MATERIALS

◆ PowerPoint presentation *Engaged Coaching Model.ppt* (in the online materials)

AGENDA

1. Begin the lesson by explaining that employee engagement involves a new model of supervision in an organization.

2. Display *Engaged Coaching Model.ppt.*

3. Say that the list highlights many of these changes that take place as engagement becomes the management philosophy in an organization. Review the first slide, which describes what this model suggests is required to create this type of work environment.

4. Explain that engagement is really all about trusting others and being trustworthy as a leader. This involves being more open about sharing information as well as listening to what others have to say. Everyone must have a greater sense of ownership concerning their jobs and be more accountable for the results. Employees need to be challenged to accept more responsibility for those aspects of their jobs, as they are the experts who know how to best perform the job. Influence should be based on knowledge, not just position or power. Those with the greatest knowledge and expertise should be the ones that are able to take the most appropriate action to ensure that the organization performs to its greatest potential.

5. Explain that employee engagement should also bring less of the following, as illustrated in the second slide.

6. Display *Engaged Coaching Model.ppt* Continued.

7. Elaborate that employee engagement will need less controls to be in place. There should be less red tape and channels that employees have to go through in order to be able to do what needs to be done to perform their jobs correctly and to the best of their abilities. Employees should not feel like they are just putting in time at work but should feel involved and engaged in their jobs. Position power should not be the only influence in the organization, but rather experience and expertise should also be important in decision making. There should be no unnecessary analysis to make the right decision, particularly when the answers are obvious to everyone. There also needs to be less bureaucracy that often causes too many of these channels and approval levels to make the right decisions.

KEY POINTS

- ◆ Two lists of leadership philosophies and approaches are presented that describe different philosophies about how to lead others. One is more of a traditional supervisory philosophy and the second is more supportive of coaching and employee engagement in the workplace.

- ◆ To describe the supervisory changes that need to take place in order to create an engaged work culture and environment.

DEBRIEF

Conclude the lesson by explaining the bottom line is that participants will be amazed at the results this simple model of engaged coaching can achieve by allowing employees to do what they do best—their jobs!

Content Module 9.12—The Real Experts

A dialog between a supervisor and an employee is presented in which the employee did exactly what he was told to do by the supervisor, which resulted in an undesirable consequence.

TIME

> ♦ 15 minutes

MATERIALS

> ♦ PowerPoint presentation *Decisions are Best.ppt.*

AGENDA

1. Begin lesson by displaying *Decisions are Best.ppt.*

2. Explain that the employee working on the job is the real expert on that job based on her experience and expertise working on the job (assuming that the employee has performed the job for enough time to gain this expertise).

3. If this is the case, then why wouldn't you go to this expert when making decisions or working on a project, as this person has more expertise and experience than anyone else in the organization?

4. Getting the right people working on the right things is critically important to the success of any endeavor and is important to creating and supporting employee engagement.

5. Emphasize that as supervisors, participants should ensure they have the right people who are the most knowledgeable about the problem actually working on the problem. Otherwise, you could experience something called *blind obedience*. This is when employees do exactly as they are told. This may sound like a good thing, but it isn't necessarily desirable. Sometimes employees follow directions or instructions to perform certain tasks just how their boss or supervisor tells them even though they know it isn't the right thing to do to solve the problem. Obviously, the result can be disastrous.

6. What you need to do is create a working environment where everyone feels that her opinions matter and that they will be listened to when sharing critical information needed to resolve a problem.

7. Display the second slide in *Decisions are Best.ppt* slide set.

8. Read the following dialog between a supervisor and employee to participants:

    Supervisor: Why did you do the job that way? This is not the way it was supposed to turn out. Now we have to redo the entire job. This is a waste of time and resources that was unnecessary.

    Employee: I just did the job the way you told me to do it.

    Supervisor: Ok, that's true, but I didn't realize at the time that there had been changes made that caused these problems. Why didn't you suggest that we do this job a different way based on these changes?

    Employee: You have told us that we also had to follow the standard operating procedures without exception unless approved by you. You never told me to do the job any other way, so I just followed the standard procedures.

KEY POINTS

*   ◆ Supervisors and employees must communicate effectively in order to ensure efficient operations and to avoid sometimes undesirable consequences for both the employee and the organization.

DEBRIEF

Explain that obviously you do not want employees to feel they can't speak up and contribute their ideas and expertise concerning their jobs. Creating a work environment based on engagement in which this employee felt empowered to either make the necessary adjustments to do the job correctly, or at least contact her supervisor to advise of the change that occurred, would have prevented this type of problem from happening.

Content Module 9.13—Helping Employees Contribute

Basic principles of creating a work climate that supports employees' feeling that they want to contribute to the overall success of the organization are presented in this lesson.

TIME

◆ 10 minutes

MATERIALS

◆ PowerPoint presentation *Helping Employees Contribute.ppt* (in the on-line materials)

AGENDA

1. Begin the lesson by explaining that people appreciate being asked for advice and asked to participate in the decision-making process, particularly when they are knowledgeable and have expertise in a particular job. They want to contribute and play an important role in the success of the team.

2. However, not everyone will demonstrate this willingness to contribute to the team in the same way.

3. Explain that as a leader or supervisor, one of each participant's most important responsibilities is to find the key to getting this commitment from each employee.

4. People often need to be given the chance to contribute to a team in different ways.

5. Often it is a matter of finding the right task or role for each employee.

6. Explain that when you get people and tasks lined up correctly, you really begin to tap into the true power of employee engagement.

7. Display *Helping Employees Contribute.ppt.*

8. Read to participants the following brief dialog between a supervisor and an employee to illustrate this point:

Supervisor: Ann, I really like the way you worked on that last project. You certainly showed a great deal of creativity and imagination in completing the job. I never realized that you are so creative!

Ann: Thanks, I really do like doing something when I can use my imagination to come up with something different. I hope you can give me other assignments in which I can utilize my creativity.

Supervisor: Now that I know how good you are at these kinds of things, I will certainly assign these types of jobs to you in the future.

Ann: Great!

KEY POINTS

◆ Reinforce employees at all levels through a supportive climate that makes them want to contribute to the overall success of the organization.

DEBRIEF

Ask participants to share their own experiences as supervisors where finding the key to an employee's real interest and talents at work helped motivate that individual to contribute to the success of the workgroup or organization.

Content Module 9.14—Spending Time With Employees

The question of what the right amount of time is that a supervisor should spend with supervisees is presented and discussed.

TIME

- ◆ 10 minutes

MATERIALS

- ◆ Handout 11.2—Spending Time With Employees (chapter 11)

- ◆ PowerPoint presentation *Spending Time With Employees.ppt* (in the online materials)

AGENDA

- ◆ Facilitate Structured Experience 11.2—Spending Time With Employees (10 minutes).

KEY POINTS

- ◆ To highlight the importance of a supervisor spending the right amount and quality of time with employees.

- ◆ The question of what the right amount of time is that a supervisor should spend with supervisees is presented and discussed.

DEBRIEF

Ask participants what they feel is the right amount of time that you should spend with employees. Ask participants what might be the results of spending more time with those who report to them. Can you spend too much time with an employee? Why or why not?

Content Module 9.15—Supervisor Ask/Tell Model

The Supervisor Ask/Tell model is presented, highlighting the extent to which a supervisor engages in either asking or telling employees concerning the performance of their jobs, and based on each person's experience and skill level.

TIME

 ◆ 20 minutes

MATERIALS

 ◆ PowerPoint presentation *Supervisor Ask Tell Model.ppt* (in the online materials)

AGENDA

 ◆ Introduce the lesson by explaining that you have to understand different employees have different needs when it comes to the type of interaction time they need or even want to have with their supervisor.

 ◆ This should be based on their experience and mastery of the tasks they perform as part of their job.

 ◆ The basic rule should be that the less job mastery an employee has, the more supervisory time should be spent with her helping perform the job correctly.

 ◆ Conversely, the greater the skill mastery, the less supervisory time you need to spend explaining or telling the employee how to perform the job. Spend more time asking for her input concerning how the job could be performed better.

 ◆ Following this does not mean that time spent communicating and building better working relationships isn't still important for any employee regardless of job skill and experience. This will always be important under any circumstances.

 ◆ Display *Supervisor Ask Tell Model.ppt.*

◆ This model can be described as the amount of time you spend either *asking* or *telling* in your communication with employees.

◆ In the model, there is a relationship between how much time you spend telling employees how to perform their jobs and their skill level in performing the job.

◆ Conversely, reversing this relationship between ask and tell as the model also depicts, the more skilled the employee, the less time you should spend telling the employee how to perform her job, and the more time you should spend asking the employee how she feels the job should be performed, consulting with the employee on improving or optimizing the job by listening to the employee's ideas, comments, or suggestions.

◆ Of course, there still may be times when a supervisor will also need to coach and direct an employee on any changes or new initiatives that may be introduced to the job. A supervisor may also need to direct an employee if their experienced performance begins to slip below acceptable levels.

KEY POINTS

◆ Supervisors need to have different supervisory approaches when dealing with employees, depending on their level of experience and job mastery.

◆ The Supervisor Ask/Tell model offers a way to gauge the best approach to use.

DEBRIEF

Discuss with participants how they feel this model can or should be applied in their workplace. Ask what would happen if this model were reversed and what the result might be in their workplace. Expect to hear that in many ways, participants are already utilizing this model and ask for examples from the group on why this approach is beneficial. Conclude the lesson by asking participants why this approach to supervising both experienced and inexperienced employees is important and even essential, particularly with new employees just learning how to perform their jobs.

Content Module 9.16—Positive Conflict

Participants are asked how they feel about conflict and if it can ever be a positive thing to exist in the workplace. Facilitator is to lead a discussion on how conflict can lead to a positive outcome if managed in a positive manner.

TIME

◆ 15 minutes

MATERIALS

◆ PowerPoint presentation *Is Conflict Always Bad.ppt* (in the online materials)

AGENDA

◆ Begin lesson by asking participants, "Do you believe that conflict is always bad?"

◆ Expect to hear responses that conflict is not always necessarily bad.

◆ Lead a discussion about how conflict can actually be productive at work by allowing different views and perspectives to be expressed that can actually lead to discovery of new ways of doing things.

◆ However, also acknowledge that conflict can become a problem if not managed or if allowed to get out of control.

◆ Explain that a good measure of whether conflict is getting out of control is if it causes people's relationships to be damaged as a result.

◆ Ask the group if they agree with this definition of conflict becoming a problem.

◆ Emphasize that a supervisor should ensure that conflict is not allowed to get to the point when it damages relationships between employees.

◆ An important part of a supervisor's responsibility is to ensure that conflict is managed and isn't allowed to become counterproductive at work.

KEY POINTS

◆ Conflict can have positive outcomes if handled correctly and is not necessarily a negative occurrence within an organization.

DEBRIEF

Conclude the lesson by explaining that some conflict is inevitable in just about any situation in which people are working together. Again, stress that conflict is not necessarily bad. Conflict can allow new or different ideas, often better ideas, to be expressed and perhaps adapted. Again, the key is to not allow conflict to damage relationships in the workplace.

Employees should feel free to express their opinions with one another and with their leadership, and even be encouraged to do so when contrary to existing ideas and workplace practices. This is part of creating an engaged workplace.

Content Module 9.17—Causes of Conflict at Work

A model of causes of conflict is presented showing some of the reasons that conflict may exist in the workplace.

TIME

- 20 minutes

MATERIALS

- PowerPoint presentation *Causes of Conflict at Work.ppt* (in the online materials)

AGENDA

- Begin lesson by asking what some possible causes are of employee conflict in your workplace. Write participants' responses on the board.

- Ask participants how these sources of conflict affect their workplace.

- Display slide *Causes of Conflict at Work.ppt.*

- Review with participants and suggest that these four sources of conflict may be responsible for much of the conflict that exists in most workplaces.

- Review each one of these potential causes of conflict at work, soliciting discussion and experiences from participants concerning how they may have caused conflict at work for them.

- Use the descriptors provided in *Causes of Conflict at Work.ppt* as prompts for discussion if necessary on the following points.

  - Miscommunication

  - Different interpretation

  - Different values

  - Opposing goals

Facilitator notes follow:

Miscommunication

The employee either did not receive the message or received only part of a message, or the message was delivered in a way that may have been misinterpreted.

Different Interpretations

The employee believes that adherence to rules, policies, or procedures should be carried out in one way, while the actual intent or the rule, policy, or procedure is something else entirely.

Different Values

The employee has less regard than others for a specific task or duty and does not attach importance to its value.

Opposing Goals

The goals of the company or supervisor are directly opposed to those of the employee.

KEY POINTS

◆ With the right approach and information, supervisors can deal effectively and positively with conflict in organizations.

DEBRIEF

Make sure that you explore in some detail the last of the two potential causes of conflict—different values and opposing goals. Ask participants why it may seem that supervisors and employees have different values or opposing goals. Emphasize that this really shouldn't be the case. Everyone should have the same ultimate values and goals concerning work. Everyone's ultimate objective should be to help their organization be successful and to contribute to the success of the team in order to have job security and a good future. Working toward these common goals is what the concept of employee engagement is really all about. When there is a disconnect between values and goals in an organization between management and employees, the reasons for this should be explored and action taken to get everyone more supportive of the overall values and goals of the organization for the benefit of everyone. Improving communication on all levels of an organization can make a big difference and can help you achieve this objective.

Content Module 9.18—Conflict Strategies

Presents four conflict strategies that are commonly used, then evaluates them for their effectiveness. Some are more productive than other but are nevertheless often utilized in dealing with conflict in the workplace.

TIME

- ◆ 20 minutes

MATERIALS

- ◆ PowerPoint presentation *Conflict Strategies.ppt* (in the online materials)

- ◆ Handout 11.3—Conflict Strategies Role Play (chapter 11)

AGENDA

- ◆ Facilitate Structured Experience 11.3 (20 minutes).

- ◆ Review Key Points.

KEY POINTS

- ◆ Some conflict strategies are more effective than others but are nevertheless often utilized in dealing with conflict in the workplace.

- ◆ Using the right conflict strategy—Win/Win; Win/Lose; Lose/Lose; and Lose/Win—is important for a successful outcome.

DEBRIEF

Discuss the differences between each of these approaches to conflict. Point out that in certain circumstances, each may be an acceptable strategy, although striving for a Win/Win solution is always the best but perhaps not always possible. Ask participants to discuss their experiences using these four types of conflict approaches and the success or lack thereof that they experienced. Finally, ask participants to comment on the last scenario depicting a Lose/ Win situation between the supervisor and the employee who was continuously tardy for work. Ask the group if there was ever a situation in which they found themselves tempted or actually did use this conflict strategy and what the results were. Ask the group what they think the chances are that this employee will be tardy for work again in the near future. The answer is that there is probably a very high likelihood of this occurring again. The supervisor who doesn't enforce the rules won't help the situation, and will only make it worse.

Content Module 9.19—Conflict Management Matrix

A matrix with continuums of assertiveness and involvement is presented showing nine different approaches to dealing with conflict. These nine strategies include: reject, confront, cooperate, resist, judge, bargain, retreat, give in, and ignore.

TIME

- 30 minutes

MATERIALS

- PowerPoint presentation *Conflict Management Matrix.ppt* (in the online materials)

AGENDA

1. Begin the lesson by explaining that conflict may sound like it is on the opposite end of the spectrum from employee engagement, but it is actually part of the process. Conflict is inevitable in any situation in which people work together. People bring many different perspectives into the workplace and this can cause conflict to exist. However, some conflict is a natural part of the team process and can actually be constructive. Conflict can help achieve better, more creative solutions to problems. Conflict can cause different perspectives to be expressed and explored by the members of a team. This can cause better ideas and solutions to be discovered and more creative solutions to be found.

2. Explain that conflict needs to be managed to ensure that it doesn't become counterproductive. Conflict must not get to the point where it damages relationships. Learning to deal with conflict constructively and positively is an important goal in creating a workplace supportive of employee engagement. Helping team members learn to deal positively with conflict should be part of your responsibility as a leader.

3. Display *Conflict Management Matrix.ppt* to participants.

4. Explain that it is a team conflict resolution matrix which can help them gain a better understanding of the different ways to deal with

team conflict. Better understanding of these different conflict strategies can help engaged employees work through conflict more productively.

5. To utilize this matrix, first look at the indexes on both the horizontal and vertical axis. On the vertical axis is the *assertiveness scale* from low to high. This indicates the level of assertiveness that one might use to deal with conflict at work. On the horizontal axis is the *involvement scale,* which reflects how involved one might be in dealing with conflict from low to high. These nine strategies are combinations of these assertiveness and involvement measures. For example, the *retreat* conflict strategy is lowest in both *assertiveness* and *involvement.* On the other extreme of the matrix, you will find *cooperate* is the highest in both *assertiveness* and *involvement.*

6. It is important to understand that each of these strategies can be an effective way to deal with conflict depending on the situation and circumstances. None of these strategies are necessarily right or wrong, but each may be conceivably the best strategy in certain situations. For example, when confronted with conflict, it might be best to *retreat.* This is what would be expected of employees if confronted by another employee in an argument or potential physical altercation. However, this strategy wouldn't be the most effective way to deal with conflict in every situation. Helping employees understand and learn how to use as many of these conflict management approaches as possible will help everyone work better together and help deal constructively with conflict.

7. Give a brief example of each of the other conflict strategies to illustrate how they can be an appropriate way to deal with conflict in certain situations, reminding participants that it isn't always possible to achieve the most desirable strategy of cooperation. For instance, you could explain that the reject strategy, which is at the top of the assertiveness continuum and lowest on the involvement continuum, is commonly used. Rejecting an idea may not always be the most pleasing but it does have the potential of resolving a conflict quickly and decisively. Emphasize that this may be the best strategy given the circumstances when a conflict needs to be quickly addressed.

8. The confront strategy may also fall into the category of not being the most pleasant but sometimes effective conflict management strategy. Explain that sometimes things left unaddressed cause conflict to continue unchecked. To simply confront the behaviors that are causing the problem can resolve the conflict. Confronting conflict and its causes is an important role of a supervisor or coach.

9. Discuss the resist strategy in terms of its frequency of use and potential effectiveness. Point out that resist is in the middle of the assertiveness continuum, which makes it more comfortable for some people to utilize. Resistance is often a warning sign that conflict exists because it can be more subtle than aggressive strategies. As supervisors, participants need to be paying attention to resistance as a possible sign of problems or conflict that may be brewing underneath the surface. However, there can be different levels of resistance ranging from passive resistance to more active resistance.

10. The ignore strategy is another complicated strategy in that utilizing this approach in the wrong situation can make it worse. However, there are certain circumstances when ignoring the situation can be the best strategy to resolving the conflict. Sometimes just letting a conflict resolve itself may be the best strategy. In some circumstances, a supervisor getting actively involved in the conflict may only make things worse. This can be especially true when two employees are having a conflict and the supervisor feels that it is best they work out their issues themselves. However, in these circumstances, a supervisor needs to keep aware of the situation and make sure that it does get resolved by itself and intervention doesn't become necessary.

11. The give-in strategy is obviously low assertiveness but high involvement and thus may sound like a poor way to resolve conflict. However, this is not always necessarily the case. Giving in can be an effective conflict strategy under some circumstances, especially when the issue isn't important to the supervisor. Sometimes we find ourselves taking a more assertive position just for the sake of argument. The point is that if something isn't really important to you, then there isn't any sense in fighting for it and the best thing to do is allow the other person to have her way or, in other words, give in. This is why it is on the high end of the involvement continuum, as it takes

a certain amount of involvement to utilize this strategy in the right situation. Supervisors need to recognize these situations and give in when it makes the most sense to do so.

12. The judge conflict strategy is in the middle of the assertiveness and involvement continuum. As its name implies, this strategy involves evaluating the conflict and making some kind of determination about which side of the conflict is right and which is wrong. This is a role a supervisor or coach may frequently find they are playing. As would any good judge, in these situations, you must remain as impartial as possible and make decisions based solely on the facts and circumstances of the situation. Also, explaining your rationale for making such judgments can be important to those involved, causing them to more readily accept your decision.

13. Negotiating typically involves each side giving something up to reach some sort of compromise concerning the desired outcome each expects or wants. As a supervisor or coach, you may find yourself playing the role of a mediator in a conflict. This sort of process is the best way to resolve a situation at work because it is perceived to be the fairest way to deal with a problem.

14. Finally, the strategy highest on the assertiveness and involvement continuums is cooperating. When everyone cooperates, they are trying their best to find acceptable ways to resolve conflicts and problems at work. They are totally engaged in the conflict resolution process and are open to all ideas and suggestions in order to resolve any conflicts that may exist. Having a cooperative attitude can resolve even the most difficult conflicts that may exist in the workplace. Perhaps one of the greatest advantages of creating an engaged workplace is that it often comes with a more cooperative spirit throughout that is supportive of this type of strategy toward resolving any problems in the workplace.

KEY POINTS

◆ The nine strategies—reject, confront, cooperate, resist, judge, bargain, retreat, give in, and ignore—on the conflict management matrix represent a wide range of possible ways to effectively deal with conflict.

DEBRIEF

Emphasize the importance of participants who can use as many of these conflict resolution strategies as possible in the many different conflict situations in which they may find themselves in their roles. Suggest that by keeping this matrix someplace where they can readily refer to it when they find themselves in challenging conflict situations can help them more consciously evaluate and determine what the best strategy is to use in each situation.

Content Module 9.20—Conflict Comfort Zones

Each person has natural ways of dealing with conflict, or has conflict comfort zones. These are similar to back-up styles that people naturally revert to when faced with a conflict situation. The lesson helps participants identify their own conflict comfort zone and how to learn to be more versatile when dealing with conflict in the future.

TIME

◆ 20 minutes

MATERIALS

◆ PowerPoint presentation *Conflict Comfort Zone Matrix.ppt* (in the on-line materials)

◆ Assessment 10.2—Conflict Comfort Zone Self-Assessment (10 minutes)

◆ Pen or pencil for each participant

AGENDA

◆ Display *Conflict Comfort Zone Matrix.ppt*.

◆ Begin lesson by explaining that each person has natural conflict resolution strategies that she may use over and over. This is their *conflict comfort zone.*

◆ A problem is created when these particular approaches are not appropriate for every situation.

◆ The point is that the more flexible or versatile you can be concerning how you deal with conflict, the better able you will be to avoid or reduce the amount of conflict experienced on the job. This could be called your *conflict versatility.*

◆ Also, the more versatile you can be in using these different approaches to dealing with conflict, the better able you will be in managing conflict in your life.

◆ By better understanding and helping others to become more versatile in dealing with conflict with one another, employees will be better able to channel their energies toward solving problems in the workplace.

◆ Facilitate Assessment 10.2 Conflict Comfort Zone Self-Assessment (chapter 10) (10 minutes).

◆ Review Key Points.

KEY POINTS

◆ Each person has natural ways of dealing with conflict or has her own conflict comfort zone. These are back-up styles that people naturally revert to when faced with a conflict situation. The lesson helps participants identify their own conflict comfort zone and how to learn to be more versatile when dealing with conflict in the future.

◆ To help participants become more versatile in the way they deal with conflict at work.

DEBRIEF

Conclude the lesson by challenging participants to move out of their conflict comfort zone the next time they have to deal with a conflict situation and evaluate the results. Ask the group what they might expect will happen.

Content Module 9.21—Conflict Role Play

A role play is conducted involving two employees who are presently having difficulty getting along with each other at work. In the role play, the participant playing the part of the supervisor intervenes to help these employees resolve their difficulty working together.

TIME

◆ 30 minutes

MATERIALS

◆ Handout 11.4—Supervisor Prompt (chapter 11)

◆ Handout 11.5—Employee A Prompt (chapter 11)

◆ Handout 11.6—Employee B Prompt (chapter 11)

AGENDA

◆ Facilitate Structured Experience 11.4—Conflict Role Play (30 minutes).

◆ Review Key Points and Debrief.

KEY POINTS

◆ There is more than one perspective concerning conflicts that employees may experience when working together.

◆ Participants get practice playing the role of the supervisor and employee as they resolve conflict at work.

DEBRIEF

Discuss how different people can perceive the same thing in such different ways. Share with the group (if they haven't already realized) that Employee A's script and Employee B's script are exactly the same and prove it if necessary by showing doubters the role play scripts. Ask the group to think about other examples of how different perceptions of the same issue can cause potential conflicts at work. Ask the group for their thoughts on how better understanding of these different perspectives can help people resolve and even prevent conflicts like the one in the role play from recurring in the future.

Content Module 9.22—Dealing With Upset Employees

Dealing with an upset employee can be a critical moment in the supervisor/ employee working relationship. The importance of acknowledging the upset employee's emotions at that moment and demonstrating empathy for the employee are reviewed.

TIME

◆ 20 minutes

MATERIALS

◆ None

AGENDA

1. Introduce the lesson by explaining that one of the most challenging situations a supervisor faces is that of dealing with an upset employee. Regardless of the reason that the person might be upset, there are a number of supervisory and coaching skills that need to be utilized to effectively manage these types of situations.

2. There are certain ways to more effectively deal with upset employees that you need to understand.

3. First and foremost, it is important to deal with an upset employee in a respectful and professional manner even if she is not doing so with you. However, this doesn't mean that an employee may not be held accountable for her inappropriate or even disrespectful behavior, but rather that a supervisor should not respond in a similar manner.

4. You need to keep in mind the best interests of the employee, the entire workgroup, and the whole organization when dealing with these situations. You should be mindful that because of the highly emotional state the employee may presently be in, she may not be totally aware of the environment in which she is expressing her frustration. Thus it is important if this situation is occurring in a location that is visible or audible to other employees or even customers, you direct the employee into a private area.

5. Throughout your interaction with the upset employee, you have to keep in mind the needs of everyone else in the organization as well. You don't want to satisfy one employee's complaint only to cause other or bigger problems. Consequently, you don't want to jump too quickly to promising solutions to the upset employee to mitigate her issue at the expense of everyone else that you supervise. In other words, be careful not to promise or make commitments to an upset employee that you may not otherwise agree to or that is inconsistent with your organization's policies.

6. Explain that there are certain needs that an employee has when upset or in a highly emotional state. How you handle these situations can have significant long-term consequences on the employee for the rest of her career.

7. Point out that whatever the problem is for an employee, it likely is the most important thing happening in her life at the moment. How you handle the problem may have a significant effect on this employee's attitude about the company for the rest of her career.

8. Ask participants how they would describe a really angry or upset employee who feels that something unjust has just happened to her and whether they have ever been faced with such a situation. What did they do at that moment to try to deal with the angry employee?

9. Ask if this is a time to try to have a rational conversation with someone when they are really upset or mad about something, and if they have ever tried to talk rationally to someone who is really mad. The obvious answer is "no," that this is not a time when you should even attempt to discuss the rationale or justification for the person being so upset at the moment.

10. This is a time to let an upset employee vent her frustrations, but in an acceptable manner. If an upset employee is beginning to act inappropriately or even disrespectfully, she should calmly be told that her behavior is becoming unacceptable and if you are going to try to help with the situation, she needs to behave in an appropriate manner. In more extreme circumstances, the upset employee may need to be

reminded that if she continues to act in a disrespectful or inappropriate manner, discipline could result.

11. Explain the steps that a supervisor should take when dealing with an upset employee in such a situation.

Dealing With an Upset Employee
   a. Allow the employee to vent. It is most important to someone who is really upset to express their emotions, which at the moment may be more important than the issue she is upset about in the first place. Making statements such as "I can see that you are really upset about this" acknowledges the other person's feelings.

   b. Avoid making any snap judgments. This is not the best time to begin expressing any opinions about how justified you think the employee's anger is or whether she was treated unfairly. This is the time to simply listen without affirming or denying the person's emotions.

   c. Try to understand exactly why the employee is angry, as it may not truly be what she initially tells you is the reason. This may not always be easy, especially if the person is in a highly emotional state.

   d. Try to look at the issue from the employee's perspective to understand why she is feeling this way at the moment. This may give you a better understanding of why the employee is really upset.

   e. Ask participants what they believe the word "empathy" means. It means that you try to understand how someone else feels. This is not the same as agreeing with someone else's actions or behaviors. Empathy is nonjudgmental. Empathy is conveying to another person, "I know how you feel" and simply means that you are trying to understand how a person feels and what she is experiencing at the moment.

   f. Showing empathy for employees is important to building trust, especially in this type of situation.

g. As mentioned, it is very difficult to have a rational discussion with someone when that person is in a highly emotional state. Thus it would typically be better to suggest another time to talk once the employee has calmed down a bit. This subsequent meeting could be later that day or on another day, but scheduling another time to talk is usually much more productive than attempting to have any kind of meaningful discussion on the issue when the employee is in this highly emotional state of mind. You could even leave the employee alone for a few minutes or however long it might take for her to be able to more rationally discuss the matter.

h. During the subsequent meeting, assure the employee that you are interested in helping her deal with the problem if possible.

i. Ask for additional information or clarifications concerning the problem.

j. Listen for any differences between what she may have told you the reasons were that she was so upset about during your initial meeting, as often the story will change when the person has a chance to think more rationally. Don't immediately confront the employee or accuse her of changing her story or even of lying to you, but try to understand why the reasons the employee is upset are being presented differently. You could ask the employee to explain these differences, but again it may be best to do so without accusing her of being untruthful to you earlier. Remember that the employee was highly emotional earlier and that things may look quite different now that she has calmed down. Your primary goal is to find out what really is occurring that upset the employee so much.

k. Provide support to the employee in resolving the problem, suggesting other resources as appropriate, that may be available either within the organization or may be outside support services in the community.

KEY POINTS

- ◆ It is important to deal with the upset employee's emotions at that moment and demonstrate empathy for the employee.

- ◆ Use tips and advice on how to deal with an upset employee in the most effective and proactive manner.

DEBRIEF

Advise participants not to promise confidentiality that they may not be able to honor. Discuss what should happen if the employee tells you that she wants what she tells you to be confidential. Explain to the employee that in order to deal with her complaint, you may need to get other people involved, but that you will only tell others what you must in order to deal with the problem. Also explain that as a supervisor, you have a responsibility to report certain types of information that you receive so you can't promise confidentiality concerning some things the employee may tell you. However, there may be things they tell that can be kept confidential and personal, and any commitments of this kind should always be honored.

Content Module 9.23—Definition of a Complaint

Participants are presented with a definition of a complaint and are provided tips on dealing with employee complaints more effectively.

TIME

◆ 15 minutes

MATERIALS

◆ PowerPoint presentation *Definition of a Complaint.ppt* (in the online materials)

◆ PowerPoint presentation *Complaint Handling Steps.ppt* (in online materials)

AGENDA

1. Begin the lesson by explaining that supervisors who learn to better deal with complaints can build stronger working relations with employees.

2. Continue the discussion by emphasizing just how important a work-related complaint is to an employee, particularly at that moment.

3. Display *Definition of a Complaint.ppt* to participants and review:

   Definition of a Complaint
   A complaint is any condition an employee thinks or feels is unjust or inequitable from her perspective. Even though a complaint may be seen from a very different perspective by other people (including yourself), this does not diminish the importance of it to the person who has the complaint.

4. Ask participants this question relating to employee complaints: "Who do you think that an upset employee will tell about the problem bothering her at work?"

5. The most likely answer to this question is—*anyone who will listen!*

6. Remind participants that an employee's work-related complaint may be all she is thinking and talking about, not only to co-workers, but also to friends and family. It is probably the most important thing

in that person's life at the time. This is even more reason to address employees' work-related complaints in a responsive but also timely manner.

7. Display *Complaint Handling Steps.ppt* and present each of the six steps as follows, starting at the bottom and moving up each step.

Complaint Handling Tips

1. Listen

   ◆ Emphasize that the first step in dealing with an employee's complaint must be to keep an open mind about this person's issue. Don't prejudge or jump to conclusions too quickly. Remember that you need to go through a process before you make any decisions concerning the employee's complaint and possible resolutions. The employee or someone else could tell you something related to this issue that could change your mind.

   ◆ Try to put the employee at ease while listening to her complaint. Be careful that your attitude, including your body language, isn't conveying the message that you either don't care or have already made up your mind about what you are going to do or not do concerning the employee's complaint.

   ◆ Don't interrupt, or do so only when absolutely necessary to get the information you need from the employee. Let the employee express her feelings as long as it is done appropriately. If the employee is not behaving in an appropriate manner, tell her that she is expected to do so or this meeting will not proceed. Tell the person firmly that there are consequences of continuing to behave in such an unacceptable manner.

   ◆ Don't argue with the employee or challenge the facts of the circumstance at this point in the process. Let the employee tell you exactly what she wants to say. Take notes if appropriate.

◆ Don't jump to problem solving too soon, especially before you have heard everything the employee wants to tell you about her complaint. This would be like going to a doctor and having her write you a prescription before you have told her about your symptoms.

2. Get the story straight.

◆ Get the other person's viewpoint and all the contributing factors that led up to the employee coming to you with the complaint. Get the names of anyone else that may have knowledge or may have contributed to the employee's complaint. Get times, dates, locations, and so forth of events that may have contributed to the complaint. Make sure that you are hearing what the employee is actually upset about, remembering that it may not always be what she initially tells you. If you don't get to the true root cause of the complaint, then you will not be able to address or resolve the problem.

◆ Restate the complaint to the person's satisfaction in order to ensure understanding. This can go like this: "Let me see if I really do understand what you are telling me— you are concerned because you didn't get the promotion that was recently posted, and you feel that the person who was selected was not as qualified as you are for the job. Do I understand you correctly?" If you heard and understood the complaint and have repeated it correctly, the employee will tell you that you got it right. If not, the employee will correct what she feels isn't correct. Repeat the process until the employee agrees that you do understand her complaint. This way the employee will at least feel that you understand what she is so upset about, and this also allows you to know that you indeed understand the complaint.

3. Investigate.

◆ Investigate the employee's complaint. Talk to other people who may have been involved in the issue. Hear both sides of the story, particularly if the employee is complaining about someone else in the organization. Gather all the facts that you can related to the matter, including any policies or rules that may govern the decision or outcome of the issues at hand.

4. Decide.

◆ Based on your investigation of the employee's complaint, you need to make a decision about what if anything needs to be done. Many times, there isn't anything that can or should be done about an employee's complaint and this is at least an answer the employee is entitled to hear. It is also very possible that was all the employee expected to hear in response to her complaint. However, it is important to make some kind of decision concerning the complaint, even if the decision is to do nothing. Not addressing or even ignoring the complaint entirely will likely only make the employee's issue worse for that individual and may cause your working relationship in the future to suffer.

5. Take action.

◆ If some action is required, either refer the problem to the appropriate person, or immediately deal with it yourself. Communicate any decisions concerning the complaint as soon as possible.

◆ Any remedies to the complaint should also be acted upon as quickly as possible. If there is going to have to be a delay, explain this fact to the employee. Avoid making a snap decision, but don't delay and do explain why there is a delay if there is one. It is important to keep in mind that taking action is the most important thing to the employee. Even if you only can take some first steps, make sure the employee is aware that you have begun the process. Communicate any follow-up actions as necessary to those who will be responsible for carrying out these actions.

6. Follow up.

◆ Explain to participants that follow-up to a complaint is the part of the process that is too often overlooked and where this process often fails. It is important to follow up to ensure that what was agreed upon gets done as expected. This doesn't always happen without some follow-up taking place.

◆ Suggest that it may be a good idea to contact the employee after a few days to ensure actions agreed upon were taken.

KEY POINTS

◆ Supervisors need effective tools and definitions of employee complaints in order to deal with them effectively.

◆ Use tips and tools that are presented to help with this key supervisory role.

DEBRIEF

End the lesson by again emphasizing just how important addressing employees' complaints and concerns is to creating a workplace environment based on employee engagement. Employees become disengaged quickly when they don't believe that anyone listens to or cares about their concerns. Going through complaint handling steps such as the ones presented in this lesson shows employees that as a supervisor, you do care about their concerns and will address them when possible or appropriate to do so.

Content Module 9.24—No Complaints

Participants are asked whether it is a good situation if a supervisor doesn't receive any complaints from supervisees.

TIME

- ◆ 10 minutes

MATERIALS

- ◆ PowerPoint presentation *Is It Good If.ppt* (in the online materials)

- ◆ PowerPoint presentation *No.ppt* (in the online materials)

AGENDA

1. Display slide *Is It Good If.ppt* and begin lesson by asking the question on the slide: "Is it good if a supervisor doesn't hear or receive any complaints?"

2. Ask participants if they agree or disagree that it is good and why they feel this way.

3. Expect to hear responses from participants that they don't believe this would be a good situation.

4. Display *No.ppt* and read it to the group, confirming that the answer to this question is "NO."

5. Review the possible reasons why a supervisor may not be hearing any complaints as described on the handout:
    - ◆ the supervisor may have walled herself away from employees

    - ◆ become too easygoing, too firm

    - ◆ been impatient with complaints that seemed unjustified

    - ◆ retaliated against complainer in the past

    - ◆ not acted upon the complaints

6. Ask participants what other reasons they can think of that a supervisor may not be hearing any complaints.

KEY POINTS

◆ The fact that no complaints are received does not mean that employee complaints do not exist.

DEBRIEF

Again assure participants that there will always be issues and complaints at work as a natural part of people working together. How the supervisor or coach responds to complaints is of the greatest importance, not the fact that she receives complaints. Again, not hearing any complaints is not a good thing, particularly for the reasons presented in the handout.

Content Module 9.25—Unsettled Complaints

The lesson describes how employees might react if their complaints are not adequately addressed, the consequences of this dissatisfaction, and why and when a complaint should be elevated to the next level.

TIME

- ◆ 15 minutes

MATERIALS

- ◆ PowerPoint presentation *Employees Reaction to Complaints.ppt* (in the online materials)

AGENDA

1. Begin the lesson by asking participants, "What happens if an employee's complaint is not adequately addressed and what then can the employee do?"

2. Display *Employees Reaction to Complaints.ppt* to participants and review.

3. Discuss these various alternatives that an employee might have if her complaint is not addressed.

4. Review the following points:
   - ◆ In response to an unresolved complaint, the employee might simply adjust to the situation and just live with it, may continue to complain, or may take some kind of action to elevate the complaint.

   - ◆ It is perhaps more likely that the employee will just live with her frustration of not getting any resolution to the complaint. This may cause the employee to be dissatisfied, to worry or brood about the problem, to be less trustful of supervision, and to become disengaged.

   - ◆ Employees can take the problem to someone else in the organization or outside the company, such as a government agency. The Equal Employment Opportunity Commission or equivalent state agency will allow an employee to file a charge of discrimination or seek legal counsel to file a lawsuit against the organization.

5. Display the next slide, *Passing a Complaint Up,* to participants and review the following:

◆ The employee might alternatively go to someone else at a higher level in the organization or utilize the organization's formal complaint process if one exists.

◆ Ask participants why a supervisor might be reluctant to pass a complaint up to someone higher in the organization.

◆ Ask if they believe that this happens because someone might be afraid that the complaint might make them look bad in the eyes of their boss or other members of management.

◆ Ask participants what additional problems might be created by not passing a complaint on up.

◆ Discuss why it is that employees want their complaints heard by higher officials in the company. They want to ensure that their issue is heard by those who might be in a position to address their concerns.

KEY POINTS

◆ The lesson describes how employees might react if their complaints are not adequately addressed and the consequences of this dissatisfaction, as well as why and when a complaint should be elevated to the next level.

◆ To show how employees might react when their complaints are not addressed by their supervisor.

DEBRIEF

Conclude the lesson by reminding participants that there will always be complaints. What is most important is how they deal with complaints. Sometimes the best way to deal with a complaint is to pass it on to a higher level, especially when it involves things that may not be in a supervisor's direct control, such as policy enforcement or interpretations.

Content Module 9.26—Complaint-Handling Quiz

A brief quiz is provided for participants to test their understanding of how to deal more effectively with employee complaints.

TIME

+ 20 minutes

MATERIALS

+ Assessment 10.3—Complaint-Handling Quiz (chapter 10)

+ Pencil and paper for participants

+ PowerPoint presentation *Decisions are Best.ppt* (in the online materials)

AGENDA

+ Facilitate Assessment 10.3—Complaint-Handling Quiz (20 minutes).

+ Use the following information for your discussion:

Complaint-Handling Quiz

1. When confronted with an upset employee, a supervisor should:
   a. Listen to what the employee has to say

   b. Allow the employee to vent some of her anger and emotions

   c. Schedule another follow-up meeting after the employee has had a chance to express what she wanted to say at another time

   d. All of the above

2. Empathy means trying to understand how another person feels about something important to her. Showing empathy does not necessarily mean you agree with the person about the issue or complaint.
   True or False?

3. Answer Yes or No if you believe that the following are examples of showing empathy.

YES_____ A supervisor listens carefully to the concerns that an employee has expressed without criticizing or becoming defensive.

NO_____ A supervisor tells an upset employee that she is wrong to feel the way she does and to get over it.

YES_____ A supervisor asks an employee how she feels about a recent decision that was made that had a possible negative effect on that person.

YES_____ A supervisor is confronted with a very angry employee who begins shouting about a decision that was recently made. The supervisor listens to what the employee has to say and then suggests that this might not be the best time to discuss this problem. The supervisor schedules a time later in the day when they can discuss this matter.

4. Which of the following would be the best thing to say to an upset employee?

"I don't care how you feel about the decision; you will just have to live with it like everyone else around here!"

"I understand how you feel about the situation, but we still have to follow the established procedures. I also understand that you are upset about this decision."

5. Do you agree with the following statement? Why or why not?

How a supervisor deals with an upset employee could be a determining factor in how that person feels about the company for the rest of her career.

YES, how a supervisor deals with an employee's complaint can determine the level of trust and respect that the employee has for the supervisor for the rest of her career with the company or organization.

KEY POINTS

- ◆ Using a consistent approach to assessing and answering employee complaints helps ensure a more satisfactory outcome.

DEBRIEF

The questions are intended to be easy to answer and their main purpose is to create a discussion on the issues presented in each question. Facilitator should ask participants why they selected the answers they did and share any experiences they may have had concerning these issues as they relate to employee complaints.

Content Module 9.27—Resolving Employee Complaints

The ultimate goal of dealing with an employee complaint is discussed in this lesson.

TIME

- ◆ 10 minutes

MATERIALS

- ◆ PowerPoint presentation *A Coaches Goal.ppt* (in the online materials)

AGENDA

1. Display *A Coaches Goal.ppt* and read to participants.

2. Ask participants what they feel is the meaning of this statement.

3. Allow discussion concerning what the possible meanings of this statement might be.

4. After discussion, explain or reiterate that supervisors need to look at an employee's complaint as something that may be valid and needs to be addressed rather than something that should not be paid serious attention. Elaborate that to some supervisors, acknowledging or giving an employee's complaint serious attention is like a "win" for the employee because she had a legitimate complaint. Supervisors need to avoid taking complaints personally or as an affront to their leadership and authority. Instead, complaints should be viewed as an opportunity to deal with an issue that is important to an employee. This helps build trust and respect, as employees feel that their supervisor is approachable and will take corrective action when appropriate to do so, regardless of any personal issues that might exist between the employee and her supervisor or coach.

KEY POINTS

- ◆ The goal of addressing an employee complaint is to deal with the issue, not necessarily "win" the complaint.

DEBRIEF

Explain that denying or ignoring employees' complaints would actually be the opposite of "winning" these complaints. In this circumstance, the supervisor will lose trust and respect and will end up with more disengaged instead of engaged employees.

Content Module 9.28—Causes of Poor Performance

Three major reasons for poor performance are presented: lack of communication, lack of conditions, and lack of consequences. Strategies for addressing each of these causes of poor performance are discussed during the lesson.

TIME

◆ 15 minutes

MATERIALS

◆ PowerPoint presentation *The Reasons for Poor Performance.ppt* (in the online materials)

AGENDA

1. Begin the lesson by asking participants what they believe to be the major reasons for poor employee performance. It is likely that you will hear responses that relate to employee motivation or even work ethic. Acknowledge that this may be true if you hear this response, but suggest that there may be other reasons that have more to do with the workplace environment than with employee motivation. In most cases, employees respond to the work environment that is created for them and come to work each day wanting to do a good job. The principles and concepts of employee engagement are based on these assumptions.

2. These three reasons for poor performance may be why this might not always happen and addressing these factors can improve employee performance overall.

3. Display *The Reasons for Poor Performance.ppt.*

4. Use the following outline to lead a discussion on these three factors that influence employee performance.

   Lack of Communication
   - ◆ Employees don't know what is expected of them.

   - ◆ Lack of clear individualized communication and direction.

 ◆ There is a lack of feedback.

 ◆ There are "mixed messages" concerning rules.

Lack of Conditions
 ◆ Employees need more help to succeed.

 ◆ Need more time to get job done.

 ◆ They need more tools/resources.

 ◆ They need more training.

Lack of Consequences
 ◆ Employees see that nothing happens one way or the other.

 ◆ They see no rewards for good work.

 ◆ They see no repercussions for poor work.

5. The first of these factors is *communication.* Explain that employees need to clearly understand what is expected of them by their supervisor or coach. If asked, most employees will say that they are not always clear exactly what their supervisor does expect of them. They need to receive clear individual communication and direction from their supervisor that pertains specifically to them and how they are expected to perform their job. Part of this communication is the need to receive feedback (both formal and informal) about how they are performing their job. This feedback needs to be the proper balance of reinforcement and opportunities for improvement, again specifically tailored to the employee's performance. This communication also needs to be clear and consistent. When there is a lack of consistency, employees receive a "mixed message" that says one thing but then does another concerning what is expected of them. This only serves to confuse employees.

6. The second factor is a *lack of conditions,* which can include such things as employees having the proper training or instruction to be able to perform the job, having the necessary tools or resources to do the job, or even having enough time to perform the job properly.

7. Finally, there need to be *consequences,* both positive and negative as appropriate, based on an employee's job performance. Too often, there are no consequences (either positive or negative) associated with an employee's job performance. This can give an employee the false impression that no one cares how she performs the job. This is counterintuitive to what employee engagement is all about. Employees need to understand the importance of their job as it relates to other employees' jobs, and that it must be performed properly. Even the smallest of details can be extremely important when it comes to meeting the goals of the organization as a whole, and each employee's contribution is important.

KEY POINTS

◆ Three major reasons for poor performance are discussed: lack of communication, lack of conditions, and lack of consequences.

◆ Strategies for addressing each of these causes of poor performance are also discussed during the lesson.

DEBRIEF

To conclude the lesson, challenge participants to remind themselves of these three points when dealing with employees' poor performance.

Ask yourself:

◆ Did I clearly communicate what I expected from this employee?

◆ Does the employee have the knowledge and training needed to complete this task?

◆ Have the consequences of the employee's behavior or performance been made clear?

Content Module 9.29—5-Step Performance-Correction Process

A 5-step performance-correction process is introduced that helps supervisors understand how to proceed when dealing with an employee's performance problem.

TIME

◆ 15 minutes

MATERIALS

◆ PowerPoint presentation *5 Step Performance Correction Process.ppt* (in the online materials)

AGENDA

1. Begin the lesson by explaining that how a supervisor addresses performance problems has a lot to do with how successful her efforts are to correct the problem.

2. By following this 5-step performance-correction process, participants can ensure that they are addressing the issue at hand in the most proactive and supportive manner as possible.

3. Introduce the 5-step performance-correction process by distributing or displaying the slide *5 Step Performance Correction Process.ppt*.

4. Review each of these five steps by reviewing the following example of a supervisor or coach correcting an employee's performance:

    Step 1—Observe—Supervisor states what she observes, in this case, the work wasn't completed when she came back at the end of the workday as expected it to be.

    > Supervisor: "Joe, I thought you would be able to complete this assignment well before the end of the day. We talked about this assignment this morning and you gave me no indication that you thought this was going to be a problem."

    Step 2—Discuss—Listen to the reason the employee gives for not getting the work completed.

Employee: "I thought I was going to be able to get the work done, but we had problems with the system all day and it caused one delay after another. I just couldn't seem to keep the job moving ahead all day."

Step 3—Correct—Tell the employee what you would have wanted her to do next time she is faced with a similar problem.

Supervisor: "Next time this happens, let me know right away so I can have you work on some other project that isn't as dependent on the system working properly. There are other projects just as critical that I would have had you work on if I had known you were experiencing this problem."

Step 4 –Advise—Give the employee directions on how to correct the problem next time just in case she may run into obstacles while following your direction.

Supervisor: "Just in case you don't see me right away, either page me or call my cell phone to let me know so I can get you working on something else right away."

Step 5—Confirm—Make sure that the employee clearly understands what you expect her to do the next time she is faced with this or a similar situation.

Supervisor: "So let's make sure you understand what you should do next time this happens."

Employee: "Sure, next time I am experiencing problems with the system, I will let you know right away. I wasn't sure that you would want me to call or page you under these circumstances because I know how busy you always are, but I will from now on."

"Supervisor: "Yes, that's exactly what I would like you to do. I'm glad we got a chance to clarify what I want you to do next time something like this happens."

 ## KEY POINTS

◆ Supervisors must understand how to proceed when dealing with an employee's performance problem.

◆ A 5-step performance-correction process is offered to help the
process.

DEBRIEF

Discuss with participants how they can utilize this 5-step approach in a manner and style most comfortable to them. It doesn't matter if they follow these
steps exactly, but most important is the concept of making clear what you
expect as a supervisor from employees and following up to ensure that there is
an understanding of these expectations.

Content Module 9.30—Setting Performance Standards

Participants are asked what message they are really sending to employees if they allow poor performance to go unchallenged or unaddressed.

TIME

◆ 10 minutes

MATERIALS

◆ PowerPoint presentation *2Basic Rules About Managing Performance.ppt* (in the online materials)

AGENDA

1. Introduce this brief lesson by explaining to participants that as supervisors, they have the right to expect nothing less than excellent performance from employees.

2. Display *2Basic Rules About Managing Performance.ppt* and share the following basic rules about managing performance:

   2 Basic Rules About Managing Performance
   1. Always expect excellent performance.
   2. Never let poor work go unnoticed or performance issues go unchallenged.

3. Emphasize the importance for participants to never let poor work go unchallenged.

4. Ask participants what message letting poor work go unchallenged sends to employees.

5. The answer is that the unintended message may be that this level of poor performance is acceptable.

KEY POINTS

◆ Supervisors need to set the performance standard for employees to reach on their jobs.

◆ It is important for supervisors not to allow poor performance to go unchallenged or unaddressed.

DEBRIEF

Discuss how other employees feel about co-workers being allowed to do poor work if they are working hard to do the job properly and the effect that this can have on employee morale as well as employee engagement.

Content Module 9.31—Discipline Role Play

In this role play, an employee is being counseled by her supervisor concerning an absentee problem that has been occurring for the past eighteen months.

TIME

◆ 30 minutes

MATERIALS

◆ Handout 11.7—Discipline Role Play Introduction Handout (chapter 11)

◆ Handout 11.8—Supervisor's Role (chapter 11)

◆ Handout 11.9—Employee's Role (chapter 11)

AGENDA

◆ If possible, use a location in which a supervisor's office can be simulated for role play exercise.

◆ Facilitate Structured Experience 11.5 (chapter 11) (30 minutes).

◆ Review the key points.

KEY POINTS

◆ In this role play, an employee is being counseled by her supervisor concerning an absentee problem that has been occurring for the past eighteen months.

◆ To provide practice to participants in dealing with sensitive employee disciplinary issues.

DEBRIEF

Discuss the issue of administering discipline for absenteeism from both the supervisor's and employee's perspective in such a situation as presented in this role play. Ask the group how they feel about the fairness or justification of disciplining an employee for things that may not be directly under that person's control. Or, on the other hand, can this amount of absenteeism be permitted to go on without being addressed? Conclude the lesson by reflecting that often a supervisor must address issues that may not always seem fair to everyone involved but are still part of a supervisor's responsibilities.

Before concluding the activity, explain that in a real-life situation, such as the one in this role play, the employee should be advised that she should contact Human Resources to see if these absences might be covered by the organization's leave policies or the Family Medical Leave Act or other programs. Also suggest that it would be a good idea for participants to contact their own Human Resources departments for guidance on these programs or benefits that might be available in these types of situations.

Content Module 9.32—Documentation

A 5 Ws model for documentation is presented to help participants think about the most important aspects of documentation each time they need to create this type of written record as part of their responsibilities as a supervisor or coach.

TIME

+ 20 minutes

MATERIALS

+ PowerPoint presentation *The 5 Ws of Documentation.ppt* (in the online materials)

AGENDA

1. Begin the lesson by discussing the importance of creating good documentation of events that occur in the workplace at times, especially for anyone who is in a leadership role in an organization. This is also true when it comes to how a supervisor or coach deals with employee performance or disciplinary problems.

2. The documentation that a supervisor creates becomes a permanent record of the events which occurred and might be used for any number of reasons at a later date, and could even become the basis for disciplinary action or termination of an employee. This documentation could also become used in the legal system to defend the organization's actions in these types of situations. Thus, for many reasons, it is important that supervisors do a good job in creating documentation and in a manner that meets the objective of creating such a permanent written record of events which occurred at work.

3. Display *The 5 Ws of Documentation.ppt.*

4. Review these 5 Ws of documentation—who, what, why, when, and where.

5. Begin by discussing *who* is going to see this documentation. Advise participants that they should assume that every time they create any form of documentation concerning an employee, particularly some-

thing concerning a disciplinary issue, they should assume that this will be seen by someone else and perhaps even used in a future legal proceeding of some kind. Thus it is very important that a supervisor only include in any documentation that she would want to be seen by others. Participants should ask themselves when creating such documentation, "Would I want this document blown up and presented as Exhibit A in a court proceeding?" Advise participants that every document they create should be made with this standard in mind.

6. Next discuss *what* should be and shouldn't be included in the documentation. A supervisor's documentation should only include the facts concerning what happened in a particular situation you are creating the document to record or include actions that were taken as a result of the event. Opinions, comments, personal feelings, or unsubstantiated information should not be included in this documentation—just the facts as they pertain to the situation and events that occurred. Some organizations have specific forms for documenting disciplinary actions that help supervisors record the right information in accordance with the company's policy. If these exist, advise participants to be sure to use these forms. Explain to participants that the documentation they create will most likely be the only permanent record of the events which occurred. Sometimes documentation is not reviewed again until years later, so it is important to create a record that clearly explains what happened at the time. In many ways, the documentation is like a snapshot of the event for someone to see again sometime in the future. Make sure that it is an accurate picture of these events.

7. Discuss *why* a supervisor should create documentation of an event that has occurred. What would the circumstances be in which such a document might need to be created? As mentioned, whenever an employee is being disciplined, a written record should be created to record the reason(s) for future reference or when an employee needs to be terminated, the reasons and circumstances that led to this need to be recorded. However, there are other times and circumstances that could warrant documentation. For example, when a supervisor believes something that occurred may become a future problem. It might also be when dealing with an employee who has had problems in the past, but the current situation doesn't rise to the level of discipline at the time. It may also be when someone else needs to know

what actions the supervisor may have taken, or something unusual occurs that is not covered by policies or rules.

8. The next step in this model is *when* you should create documentation. Obviously, the sooner the better after the event has occurred. The greatest benefit of documentation is that it captures the circumstances and events that have just occurred. Waiting too long to create this documentation can cause critical information to be lost forever. Participants should make it a habit to sit down and document events as soon as possible after the event they are recording occurred rather than relying solely on memory to capture the facts of the situation or circumstance. Also, *when* exactly the event or situation occurred (the precise time and date) should be clearly documented.

9. The last thing to think about concerning documentation is *where* you are going to store this document as well as how long. Obviously, you will want to keep the document in a location where you can find it if needed at a later date and in a secure location. This may be in the employee's personnel file depending on your organization's policies or record retention guidelines that may exist.

KEY POINTS

◆ The 5 Ws model helps participants understand how to create better documentation as part of their job as supervisors or coaches.

DEBRIEF

As you conclude the lesson, remind participants that documentation is an important part of any coach or supervisor's job. Documentation can have an historic significance as it can provide a solution to a current problem by understanding what was done in past similar situations. Documenting your actions also lets others know what you've done, either showing a consistency in the actions you have taken or indicating how something is being done differently and why. Remind participants that they should direct any specific questions concerning documentation issues to their organization's Human Resources department. Also, their organization may have specific policies on electronic record keeping that you should also make sure are understood. How are they stored? Participants should check within their organization for policy guidance on this subject.

Content Module 9.33—Documentation Role Play

A role play involving a supervisor and an employee who has an attendance problem is observed by the group and then each participant is asked to create documentation about this meeting.

TIME

* 30 minutes

MATERIALS

* Handout 11.10—Role Play Script—Supervisor's Part (chapter 11)

* Handout 11.11—Role Play Script—Employee's Part (chapter 11)

* Handout 11.12—Role Play Documentation Example (chapter 11)

* Paper and pencil/pen for each participant

* Simulated office environment for role play (two chairs in front of room will suffice)

AGENDA

1. Explain that in this lesson, two participants will enact a role play involving a supervisor and an employee who is currently having an absentee problem.

2. Ask for volunteers (or select participants) to play each of these roles.

3. Facilitate Structured Experience 11.6—Documentation Role Play (30 minutes).

4. Review Key Points of the exercise.

KEY POINTS

* Provides participants practice in creating documentation.

* Documentation is an important part of ongoing dialog between a supervisor and an employee.

DEBRIEF

Ask participants how they feel this documentation example could be helpful, particularly if this absenteeism with the employee continues in the future. The answer is that this documentation could be very useful in the event of future problems with this employee's absenteeism. Conclude the lesson by again emphasizing the importance of supervisors creating good documentation concerning significant events that occur in the workplace. As shown in this example, this documentation doesn't have to be extensive, just be sure to cover the important points that occurred. In this role play example, the documentation was only a page long but provided all of the pertinent facts that may need to be reviewed at a later date.

Note: Please see Content Module 9.32 for more information on creating effective documentation and consider reviewing or presenting it prior to this lesson.

Content Module 9.34—Performance-Improvement Process Plan

An example of a Performance-Improvement Process Plan (PIPP) is presented. During the lesson, the objectives, design, and implementation of performance-improvement process are reviewed.

TIME

+ 45 minutes

MATERIALS

+ PowerPoint presentation *Reasons for Performance Problems.ppt* (in the online materials)

+ Handout 11.13—Performance-Improvement Process Plan (chapter 11)

+ Handout 11.14—Performance-Improvement Process Plan (chapter 11)

AGENDA

1. Begin the lesson by discussing that sometimes there is a need to address an employee's poor job performance in a formal manner. One way to address this need is to utilize a PIPP in which the employee is formally counseled that her performance is unacceptable and must improve or some consequence will occur, possibly even termination of her employment.

2. Explain to participants that in this lesson, an example of a PIPP will be presented. Before presenting the PIPP form, including a completed example that will be used in the role play, review the following about using such a plan and when it may be most appropriate and necessary. First review some of the possible reasons for poor performance as described below:

3. Display *Reasons for Performance Problems.ppt.*

Reasons for Performance Problems
+ Job fit

+ Motivation

◆ Ability

◆ Training

◆ Job itself

◆ Supervision

◆ Other reasons?

◆ Facilitate Structured Experience 11.7—Performance-Improvement Process Plan (chapter 11) (30 minutes).

◆ Review Key Points.

KEY POINTS

◆ A Performance-Improvement Process Plan (PIPP) is necessary to address poor job performance and provide a structured way toward improvement for the employee.

DEBRIEF

Conclude the lesson by commenting that if a manager does a good job managing poor performance, one of two things will happen:

1. Goal is achieved. The performance will be improved and there is a win/win result.

2. The manager has helped support a defensible and documented case for termination.

In either case, you have addressed the poor performance and brought it to resolution. This is much more desirable than simply allowing poor performance to go unaddressed or without consequence. Following such a process as this not only documents poor performance and efforts to help the employee improve her performance, it also eliminates reasons or excuses for poor performance or the claim by an employee that "I was never told what was expected of me!" It is also the fairest way to deal with employee performance problems.

Again remind the group that a process such as the one described in this lesson is not the answer to every employee performance problem. It should only be utilized when there is a reasonable expectation that it can be successful in improving an employee's poor performance. In some cases, such as when the employee just doesn't have the ability to perform the job satisfactorily, other alternatives should be considered to deal with this type of problem, such as reassignment to a different job, layoff, or termination of her employment. Remind participants before making any decision to place an employee on a PIPP or discipline up to and including discharge that they should seek the advice of their Human Resource or legal department in their organization.

Content Module 9.35—Performance-Improvement Process Plan Role Play

The same PIPP templates are utilized in this lesson as the previous one (lesson 34). In this lesson, teams of two participants are assigned either the role of supervisor or employee. Each participant is provided background information for her role to review before this exercise begins. The participant playing the role of supervisor will present and review the PIPP to the participant playing the role of the employee.

TIME

◆ 30 minutes

MATERIALS

◆ Handout 11.14—Performance-Improvement Process Plan (chapter 11)

◆ Handout 11.15—PIPP Role Play Background-Supervisor (chapter 11)

◆ Handout 11.16—PIPP Role Play Background-Employee (chapter 11)

◆ A private area for each two-person team to conduct role play

AGENDA

1. Facilitate Structured Experience 11.8—Performance-Improvement Process Plan Role Play (chapter 11) (30 minutes).

2. Review Key Points.

KEY POINTS

◆ Participants gain practice with the Performance-Improvement Process Plan (PIPP).

◆ Learners gain experience from both the employee and the supervisor point of view.

DEBRIEF

Discuss the fact that in the employee's role play background, there were instructions that this person wasn't in complete agreement with what was to be presented to her on the PIPP. Ask the group how significant a factor this might be in the actual implementation and results of such a plan. Expect to hear comments that if the employee isn't committed to the success of the plan, the likelihood of its success will be significantly less. Part of the challenge of any supervisor presenting such a plan to an employee is to help that person under-stand the seriousness and eventual consequences of not accepting ownership for the success of the performance-improvement process.

Content Module 9.36—A World Without Feedback

The importance of feedback is emphasized using a sports analogy in which participants are asked to envision participating in a sport without any feedback on their performance. Different levels of feedback are presented and discussed.

TIME

+ 15 minutes

MATERIALS

+ PowerPoint presentation *Levels of Feedback.ppt* (in the online materials)

AGENDA

1. Introduce the lesson by emphasizing the importance of feedback, in any activity that someone might engage in, day-to-day or even pursuing their favorite pastime.

2. Explain that we all learn from feedback. Without feedback, we wouldn't be able to know if we are doing things right or wrong. Everyone needs feedback to grow and develop both personally and professionally.

3. Ask the group how many are golfers. Acknowledge anyone who responds and ask them in particular to envision the following scenario.

4. Present the following scenario called Blindfolded Golf. Read the following to participants:

   Blindfolded Golf

   Just think what it would be like to receive no feedback at all about how well you did things.

   Imagine what some of your favorite activities might be like without feedback, such as playing a round of golf.

   What if every time when a golfer went to hit the ball, that she was blindfolded and couldn't see where it went? How do you think the golfer would be able to perform during this round?

What if the golfer wasn't allowed to keep score during the round? Or what if the golfer's score was sent to her in the mail at the end of the quarter or calendar year?

How would these things affect the golfer's ability to improve her performance during that round or even subsequent rounds if this blindfolding process would continue?

5. As you read this description of blindfolded golf, allow participants to have some fun with this different version of the game of golf. Expect to hear statements that their golf would probably be better if they didn't see the results of the shots!

6. Emphasize the importance of getting feedback right away. Ask how much good it would be to get your score for holes you played that day in the mail a month or later. Would that help you play golf that afternoon? Ask how much a golfer would really enjoy the game without these types of immediate feedback being part of the experience.

7. How does this relate to the way we often get feedback about our performance at work?

8. Just like the golfer, employees need immediate feedback on their performance.

9. They need to know their *score* concerning how well they are performing their jobs in real time.

10. They also need to receive this feedback on an ongoing basis and not just once a year.

11. Discuss how often the group thinks that those who work for them want to receive feedback about their work performance. Can you give someone too much feedback? Go back to the golf analogy and ask the golfers in the group how they feel when someone constantly tries to correct or change their golf swing during the round. Finding the right balance of feedback is something that requires some thought and consideration. Different people have different needs concerning feedback. Tailoring the amount of feedback that participants give to those who work for them is something that each supervisor should work toward achieving.

12. Continue the lesson by stating that *feedback is key to learning in all of life.* The purpose of feedback is to promote learning and thus enhance performance. Coaching is a process which includes giving employees feedback and helpful suggestions that will allow them to grow and develop in their jobs.

13. Display *Levels of Feedback.ppt,* which shows four levels of feedback that an employee might receive from her supervisor:

Levels of Feedback

   ◆ None at all

   ◆ Negative only

   ◆ Positive only

   ◆ Balanced

Point out that each is better than the previous one. Begin the discussion by pointing out the possible problems with each one except the last one—balanced feedback.

14. Ask participants what problems are created if an employee receives no feedback at all about her performance. Unfortunately, this is all too common of an occurrence in many workplaces.

15. Display the second slide in *Levels of Feedback.ppt* slide set, which reads:

The Default Performance Feedback System

   "If you don't hear anything, you are doing just fine. But if you screw up, we'll let you know!"

16. Suggest that this default feedback system is what, unfortunately, many employees work under. Ask participants what problems are created by such a system. Expect to hear responses such as the employee won't know if she is performing the job correctly or not, and so will not have any opportunity to grow if there is no feedback, or it simply isn't fair to hold someone accountable for things that you never discussed with her. If not brought up by the group, review these possible problems with this lack of performance feedback.

17. Next discuss what happens if an employee only receives negative feedback, also a common occurrence in many work situations. The obvious problems that this situation creates include affecting the employee's self-esteem, creating a negative work environment, lack of reinforcement to motivate the employee, and the supervisor creating a poor working relationship with the employee.

18. Ask participants what happens if an employee only receives positive feedback, assuming there are also negatives that should be discussed. The problem is that if employees don't hear about those aspects of their job performance that are lacking, they won't be able to address these problems and grow in their jobs and careers. In many ways, a supervisor is doing an employee an injustice by not communicating where the employee needs to improve and only telling her the positives about her performance. Often, it is this type of feedback that is the hardest to hear that can ultimately be the most beneficial to an employee's growth and development on the job.

19. Balanced feedback, which is an appropriate amount of both positive and negative information provided to the employee, is the optimum level of feedback an employee should receive from her supervisor or coach. Balanced feedback means that the person receives both positive and constructive feedback on how she can improve performance. The ratio of positive to negative should be determined by the employee's actual performance, but there should typically be much more positive than negative feedback presented to the employee. Typically an employee's strengths are first presented and then any areas that she could possibly improve in should be reviewed in a constructive developmental way.

KEY POINTS

- ◆ Feedback is important to people in any situation in life, including in our jobs.

- ◆ This module asks participants to envision participating in sports without any feedback on their performance.

DEBRIEF

Tell the group about a management philosophy that was practiced for many years, but fortunately is no longer recommended. It was called the "Sandwich Technique," which suggested that you start by telling the employee something positive, then insert any negative feedback in the middle of the discussion, and then end with something else positive. The thinking at the time was that the negative feedback would be more readily accepted if inserted between the positive comments. In reality, all this approach may do is confuse the employees and have them leave the discussion not knowing if they were being commended or reprimanded. Ask the group what they think of this "sandwich technique." This is different than balanced feedback, in which both types of feedback are presented independently and at different times. Balanced feedback doesn't try to minimize any negative feedback an employee receives by immediately presenting something positive.

Ask participants to share some of their experiences providing balanced feedback to employees and how to best present each type of feedback. Ask the group if the common practice of putting any areas of improvement at the end of a formal counseling or appraisal session is really the best way to present this information. Is there a better way to provide this type of balanced feedback?

Content Module 9.37—Formal and Informal Feedback

Formal and informal feedback are defined and discussed, with guidance provided on when each type of feedback may be most applicable and beneficial.

TIME

◆ 10 minutes

MATERIALS

◆ PowerPoint presentation *Types of Feedback.ppt* (in the online materials)

AGENDA

1. Begin presentation by displaying *Types of Feedback.ppt*.

2. Review the definitions of both types of feedback.

3. Explain that formal feedback is typically provided as part of the organization's established performance appraisal system or process. Formal feedback is usually provided annually, and sometimes with midyear update reviews. There is usually a standard form that is required by the organization and an evaluation system that requires supervisors to rate each employee. This rating typically determines such things as the amount of raise an employee may receive for the past performance year, bonuses, consideration for promotions, or even disciplinary actions if rated below acceptable levels of performance. The formal performance evaluation form is usually kept in the employee's personnel file for some prescribed period of time as an official company document, according to the organization's policies and procedures for record keeping. Participants should check with their Human Resource department for guidance on their organization's policy. (See Lesson 40 for an example of a performance evaluation document).

4. Next explain that informal feedback is not typically documented, but is usually presented verbally by a supervisor to an employee. The best coaches do a good job providing this informal or day-to-day feedback and direction to employees.

5. There is no limit on the amount of informal feedback that a supervisor can provide to employees, and it could be as frequent as daily. Informal feedback can be positive or may address any performance issues that might need correcting. Informal feedback doesn't have to take a lot of time. It can be just a passing comment or even a thank you to an employee in recognition of completing a job or task. It could also include instruction or guidance on how to perform a particular task more effectively.

6. Ask participants the question, "Which do you think is most important to performance—informal or formal feedback?"

7. Most likely the response will be that you need to have both to effectively provide the right amount and type of feedback employees need to be better able to perform to the best of their ability. A supervisor's goal should be to provide a balance of both formal and informal feedback to each employee who works for her.

KEY POINTS

◆ Formal and informal feedback are defined and discussed. Formal feedback is annually or semiannually documented and informal feedback is provided day-to-day.

◆ Participants are provided descriptions of both formal and informal feedback and the proper applications of both types of feedback.

DEBRIEF

Discuss what happens if either formal or informal feedback is not provided to employees. The answer is that if either is lacking, there will be a serious gap in the feedback that employees receive. Employees want and need to receive both formal and informal feedback. Each should support the other. If a supervisor provides regular informal feedback to an employee, then there should be no surprises at the end of the year when the formal feedback includes how the individual's performance is rated for that year. Informal feedback should also be an extension of the formal feedback process, reinforcing and continuing the topics presented during the employee's annual performance review.

Content Module 9.38—Coaching Time

The question of how much time participants in the lesson should spend coaching their employees is presented and discussed during the lesson.

TIME

- ♦ 10 minutes

MATERIALS

- ♦ None required

AGENDA

1. Begin the lesson by asking participants how much time they think they should spend coaching their employees on a daily basis. Coaching in this case can be defined as providing some kind of informal feedback (see lesson 37 for definition) to employees under their supervision. This isn't necessarily the same as any time spent interacting with employees but includes the amount of time spent coaching employees.

2. Suggest that they spend at least one hour a day coaching their employees. This one hour is the total time spent each day, not time spent with each employee.

3. Suggest if participants are not already doing so, they should set a goal of spending at least one hour a day coaching their employees. Ask what they believe would be the benefit of achieving this goal.

KEY POINTS

- ♦ The question of how much time participants in the lesson should spend coaching their employees is presented and discussed during the lesson.

- ♦ Spending more time coaching employees is a good investment of a supervisor's time.

DEBRIEF

Expect to hear responses from participants that they don't have enough time in their busy schedules to spend even this amount of time collectively coaching their employees on a daily basis. In response, ask participants how much time developing this work habit might ultimately save them on a daily basis in the future.

Content Module 9.39—Coaching Tips

This lesson provides advice on how to most effectively correct poor performance when observed, as well as how to reinforce effective performance when observed.

TIME

◆ 10 minutes

MATERIALS

◆ PowerPoint presentation *Coaching Performance Tips.ppt* (in the online materials)

AGENDA

1. Introduce the lesson by discussing the fact that how a supervisor or coach corrects poor performance very often determines just how successful she is in helping that person improve her performance in the future.

2. This lesson introduces a simple model for correcting ineffective behaviors in a manner most productive and acceptable to the employee being coached.

3. Display *Coaching Performance Tips.ppt* to participants:

Coaching Performance Tips
1. Observe and assess the specific job performance behavior(s) of an employee.
2. Decide whether it is effective or ineffective job performance.
3. If it is effective behavior:
    ◆ Point out what is effective about the behavior.

    ◆ Say why it should be continued and the benefits of doing the job right.

    ◆ Praise or compliment the employee for this effective behavior as appropriate.

Read the following example of a coach pointing out effective behavior to an employee:

Coach: I notice that you always follow the correct procedures for this job every time you perform it. Ensuring that you use the most updated data will ensure you get the results we expect and that the process operates correctly. I appreciate the extra effort you put forth every time to make sure that you perform this job correctly. Thanks.

4. If it is ineffective behavior:
   a. Tell the employee to stop the behavior and explain why it is ineffective.

   b. Explain what an alternative behavior would be and why the alternative behavior would be better.

   Read the following example of a coach pointing out ineffective behavior to an employee:

   Coach: I noticed that you didn't check to make sure that you had the most current information before beginning this part of your job. The problem that this could create is that without inputting the most current information, not all of the results are always going to be accurate, which causes other problems later on. I need you to make sure that there haven't been any changes before you go ahead with the job so we will know in the future that the results are always accurate and up-to-date. Do you have any questions how to do this or where to get the most current information?

5. Reinforce the correct behavior when observed in the future.
   Coach: I have been noticing that you have been consistently following the correct procedures for ensuring that the most current data is entered into the system. This is helping ensure that the process operates correctly and I appreciate you taking the time to do this. Thanks.

6. Review these five steps for addressing both effective and ineffective performance. Emphasize that it is important to not only point out that the employee is doing something wrong but also tell why it is wrong, why it is ineffective to do it that way, what the desired performance is, and why it is better to do the right way. This way the employee understands why you are asking her to change the performance behavior and why it is important to perform the task correctly.

KEY POINTS

- ◆ This lesson provides advice on how to most effectively correct ineffective performance when observed as well as how to reinforce effective performance.

- ◆ Tips on how to correct ineffective performance.

DEBRIEF

Explain that too often, we only point out when we see someone doing something wrong or incorrectly. Explain that we should point out both good and unsatisfactory performance as we see it. The ratio should be at least 4:1, that is at least four positives to every one negative comment.

Content Module 9.40—Performance-Appraisal Role Play

Groups of three participants act in a role play where each is assigned one of the following roles: supervisor, employee, or observer. Each role is given specific instructions and background information concerning their responsibilities during the lesson. After each role play is completed, the observer should provide feedback to the person playing the role of the supervisor as well as to those playing the employees. Participants could also take turns playing each role as time permits.

TIME

◆ 45 minutes

MATERIALS

◆ Handout 11.17—Background Data Sheet—Supervisor's Role

◆ Handout 11.18—Background Data Sheet—Employee's Role

◆ Handout 11.19—Observer's Role Play Responsibilities

◆ Simulated office environment for the role plays to take place

AGENDA

1. Introduce this lesson by explaining that today's workplace is rapidly changing and so too are the roles a supervisor must play. This is especially true in workplaces where the concepts of employee engagement are being introduced and applied. The supervisor must be a coach, counselor, technical expert, teacher, resource person, judge, confidant, quality expert, inventory coordinator, customer relations representative, and disciplinarian, as well as play many other roles.

2. As engaged employees are given greater responsibility and decision-making ability, the leadership challenges for supervisors also increase. In the past, the supervisor's role was one of telling others who work for her exactly what they were to do and ensuring that the work got done. Today, as the concepts of employee engagement are introduced, this role is changing. Supervisors must help employees make decisions on their own, when appropriate, concerning how they can

perform their jobs more efficiently and effectively. Supervisors must lead their employees to become more engaged and to accept more accountability for the results of their work.

3. Facilitate Structured Experience 11.9 (chapter 11).

4. Review Key Points.

KEY POINTS

♦ Groups of three participants act in a role play where each is assigned one of the following roles: supervisor, employee, or observer. Each role is given specific instructions and background information concerning their responsibilities during the lesson. After each role play is completed, the observer should provide feedback to the person playing the role of the supervisor as well as to those playing the employees. Participants could also take turns playing each role as time permits.

♦ To give participants practice and experience in conducting a performance appraisal.

DEBRIEF

Ask participants how effective they feel their role play was in helping this employee improve her performance in the future. Ask those people playing the roles of both the supervisor and employee what they learned from participating in this role play and how they may be able to conduct better performance appraisals in real time in the future. Also, give observers an opportunity to provide comments on what they noted during the role plays that could be beneficial for the group to hear to help them perform this challenging supervisory responsibility in the future.

Discuss how important it is to receive accurate feedback concerning job performance from your supervisor and how it can potentially improve future performance if done effectively. Ask the group what they believe makes the difference between going through the motions of performance appraisals and really providing meaningful information that can help an employee improve her performance.

Conclude the lesson by discussing the importance of follow-up to a performance appraisal. Explain that one of the most important aspects of a performance appraisal is the follow-up, which may need to take place after the appraisal has been completed. This follow-up may need to be on a regular basis or on an intermittent basis between the supervisor and the employee, depending on the situation. Many times, this follow-up is referred to as performance coaching, which is typically more frequent than more formal feedback processes. This type of coaching, designed to support a performance appraisal, helps both the employee and supervisor stay focused throughout the year on the goals and objectives established during the annual or semiannual performance appraisal. It also gives the employee the opportunity to receive regular feedback on how she is performing and progressing toward the goals established during the performance appraisal rather than deferring this feedback until the actual appraisal occurs.

Content Module 9.41—Recognition

Different types of recognition are reviewed in the lesson with a discussion concerning which ones are the most effective.

TIME

- ◆ 15 minutes

MATERIALS

- ◆ PowerPoint presentation *Potential Reinforcers.ppt* (in the online materials)

AGENDA

1. Begin the lesson by asking the group, "What do employees find reinforcing?"

2. The goal of recognition is not only to acknowledge someone for her significant contributions but also to reinforce these behaviors so that they will be repeated in the future.

3. Understanding what your employees perceive to be reinforcement is important to making sure that what you think is reinforcing to employees really is doing what you are hoping to accomplish with the recognition.

4. Explain that sometimes we think we are reinforcing or rewarding someone when we are actually doing just the opposite.

5. Provide examples of when you thought you were reinforcing someone when you actually were doing the opposite. An example might be giving someone the chance to speak in front of a large group as recognition when they are actually petrified of public speaking.

6. Display *Potential reinforcers.ppt*.

7. Ask participants to review this list and place a check mark in front of those that they feel would be perceived as positive rewards for employees they supervise.

8. Once everyone has had a chance to choose the ones they believe would be received as positives in their work group, ask for participants to comment on why they made the selections they did.

9. Emphasize just how important it is to give some careful thought to the effectiveness of your reward and recognition programs. The point is that even the best of intentions can have the opposite effect if you get this wrong. Instead of providing a positive recognition experience, you could actually be creating a punishing experience, one that employees would prefer not to have to repeat. This could be counter to your efforts of creating a more engaged workplace and reinforcing the behaviors you want to see continued in the future.

KEY POINTS

◆ Different types of recognition are reviewed in the lesson with a discussion concerning which ones are the most effective.

◆ To highlight that recognition must be personalized and tailored to each employee's individual needs.

DEBRIEF

Ask participants if they have ever had any personal experiences with what was intended to be a sincere recognition effort having the opposite affect and actually causing a negative reaction? Discuss why this may have happened and how it could be avoided in the future.

One way to prevent this recognition-gone-wrong scenario is to ask employees what they would want to receive as recognition. You might just be surprised how inexpensive and easy it may be to provide these types of reinforcement to employees as a reward for their hard work and accomplishments.

Content Module 9.42—Recognition Role Play

This role-play lesson actually consists of two different exercises about providing recognition for employees. In the first role play, a supervisor presents a group of employees with a formal award for a special project they recently completed. In the second role play, the supervisors present informal recognition to an employee for excellent job performance.

TIME

- ◆ 20 minutes

MATERIALS

- ◆ Handout 11.20—Team Award Presentation (chapter 11) (10 minutes)

- ◆ Handout 11.21—Individual Recognition (chapter 11) (10 minutes)

AGENDA

1. Explain to participants that providing recognition can be tricky.

2. Recognition given incorrectly can actually have a negative effect on an organization if presented improperly or to the wrong recipient(s). Thus it is important that you ensure your recognition efforts are fair and delivered to the right people.

3. Recognition can be formal and involve awards, compensation, job privileges, advancement, and so forth.

4. Recognition can also be informal in the form of a simple "thank you," a mention in front of peers, a cup of coffee or invitation to lunch with the boss, or any number of other things that wouldn't cost a lot of money or need higher-level approval to provide to employees.

5. Facilitate Structured Experience 11.10 (chapter 11) (20 minutes).

6. Review Key Points.

KEY POINTS

◆ This role-play lesson actually consists of two different exercises about providing recognition for employees. In the first role play, a supervisor presents a group of employees with a formal award for a special project they recently completed. In the second role play, the supervisors present informal recognition to an employee for excellent job performance.

DEBRIEF

Discuss the benefits as well as possible problems that can exist when giving recognition to a group or a single employee. Some of these potential problems could be resentment among others who feel that they deserved recognition instead, the intended reinforcement actually being punishing to the recipient if not perceived to be of value or embarrassing, or simply omitting worthy recipients from inclusion in the recognition. Emphasize that despite all of these potential pitfalls, it is still very important to continue to recognize and reinforce employees for deserving accomplishments, even if you don't always get it perfect.

Content Module 9.43—When Teams Are Most Effective

This lesson involves a discussion concerning the appropriate use of teams and when and when not to utilize them in the workplace.

TIME

♦ 15 minutes

MATERIALS

♦ PowerPoint presentation *Deciding When Teams Can Be Effective.ppt* (in the online materials)

AGENDA

1. Introduce the lesson by stating that a great deal of time, money, and energy are invested in teams in many workplaces today. Often supervisors are asked to serve as the leader of these teams as part of their expanding role in the organization. The role of a team leader is to maximize these resources to get the best results possible. As the leader of a project team, it is important to keep in mind just how much the organization has invested in establishing the team you have been assigned to lead. Employees are typically paid for the time they serve on teams, including attending meetings.

2. Learning to lead teams more effectively is a worthwhile goal for anyone in a leadership or supervisory position at work. The ability to effectively lead teams can play an important part in your career development and success in the organization.

3. Utilizing teams to solve problems at work can be an important part of creating a workplace based on employee engagement. However, contrary to some popular opinions, teams are not always the solution to every problem or always the best way to address an issue.

4. Ask participants to think of a time when they may have been part of a team at work that fell short in some manner of achieving the goals or objectives it was assigned. The sponsor of the team probably didn't feel very satisfied that the resources committed to the team didn't yield the expected or desired results. It is also likely that you didn't

feel very satisfied with what that team accomplished, or in this case didn't accomplish.

5. As leader of a team, you need to ensure that the organization gets the greatest return possible on this investment and that the expectations for the team are met. When these goals are achieved, everyone feels good about being part of the team and the project gets completed to the satisfaction of the sponsors of the team.

6. Distribute a copy of Handout 43.0 to participants. Tell the group these are questions that should be asked whenever they are considering establishing a team to work on a project or solve a problem at work.

7. Suggest that before you consider establishing a project team, it is a good idea to check to make sure that the problem or issue that will be the focus of this effort lends itself well to a teamwork approach. There are certain things that should exist before a team is considered as the best way to address a problem or tackle a project that needs to be completed. Review each of the four bullet points outlined in Handout 43.0, elaborating each as follows:

Deciding When Teams Can Be Most Effective

1. *When teamwork can unblock creativity.*
    Teams often come up with more creative and innovative solutions to problems or projects. The collective experience of the team helps find these creative approaches to the issues that need to be addressed. If there isn't any interest in finding more creative or innovative solutions to problems, a team may not be the best way to address the issue or problem.

2. *When there is no obvious solution.*
    There really isn't any reason to form a team if there is only one obvious solution to the problem or issue. You simply don't need to get a group of employees together to decide what could easily be decided by one person. If this is the case, just make the decision.

3. *When team decision-making is most effective.*
    There are many situations where it is best to get the perspective of a number of different stakeholders. This allows more

employees to have a say in the possible solution or recommendations. Each brings a unique viewpoint concerning the problem or issue and represents the interests of those they work closest with on a daily basis.

4. *There is a willingness to accept the team's recommendations.* If you are going to ask a team to make recommendations concerning a problem or issue, there must be a willingness to accept the recommendation of the team. You don't necessarily have to agree with every recommendation of a team, but you do need to listen to what they suggest. Don't ask the team for their recommendations or solutions if you aren't going to at least consider them as viable options. This will only frustrate the team. They want to know if their recommendations will really be listened to by management. Decision parameters need to be established and communicated clearly to everyone involved in the team from the very beginning. As the team leader, you should find out from the team's sponsor exactly what the parameters are of the team's decision-making authority. It should be clear to everyone exactly what the team has been authorized to decide and what they are expected to make recommendations about. The clearer the team's decision-making authority and parameters, the fewer misunderstandings and unmet expectations will follow on the part of team members when the team has completed its work.

KEY POINTS

◆ This lesson involves a discussion concerning the appropriate use of teams and when and when not to utilize them in the workplace.

◆ To describe when the use of teams can be the most productive and effective.

DEBRIEF

Reemphasize the fact that the value of teams and teamwork is undeniable and an important part of creating and maintaining a work climate supportive of employee engagement. As you conclude this lesson, point out again that this presentation is not trying to diminish the usefulness or value of teams, but rather to ensure that they are used when they can be of the greatest benefit.

Content Module 9.44—Reaching Consensus

The meaning and importance of reaching consensus as a team is reviewed during the lesson.

TIME

◆ 15 minutes

MATERIALS

◆ PowerPoint presentation *Definition of Consensus.ppt* (in the online materials)

AGENDA

1. Begin the lesson by explaining that consensus means everyone on the team understands each other's position and feelings about the problem and the solution, and feels that the team should take a particular course of action even though everyone may not personally agree.

2. Continue defining consensus, explaining that it is different than agreement. Agreement implies that everyone feels the same way about something. This is not an easy objective to achieve and might not be possible in many (or even most) situations.

3. People often have very strong beliefs and convictions on just about any topic or problem they may face as members of a team. Reaching consensus is a much more realistic objective.

4. Explain that the concept of consensus is very important in teamwork. Teams must strive to reach consensus on whatever they decide should be the best course of action to take or decision to make. Everyone on the team must be able to at least support the decisions of the group and work toward the team's goals and objective even if they might not personally agree.

5. Everyone on the team must be committed to work toward consensus from the very beginning when the team is established. If team members aren't willing to at least work toward consensus, the chances of the team being successful and reaching its objectives will be greatly diminished.

6. Display *Definition of Consensus.ppt* to participants.

   Team Member's Definition of Consensus

   "This decision was not my idea or even my first choice concerning the decision of the team, but I do agree to support and work toward the success of this decision just as if it were my own."

7. Ask participants how sharing this definition of consensus with teams they lead in the future could help the team become more successful. Expect to hear responses such as this would be a more realistic and practical objective when it comes to the team members working together toward a common goal rather than trying to achieve 100 percent agreement.

KEY POINTS

- ◆ The meaning and importance of reaching consensus as a team is reviewed during the lesson.

- ◆ To introduce the concept of consensus and its importance as it relates to working as a member of a team.

DEBRIEF

Ask participants if anyone has ever personally worked on a team that couldn't seem to agree on anything and how this concept of consensus could have helped that team work together more effectively.

Content Module 9.45—Synergy

First, the definition of synergy is presented. Then participants are asked to complete a brief quiz individually and then work together as a member of a team to complete this quiz. The participants should compare results.

TIME

◆ 10 minutes

MATERIALS

◆ PowerPoint presentation *Synergy.ppt* (in the online materials)

◆ Handout 11.10—Synergy Trivia Quiz for participants (chapter 11)

◆ Pencil/pen for each participant

◆ Space enough for participants to meet and work together in small teams

AGENDA

1. Discuss Key Points.

2. Facilitate Structured Experience 11.10—Synergy Trivia Quiz (chapter 11) (10 minutes).

3. Debrief material.

KEY POINTS

◆ Working together is more powerful than working alone.

◆ Synergy can be a powerful and efficient way to build engaged and productive teams.

DEBRIEF

Ask participants how the concept of synergy could be utilized more often in their workplace and with their employees. What would be the benefit of increasing the amount of synergy in their workplaces and how could this increase employee engagement?

Content Module 9.46—Designing Engagement Into Your Organization

An example of a production measurement system which was actually unintentionally discouraging employees from working together toward a common goal is presented with a discussion about how to prevent this from occurring in participants' workplaces.

TIME

- ◆ 10 minutes

MATERIALS

- ◆ None required

AGENDA

1. Begin the lesson by explaining that one way to establish more engagement is to design it into your organization. This isn't really as hard as it might sound. If you look, you may even find that you have many competitive systems in place that actually inhibit or prevent employee engagement from occurring.

2. For instance, in many organizations there are contests or competitions established that present those who reach a certain goal with rewards such as bonuses, special privileges, recognition, promotions, special assignments, extra time off, and more. When these incentives are designed as a winner-take-all contest, one in which there is one winner or group of winners, there is likely to be less teamwork and cooperation between groups of employees in the organization and thus less engagement. Everyone wants to win the reward, so naturally they won't be motivated to help their competition take away the prize. This is obviously not the ultimate goal of the sponsors who create these contests. They may have believed that they could motivate everyone to perform better if they were striving to win the competition and receive the reward. Unfortunately, it doesn't always work out that way.

3. Share the story of a manufacturing facility where a contest was established that pitted each production crew against the other to see who could produce the most product during the month. Contrary

to what the plant manager really expected to occur, what was actually happening was that each crew did everything they could to keep the other crew from performing better than they did when they took over at shift change. They had no motivation to help the other crews, and in fact the contest provided a disincentive. The result was increased scrap, especially during these shift change times when the oncoming crew, took over the production from the previous crew, which resulted overall in the factory producing fewer products rather than more as a direct result of this contest. The ongoing crew received no credit for the product that was begun during the previous crew, so when they took over, they only wanted to work on that product that they produced from the beginning of the process. To avoid helping the previous crew achieve higher production numbers, they were actually scrapping the previous crew's product that was still in process when they took over the production for their shift. Once the plant manager discovered what was happening, he changed the contest's measurement system from what each crew produced and instead established a production goal for the entire plant to reach as a whole. Under these new rules, crews were motivated to help one another perform more efficiently and productively. Under this new production reporting procedure, they were able to easily reach the contest's production goals established by working together as a team and helping each other increase their production rates rather than competing with each other.

KEY POINTS

◆ An example of a production measurement system which was unintentionally discouraging employees from working together toward a common goal is presented with a discussion concerning how to prevent this from occurring in participants' workplaces.

◆ To describe better ways to support engagement by the design of programs, systems, functions, and more that can encourage or unintentionally discourage engagement in an organization.

DEBRIEF

Conclude the discussion by emphasizing that system design can have a great deal of influence concerning the amount of engagement that exists in an organization. Reviewing your current organization and systems design to see where teamwork and cooperation might actually be limited can help you achieve greater engagement. Suggest that participants take a close look at the organizational structures currently in place in their organization. Are they supportive or do they actually discourage teamwork from happening in the workplace? Ask if anyone would share any real-life examples of system design actually becoming counterproductive, and what was done to correct this problem.

Content Module 9.47—Helping Teams Get Things Done

This lesson provides tips and advice to help participants be better able to help others work together and accomplish their goals as a team.

TIME

◆ 15 minutes

MATERIALS

◆ PowerPoint presentation *Team Leader's Responsibilities.ppt* (in the online materials)

AGENDA

1. Introduce the lesson by explaining that one of the key responsibilities of any team leader is to ensure that the work of the team she is responsible for actually gets done. However, just ordering employees to get the work done is not the most effective way to motivate them or to create an engaged workplace.

2. Display *Team Leader's Responsibilities.ppt*.

3. Review the following explanations of these team leadership responsibilities.

Team Leaders' Responsibilities
1. *Train team members to work together*—As team leader, you need to ensure the members of your team have the training necessary to be productive members of the team. Provide any instruction necessary to ensure they have these skills. It is not fair to ask someone to do a job or task that she has not been properly trained to perform.
2. *Identify potential obstacles*—There are a number of potential obstacles that could interfere with the work of the team. The leader is responsible for dealing with and hopefully removing as many of these obstacles as possible so each employee as well as the team as a whole can do their work. The team leader may need to appeal to top management of the organization to get help in dealing with these potential obstacles, as well as to address any issues within her control.

3. *Suggest procedures or ideas for solving a problem*—The leader should help the team get started by suggesting ways the problem they are dealing with might be solved. The leader must find the right balance between providing guidance and direction to the team and being too dominating. The leader should suggest tasks and goals for the team, but not do all the work of the team.

4. *Help get information*—Information can be critically important to solving problems in an organization, but one needs to know where to go to get this information. The leader needs to help the team find any information they need to resolve their assignment. The leader may need to direct team members where to request data and seek relevant information.

5. *Give input*—The leader should give her opinions concerning issues important to the team. Team members need this guidance to ensure they are moving in the right direction toward accomplishing their task or goals. At critical decision points, the team leader should give suggestions or ideas concerning how the team should proceed. However, the leader still needs to allow the team to make decisions on their own. If not, the talent and experience of the team members are not being fully utilized.

6. *Help the team progress*—The leader needs to pull together related ideas of the members, restate suggestions, and offer a decision or conclusion for the team to accept or reject. The leader should elaborate, interpret, or redirect ideas and suggestions into actionable steps or tasks for the members to perform. The leader should also help clarify points about which there may be confusion, providing explanations why something may not be possible and finding more acceptable alternatives when the team is heading in an unacceptable direction.

7. *Monitor progress*—One of the leader's most important responsibilities is to evaluate progress; set standards for team achievement; establish timetables for reaching goals and milestones; and measure and communicate the progress and results of the team.

8. *Recognize and reward results*—Perhaps most importantly, as the leader, you must recognize the accomplishments of the

individuals and the team as a whole. You need to ensure that participating on the team was a rewarding experience, one that the members would want to experience again in the future. This doesn't have to cost a lot of money. This recognition could be a note or letter, certificate, and so forth, presented to each participant at the conclusion of the team project.

KEY POINTS

- ◆ This lesson provides tips and advice to help participants be better able to help others work together as a team and accomplish their goals as a team.

- ◆ To provide guidance on how coaches can help teams they lead get the work done.

DEBRIEF

Explain that these team leadership responsibilities can help participants in this lesson lead their employees to do a better job and feel more engaged not only when working as a member of a team but also when working together on their jobs as they interrelate with one another.

Content Module 9.48—Dealing With Difficult Team Members

Various descriptions of challenging and difficult types of personalities of team members that can be disruptive to the team's work and progress are presented with strategies suggested for dealing with each of these problem team members.

TIME

◆ 20 minutes

MATERIALS

◆ PowerPoint presentation *Types of Difficult Team Members.ppt* (in the online materials)

AGENDA

1. Begin the lesson by explaining that sometimes certain team members can pose a particular challenge to the team leader. They may be difficult to deal with and at times even disruptive to the team's work and progress.

2. Emphasize to participants that as the team leader, it is their responsibility to effectively deal with these difficult team members, as they can be disruptive to the progress of the entire team. Just ignoring these behaviors may not be the best strategy and may be counterproductive to correcting the problem.

3. The following are brief descriptions of some of the more common characteristics and behaviors of difficult team members, as well as advice on how to deal with each of them.

   The Reluctant Team Member
   How to identify:
   Team member acts like she doesn't really want to participate on the team. This person will avoid assignments and generally not participate in the team's functions and may even tell you that she was forced to be on the team but didn't want to be.

How to deal:

To deal with this type of team member, you should first assure this person that her contributions are important to the team. If you don't see any significant improvement in the person's attitude, then you might ask her to stop being a member. This may shock the person into becoming more participative or it may give her the opportunity to leave if that's what the person really wants. In this case, the team won't be any worse for this person leaving.

The Defiant Team Member

How to identify:

Team member appears to oppose most or all ideas, suggestions, or decisions of the team. This type of individual is one who is constantly negative about everything related to the team. This person may challenge your authority as leader of the team, usually in front of the others.

How to deal:

To deal with this type of team member, you might first talk privately to this individual about her attitude and how it is affecting the rest of the team. Find out if there is a reason for her attitude. Try to determine if there is a legitimate reason for this person's attitude that you could address and correct. You might also challenge this person to come up with other, better ideas and suggestions than yours, and if legitimate, consider adapting with credit given to this person.

If none of these approaches seems to work and you don't see any improvement, you might consider telling this person not to participate any longer on the team if this behavior is too distracting to the progress of the team.

The Dominant Team Member

How to identify:

Team member tries to influence or dominate every discussion or decision of the team. This is another example of a team member that may challenge your authority as the leader, but in a less critical manner. In this case, the challenge is that this person may try to take over your role rather than being overly critical of the way you are leading the team.

How to deal:

This is someone who can potentially be helpful to the team as long as she doesn't dominate everyone else. The best strategy is to find ways to exercise your leadership authority in a way this person can't interfere with. For instance, to ensure that others have a say and role in the team's functions, you could assign roles and tasks to other members one on one without this dominant member present.

After giving specific responsibilities to others, ask them to report back during meetings. If this dominant member tries to get involved during these reports, ask her to give the person assigned the task a chance to present her report. You may want to appeal to this type of team member to not be so dominating and to let others participate more actively on the team.

The Absentee Team Member

How to identify:

Team member doesn't come to meetings, or when present, doesn't participate or contribute in any manner. This is the type of member who either doesn't show up or is not prepared, or doesn't help the team function.

How to deal:

To deal with this type of member, you could set attendance requirements for remaining an active member of the team. This may get the person to come to the meetings but not to participate. You could try to draw this person out with questions or by requesting her feedback during the meetings once she is attending again. Let this person know that her attendance as well as active participation when present is important to the team.

The Vacationer Team Member

How to identify:

Team member seems only interested in getting out of work rather than contributing to the work of the team. This person is usually easy to spot as she is constantly volunteering to join teams, especially ones that meet during working hours.

How to deal:

There are several possible approaches to this type of team member.

This person obviously wants to stay on the team, so setting certain rules for continued team membership could be a good way to get her positively involved on the team. You should also remind the employee that she is still being paid while serving on the team, and this is part of her job while serving on the team. Remind the employee that this is work, not a vacation.

KEY POINTS

- ◆ Various descriptions of challenging and difficult types of personalities of team members that can be disruptive to the team's work and progress are presented along with suggested strategies for dealing with each of these problem team members.

- ◆ To help participants learn to deal more effectively with difficult or challenging members of teams they lead in the future.

DEBRIEF

Conclude the lesson by emphasizing the importance of a leader who deals with disruptive team members' inappropriate behavior in a proactive and constructive manner. Explain that if a leader can turn around the inappropriate behavior of a difficult team member in such a way that it can result in an overall change in that employee's overall attitude and work performance, a disengaged employee can turn into an engaged employee. This can also have a significant positive impact on the rest of the team.

Content Module 9.49—Characteristics of an Engaged Team Player

A list of 10 characteristics of an engaged team player is presented and discussed during the lesson.

TIME

◆ 20 minutes

MATERIALS

◆ PowerPoint presentation *Characteristics of Engaged Team Player.ppt* (in the online materials)

AGENDA

1. Display slide *Characteristics of Engaged Team Player.ppt.*

2. Begin the lesson by stating that in contrast to the descriptions of difficult team members (see Content Module 9.48), more typically you will find that most people are good team players. They will work hard to be positive and productive team members and will want to help the team reach its goals.

3. Explain that sharing these characteristics of engaged team members with your team can help remind and guide them concerning what it takes to be a contributing member of the team.

4. This could serve as a reminder about how team members need to work together, especially when working together gets to be more challenging and difficult.

KEY POINTS

◆ Team members who share feelings, listen, cooperate, show trust and respect, use good decision-making techniques, and seek win-win solutions and consensus are positive forces toward productivity.

DEBRIEF

Suggest that participants might consider posting these characteristics in the meeting room to serve as a constant reminder of how team members should interact with one another when working together.

Content Module 9.50—Creating a Team Project Plan

An example of a team project plan is presented to show how such a plan can help everyone on the team understand her role and responsibilities.

TIME

- 20 minutes

MATERIALS

- PowerPoint presentation *Project Plan Example.ppt* (in the online materials)

- Handout 11.21—Project Plan Example

- Handout 11.22—Completed Project Plan

AGENDA

1. Begin the lesson by explaining how important it is for a team to create a project plan.

2. Review PowerPoint presentation *Project Plan Example.ppt*.

3. Facilitate Structured Experience 11.11 Creating a Team Project Plan (15 minutes).

4. Lead the group through the exercise.

5. Review Key Points (5 minutes).

KEY POINTS

- A project plan helps everyone on the team understand her role and responsibilities.

- A project plan also helps team members stay organized and focused on their objectives and goals.

DEBRIEF

Conclude the lesson by explaining that this project plan should be updated and reviewed during each team meeting by sending it out as regular updates to team members. This will help keep everyone focused on the team's progress toward its goals. This way, each team member understands what follow-up responsibilities she has to complete and by when. This keeps everyone on track and contributing to achieving the team's overall goals and objectives.

Another suggestion would be to also send these updates to others sponsoring or supporting the team. This can serve as a good communication tool concerning the progress of your team to these key stakeholders.

◆ Assessments and Training Instruments

- ◆ Instructions for using assessments and instruments
- ◆ Assessments 10.1 through 10.3

Assessments and Training Instruments

- ◆ Assessment 10.1—Communicating Assignments Quiz
  This assessment provides insight into how well participants assign tasks.

- ◆ Assessment 10.2—Conflict Comfort Zone Assessment
  Participants use this assessment to identify their own conflict comfort zone and how to learn to be more versatile when dealing with conflict in the future.

- ◆ Assessment 10.3—Complaint-Handling Quiz
  Participants gain an understanding of how to deal more effectively with employee complaints.

Many worksheets and data-gathering instruments are available to the facilitator or trainer using this program. This chapter includes assessments and training instruments that rate relevant traits, competencies, and practices, as well as other tools to assist in the learning process.

An assessment differs from a test because the responses to the questions in an assessment are not considered right or wrong. Most of the assessments are designed to increase self-awareness; this process helps participants focus on learning objectives to which they can willingly commit.

Please note that we have included these training instruments for their usefulness, not for their predictive power. They have not been tested for reliability or validity, but they were designed primarily to generate data for action planning and personal commitment, as well as to promote learning about what is important. Participants can use some of the training instruments during the actual learning process.

Assessment 10.1—Communicating Assignments Quiz
INSTRUCTIONS

◆ Provide each participant a copy of the communicating assignments quiz and ask them to spend a few minutes to complete it. Answer any questions they may have about the quiz but tell them not to over-think the questions too much, but to answer them as honestly as they can. Instruct participants to add up the totals of each column and then add all columns for a total final score on this quiz.

◆ After everyone has completed the quiz, present or distribute the scoring for the quiz.

Table 10–1 Communicating Assignments Quiz

	1 point Never	2 points Sometimes	3 points Often	4 points Usually	5 points Always
1. How often do you make your expectations clear when giving an assignment?					
2. Do you make sure that employees have all the information needed to complete the assignment?					
3. Do you give employees a chance to ask for clarification or ask questions about assignments?					
4. Do you explain why it is important to complete the assignment correctly?					
5. Do you tell employees what others will be working on relating to the assignment?					
6. Do you check on employees after giving an assignment to see if they have any other questions?					

Table 10–1 Communicating Assignments Quiz cont'd

7. Do you ask employees for any feedback on the instructions you gave on the assignment, such as "Do you understand what to do based on these instructions?"					
8. Do you ask employees for their input concerning how the assignment should be completed before beginning?					
9. Do you listen to any suggestions employees may have about how the assignment could be completed more effectively?					
10. Do you ask employees if they are comfortable with being able to complete the assignment?					
Add column totals					

Final Score_____

SCORING

10–20	Need improvement in communicating assignments
20–30	Need to work on better communication in assigning work
30–40	Meeting most of the communication needs of employees when assigning work
40–50	Doing a great job communicating assignments to employees

Assessment 10.2—Conflict Comfort Zone Self-Assessment

INSTRUCTIONS

◆ Distribute a copy of *Assessment 10.2 —Conflict Comfort Zone Self-Assessment.*

◆ Ask participants to mark on the *Conflict Comfort Zone Matrix* which quadrant (A, B, C, or D) would best represent how they typically respond to conflict by factoring in both their tendencies to fight or flight and their tendency to use logic or emotion when presented with a conflict situation.

◆ Explain that this matrix could also help their employees better understand how potential work-related conflicts may be resolved in different ways than they may have tried unsuccessfully in the past.

◆ Next ask the participants to complete the second part of the Assessment 10.2—Conflict Comfort Zone Self-Assessment. This should take no more than 5 to 10 minutes.

◆ Ask participants if they would share some of their responses on this self-assessment concerning how their particular conflict comfort zone approach to conflict has served them well and when not so well.

◆ Discuss the advantages of increasing one's conflict versatility and emphasize again that conflict can be resolved in many different ways. Ultimately what is most desirable is to be able to choose the best conflict strategy for a given situation and not just automatically respond according to your natural conflict comfort zone.

◆ Stress that it is important the leaders learn to become comfortable with as many of these strategies as possible and choose which is appropriate for any given situation.

Figure 10-1 Conflict Zone
Assessment 10.2—Conflict Comfort Zone Self-Assessment
Conflict Comfort Zone Matrix

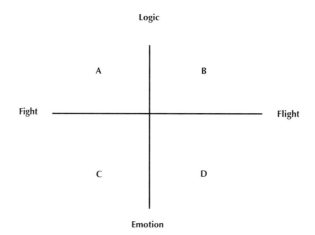

Table 10–2 Conflict Comfort Zone Self-Assessment

How has your conflict strategy and style been useful to you on your job?

_____

_____

_____

In what ways has it served you not so well? What are some examples?

_____

_____

_____

How might a different conflict comfort zone quadrant have been a more appropriate response to the situation you described above and how might have the results been different?

_____

_____

_____

What quadrant would you like to be able to utilize more comfortably in conflict situations and how could you learn to use this approach in the future?

_____

_____

_____

How do you think increasing your conflict versatility by being able to utilize all or most of the quadrants would make you a more effective supervisor or coach?

_____

_____

_____

Assessment 10.3—Complaint-Handling Quiz
INSTRUCTIONS

1. Distribute a copy of the complaint-handling quiz to each participant and ask them to spend a few moments completing the complaint-handling quiz.

2. After everyone has completed the quiz, review each question and discuss the correct answers along with the issues presented in each question.

Complaint-Handling Quiz

1. When confronted with an upset employee, a supervisor should:

    a) Listen to what the employee has to say

    b) Allow the employee to vent some of her anger and emotions

    c) Schedule another follow-up meeting after the employee has had a chance to express what she wanted to say at another time

    d) All of the above

2. Empathy means trying to understand how another person feels about something important to her. Showing empathy does not necessarily mean you agree with the person about the issue or complaint.
    True or False?

3. Answer Yes or No if you believe the following are examples of showing empathy.

    _____A supervisor listens carefully to the concerns that an employee has expressed without criticizing or becoming defensive.

    _____A supervisor tells an upset employee that she is wrong to feel the way she does and to get over it.

    _____A supervisor asks an employee how she feels about a recent decision that was made that had a possible negative affect on that person.

_____A supervisor is confronted with a very angry employee who begins shouting about a recently made decision. The supervisor listens to what the employee has to say and then suggests this might not be the best time to discuss the problem. The supervisor schedules a time later in the day when they can discuss the matter.

4. Which of the following would be the best thing to say to an upset employee?

   "I don't care how you feel about the decision, you will just have to live with it like everyone else around here!"

   "I understand how you feel about the situation, but we still have to follow the established procedures. I also understand that you are upset about this decision."

5. Do you agree with the following statement? Why or why not?

   How a supervisor deals with an upset employee could be a determining factor in how that person feels about the company for the rest of her career.

Chapter 11

Structured Experiences

- Explanation of structured experiences
- Step-by-step instructions for using structured experiences
- Structured Experiences 11.1 through 11.11
- Handouts 11.1 through 11.22

This chapter contains 11 structured experiences to aid your training programs. A structured experience provides step-by-step directions and includes the following elements:

Goals. The learning outcomes that the structured experience is designed to achieve.

Materials. A listing of all materials required to facilitate the experience.

Time. Approximate time to allow for each experience.

Instructions. Step-by-step instructions to facilitate the experience.

Debriefing. Suggest debriefing topics and questions. You can modify these for a particular group of participants.

Structured Experiences

Each of the following designs is self-contained. Although some of the experiences are designed specifically for learning outcomes associated with the module they support, others can be used in a variety of modules associated with them.

- ◆ **Structured Experience 11.1—The Rumor.** This experience explores how rumors spread throughout organizations and the potential impact of rumor mills.

- ◆ **Structured Experience 11.2—Spending Time With Employees.** This experience highlights the importance of a supervisor spending the right amount and quality of time with employees.

- ◆ **Structured Experience 11.3—Conflict Strategies.** This experience explores four conflict strategies that are commonly utilized and discusses these strategies for their effectiveness, some of which are more productive than others but nevertheless are often utilized in dealing with conflict in the workplace.

- ◆ **Structured Experience 11.4—Conflict Role Play.** This experience gives learners practical experience in dealing with conflict and explores roles of both the employee and the supervisor.

- ◆ **Structured Experience 11.5—Discipline Role Play.** This experience provides practice to participants in dealing with sensitive employee disciplinary issues.

- ◆ **Structured Experience 11.6—Documentation Role Play.** This exercise gives participants practice in creating documentation involving a supervisor and an employee having attendance problems.

- ◆ **Structured Experience 11.7—Performance-Improvement Plan Process.** This experience demonstrates the use of a Performance-Improvement Process Plan (PIPP) and why it is necessary to address poor job performance and provide a structured way toward improvement for the employee.

- ◆ **Structured Experience 11.8—Performance-Improvement Plan Process Role Play.** This experience allows participants to practice the PIPP and experience it from both the employee and the supervisor points of view.

- ◆ **Structured Experience 11.9—Performance Appraisal Role Play.** This experience has groups of three participants act in a role play where each is assigned one of the following roles: supervisor, employee, or observer. Each role is given specific instructions and background information concerning their responsibilities during the lesson.

◆ **Structured Experience 11.10—Synergy.** This experience demonstrates how groups of individuals working together are more successful than working alone through the use of a brief quiz.

◆ **Structured Experience 11.11—Creating a Team Project Plan.** This experience demonstrates how a project plan helps everyone on the team understand her role and responsibilities, and offers ways that a complete project plan also helps team members stay organized and focused on their objectives.

The Handouts

Many of the handouts offered here (in the online materials) are part of the content for the activities. Adapt them as needed for your training program.

◆ **Handout 11.1: Part of Structured Experience 11.1— The Rumor.** This handout provides a graphic example of the impact of rumors in organizations.

◆ **Handout 11.2: Part of Structured Experience 11.2— Spending Time With Employees.** This handout uses a hands-on exercise to help participants determine the right amount of time to spend with employees.

◆ **Handout 11.3: Part of Structured Experience 11.3—Conflict Strategies.** These handout uses a dialogue to explore conflict strategies.

◆ **Handouts 11.4, 11.5, and 11.6: Part of Structured Experience 11.4—Conflict Role Play.** These handouts will give participants practical experience in resolving conflict from the supervisor and employee points of view.

◆ **Handouts 11.7, 11.8, and 11.9: Part of Structured Experience 11.5—Discipline Role Play.** These handouts allow participants to gain understanding in how to deal with sensitive employees from both the supervisor and employee perspective.

◆ **Handouts 11.10, 11.11, and 11.12: Part of Structured Experience 11.6—Documentation Role Play.** These handouts allow participants to create relevant documentation and understand both the supervisor and employee perspective.

◆ **Handouts 11.13 and 14: Part of Structured Experience 11.7—Performance-Improvement Process Plan.** These handouts allow participants to use example performance plans and learn a useful process.

◆ **Handouts 11.14, 15, and 16: Part of Structured Experience 11.8—Performance-Improvement Process Plan Role Play.** These handouts add another practical dimension to understanding the PIPP.

◆ **Handouts 11.17, 11.18, and 11.19: Part of Structured Experience 11.9—Performance Appraisal Role Play.** These handouts are part of a highly interactive role play that gives participants real experience in dealing with performance appraisals.

◆ **Handout 11.20—Part of Structured Experience 11.10—Synergy.** This handout graphically shows the power of working together.

◆ **Handouts 11.21 and 11.22—Part of Structured Experience 11.11—Creating a Team Project Plan.** These handouts are part of an exercise which demonstrates how understanding roles is important to successful teams.

Structured Experience 11.1—The Rumor

GOALS

The goals of this experience are to:

◆ Explore how rumors spread throughout organizations.

◆ Demonstrate the potential impact of rumor mills.

MATERIALS

◆ Handout 11.1—Rumors for all participants

TIME

◆ 15 minutes

INSTRUCTIONS

1. Facilitator should tell the group that she is going to begin a rumor concerning a message that was just received from the *main office* of the organization (or appropriate terminology for the organization).

2. The Facilitator should show the first person to receive the message Handout 11.1, which contains the message in written format.

3. After this first person reads the message, the facilitator should take back the written message and instruct that person to verbally tell the person nearest her what the message said. This should be done in a manner in which no one else can hear. This could even be done outside the room if the facilitator chooses.

4. This communication process should continue until everyone in the session has had a chance to hear the message told verbally.

5. If the group is large, the facilitator may choose to go on to some other lesson while this communication exercise continues, instructing the last person to receive the message to let her know the process is complete.

6. Facilitator should ask the last person to hear the message to repeat what she heard. Compare how accurate this is to the original written message shown to the first participant by reading the original message to the group.

7. Discuss the reliability of information typically contained in rumors and how this exercise illustrates what happens to information when spread in rumors. Point out that with time, information being spread throughout an organization as actual rumor would be even less accurate than in this exercise. Rumors spread in a variety of patterns in real situations.

   For example, not everyone who hears a rumor passes it on and others pass rumors on to many other people. However, sooner or later just about everyone participates in the rumor in some manner. Rumors usually begin in the absence of factual information and are born out of the necessity for people to have information. That is why it is important for supervisors to provide accurate and timely information to employees before the rumors take over and fill this information void.

8. Explain that studies have shown types of informal communication such as the "grapevine" or "rumor mill" are about 75 percent accurate at times. At first, this might seem to be more accurate than expected. But just imagine if all the information you received was only 75 percent accurate. What if information you needed for an important report to your boss was only 75 percent accurate? Would that be acceptable? Obviously not.

9. One of the biggest problems with rumors is that many people tend to believe them, sometimes more than the information they receive from their employer. In this case, people are forming opinions and maybe even making decisions based on inaccurate information. Emphasize to participants that as supervisors, their goal should be to be perceived by their employees as a source of accurate and timely information, so that employees don't have to resort to relying on rumors as the main source of information concerning what is going on in their workplace.

DEBRIEF

Allow participants to have some fun and laugh about what just happened in this lesson, as it will be very likely that what the last person heard was very different than the original written message. The larger the group, the more the original message will change as the rumor spreads during this lesson. As facilitator, you might joke that the last sentence of the rumor said that this information should be kept confidential at this time, which only makes it more tempting for some to tell others about it!

Structured Experience 11.2—Spending Time With Employees

GOALS

The goal of this experience is to:

◆ Highlight the importance of a supervisor spending the right amount and quality of time with employees.

MATERIALS

◆ Copies of Handout 11.2—*Spending Time With Employees* for all participants

◆ Pad board or whiteboard, and pencils or pens for participants

◆ PowerPoint presentation *Spending Time With Employees.ppt* (in the online materials)

TIME

◆ 10 minutes

INSTRUCTIONS

1. Distribute a copy of Handout 11.2 to each participant. Display *Spending Time With Employees.ppt*

Figure 11–1

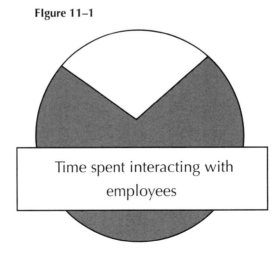

Time spent interacting with employees

2. Ask participants to draw the percentage of their time they spend directly interacting with those who report to them in relation to their total working time on the job. For instance, if a participant estimates that she spends 75 percent of her time interacting with employees, the pie chart would look like the one shown.

3. Draw this example on a pad board to illustrate how participants should complete Handout 11.2.

DEBRIEF

Ask participants if they feel this is the right amount of time they should spend with employees. Ask participants what might be the results of spending more time with those who report to them. Can you spend too much time with an employee? Why or why not?

Structured Experience 11.3—Conflict Strategies

GOALS

The goals for this experience are to:

◆ Explore four conflict strategies that are commonly utilized.

◆ Discuss and evaluate these strategies for their effectiveness, some of which are more productive than others but nevertheless are often utilized in dealing with conflict in the workplace.

MATERIALS

◆ PowerPoint presentation *Conflict Strategies.ppt* (in the online materials)

◆ Copies of Handout 11.3—Conflict Strategies Role Play

TIME

◆ 10 minutes

AGENDA

1. Introduce the lesson by displaying Handout 11.3 and reviewing these four common conflict resolution strategies. Emphasize that although all four may be utilized frequently, some may be more counterproductive to developing and maintaining a workplace culture based on employee engagement.

2. Explain that obviously, Win/Win is the most desirable goal in most conflict situations, but it may not always be possible to reach this level. The other strategies may be used more out of frustration than trying to use the most effective conflict resolution strategy.

3. Review the following **Win/Win** discussion between a supervisor and two employees who are experiencing a conflict at work. You could assign the parts of each of these three brief roles to participants (substituting gender-appropriate names if necessary) in the lesson by copying this brief script and highlighting these three parts for each role player:

Supervisor: John and Frank, I wanted to talk to you both concerning you two have been having a problem working together lately and to come to some kind of resolution concerning this problem. Would that be ok with both of you?

John: Yeah sure.

Frank: Sounds ok to me.

Supervisor: Let me start by asking both of you to explain what the problem is between you two. John, why don't you go first and tell me what is going on from your perspective?

John: Well, I just don't appreciate Frank making changes to my work without telling me first. When he does this, sometimes I don't find out until days later and it causes problems for me because I am working under the assumption that nothing has been changed. This has caused me to have to redo a lot of work recently when I am already struggling to stay on schedule.

Supervisor: Ok, Frank can you comment on what John just brought up?

Frank: Yes. John, first I just want to tell you that I am not intending to make your job any more difficult than it already is. I appreciate all the things you have going on right now and how hard it is to manage everything you have to do. I admit I have made a couple of changes to things you previously worked on but that was only because I had knowledge of other things that you may not have been aware were important to what you were working on. I just went ahead and made these changes when you were gone, intending to bring you up to speed on why they were necessary, but never got a chance to do this before you got back and saw the changes for yourself. I do want to tell you that they were necessary or I wouldn't have made them and I am sorry that I wasn't able to tell you first.

John: I am not disagreeing that the changes weren't necessary or correct— just that I didn't know they had been made.

Frank: Again, I apologize that I didn't make sure you knew about them. I am just so busy myself that I forgot to tell you or thought that I would when I saw you next time.

Supervisor: Ok, I think we all have a better understanding about how and why this occurred. What can we do to prevent this problem from occurring in the future?

Frank: Well, I could set up a procedure that automatically notifies John when any changes are made relating to what he is working on and explaining the reason for the change. Also, I could set it up so that John gets the same updates that I receive so he will know when these types of changes are made. That way he'll know right away about the changes going forward and not be working on old information, and I don't have to try to remember to tell John about each change every time they occur, which has been more frequently lately. I think such a system could be put in place pretty easily.

John: That would be great. There have been many times when I simply didn't know about these types of updates in the past. Receiving these in real time in the future would prevent many problems and rework for me.

Supervisor: Sounds like we have a good solution that will benefit everyone and prevent this type of problem from occurring in the future. Thanks to both of you for being willing to openly discuss this issue and work toward an acceptable solution to each of you.

Review with participants how and why this was a Win/Win solution to this problem, emphasizing how each person gained something as a result of the agreed upon solution.

4. Next discuss what a **Win/Lose** scenario might look like. A Win/Lose situation between a supervisor and an employee might exist when the employee's complaint or request is denied without adequate reason. Review this Win/Lose situation by presenting the following dialog to participants or again assigning role play parts:

    Employee: I would like to talk to you about the assignment you recently gave me. I don't think it's fair that I get stuck with this work when other employees don't do half the things I do. There should be some way to make sure that everyone pulls their weight around here, not just me all the time.

    Supervisor: I am not going to discuss other employees with you or their workloads. I believe that I am always fair in giving out assignments with everyone. The assignment I just gave you is part of your job, not other employees', and I expect you to get it done. If you have any questions about the assignment I will discuss it with you; otherwise you need to get to work on completing this. Do you have any other questions?

Employee: No, I guess not.

5. Next discuss what a **Lose/Lose** scenario might look like. In a Lose/Lose situation, both parties fail to achieve their objectives. The following is a Lose/Lose dialog between a supervisor and an employee:

Employee: I would like to talk to you about some of the problems I am still having concerning my job. It still isn't any better than the last time I talked to you about these issues. If things don't get any better, I am just going to have to quit and find another job, which is too bad, because I would like to keep working here.

Supervisor: Well, I don't really know what else I can tell you or do about it. We have already talked about it several times and I don't have a solution to your problem. I suppose if things aren't getting any better, then maybe you had better move on to another job if that's what you want to do. However, I would hate to see you leave because you do a good job here.

Employee: Well, I guess that's what I am going to have to do.

6. Finally, review what a **Lose/Win** scenario might look like when a supervisor gives in and doesn't enforce the rules by presenting or role playing the following dialog:

Supervisor: I see that you have been late for work again this morning. This is the fifth time that you have been late since the last time we talked about this not that long ago. I told you at that time that this needed to improve, but obviously it hasn't. No one else who works for me has nearly as many problems getting to work on time as you. I told you before if this continues that you would receive a disciplinary notice, and that's what I called you into my office this morning to discuss with you.

Employee: Please just give me one more chance. I promise you that I will stop being late so much. As I told you before, I can't help it sometimes. I know it is against the rules and other employees get upset when I am late and they have to cover for me. I just can't afford to get another discipline on my record or it could cost me my job, which I do need to hang onto right now. You'll see, it will be different this time. I really mean it!

Supervisor: Ok, I will let it slide this one last time. But remember, if you have any more tardiness or unexcused absences, you will receive discipline and whatever consequences may come with it. Do you understand?

Employee: Yes, thank you, and I won't let you down this time.

KEY POINTS

◆ These four conflict strategies that are commonly utilized are discussed and evaluated for their effectiveness, some of which are more productive than others but nevertheless are often utilized in dealing with conflict in the workplace.

◆ The common conflict strategies of Win/Win, Win/Lose, Lose/Lose, and Lose/Win are presented with a discussion on the advantages and disadvantages of each one.

DEBRIEF

Discuss the differences among each of these approaches to conflict. Point out that in certain circumstances, each may be an acceptable strategy, although striving for a Win/Win solution is always the best though not always possible. Ask participants to discuss their experiences utilizing these four types of conflict approaches and the success or lack thereof that they experienced. Finally, ask participants to comment on the last scenario depicting a Lose/Win situation between the supervisor and the employee who was continuously tardy for work. Ask the group if there was ever a situation in which they found themselves tempted or actually did use this conflict strategy and what the results were. Ask the group what they think the chances are this employee will be tardy for work again in the near future. The answer is there is probably a very high likelihood of this occurring again, and the supervisor who doesn't enforce the rules will only make the situation worse.

Structured Experience 11.4—Conflict Role Play

GOALS

The goals of this structured experience are to:

- ◆ Give learners practical experience in dealing with conflict.

- ◆ Explore roles of both the employee and the supervisor.

MATERIALS

- ◆ Handout 11.4—Supervisor Role for all participants

- ◆ Handout 11.5—Employee A for all participants

- ◆ Handout 11.6—Employee B for all participants

TIME

- ◆ 30 minutes

INSTRUCTIONS

1. Introduce the role-play scene as that of a meeting between two employees who have not gotten along with one another at work for some time. Read the general background to participants as follows:

   Conflict Role-Play Background

   In this role play, there are two employees who for years have not gotten along with each other. This conflict has at times caused some problems, but basically has been tolerated by everyone in the workplace. They have been kept as far away from one another as possible to prevent this conflict from flaring up on a daily basis. However, today, with the concepts of engagement being introduced in to the workplace, these two individuals must work more closely together and share information with one another. This of course has resulted in renewed problems between these individuals that presently are causing a major problem in the workplace.

   There seems to be a personality conflict between these two employees that has existed for many years. They both are very strong-willed in-dividuals who take a great deal of pride in their work. Recognition for good job performance is important to each of them. They both have their own way of performing their job and both do good work. They even sometimes appear to compete with one another to see who could do the job the best. The situation has gotten to the point where other employees are concerned that this conflict is interfering with the entire group's effort to work together effectively as a team.

Today, their supervisor plans to sit down with both these individuals and have them begin to resolve their problems.

2. Divide participants into groups of three. Assign at random the parts for employee A and employee B and supervisor to each person in each group. If the group size doesn't divide evenly in threes, you could serve as the supervisor's role, assign two supervisors to a group, or just ask one of the participants to be an observer to one of the role plays. Allow them time to read their role-play instructions.

3. Note that both employee A's script and employee B's script are ex-actly the same. Do not disclose this to any of the participants in the role play at this time.

4. After participants have had time to review their parts, announce that they are to sit down to try to resolve their differences and inability to work together.

    Provide a location in which each trio of participants can conduct the role play in relative privacy. This could be in a corner of the training room or in an unused office or lobby area.

5. Ask the supervisor role players to try to help these two make commit-ments to get along better in the future.

6. Provide these instructions to those playing the supervisor role:

    As you know, these two employees do not get along very well and this situa-tion has existed for a number of years, although as you understand it, they were actually friends one time long ago. Each employee has the potential of contributing to the success of the entire team, but only if they can get past this conflict they have with one another, as it has the potential of interfer-

ing with the teamwork in your entire group. This is something about which you should remind each of these individuals as you conduct this coaching session with them. As supervisor in this conflict role play, encourage each employee to express to one another what she feels is the real reason for their conflict. Encourage them to develop areas of agreement and common goals or objectives. Each employee should seek feedback from the other on how they could improve their relationship and make commitments to change her behaviors to help achieve this goal.

7. Before the role play ends, try to have each employee state her commitment to improving their relationship and schedule a follow-up meeting sometime in the near future to monitor their progress. As well as committing your support, you may also suggest that they ask others on the team for their support in helping these two employees work better together in the future.

8. Monitor the progress of each group as they conduct their role plays. When everyone has completed the role play, reconvene the group to discuss their role-play experience.

9. Ask each supervisor how the role play went from her perspective. Did the supervisor help coach these employees to reach some sort of agreement toward resolving their conflict?

10. Next, ask participants how they feel the meeting went and if they felt that they were encouraged to work together better with less or no conflict in the future.

DEBRIEF

Discuss how different people can perceive the same thing in such different ways. Share with the group (if they haven't already realized) that employee A's script and employee B's script are exactly the same and prove it if necessary by showing doubters the role-play scripts. Ask the group to think about other examples of how different perceptions of the same issue can cause potential conflicts at work. Ask the group for their thoughts on how better understanding of these different perspectives can help people resolve and even prevent conflicts like the one in the role play from recurring.

Structured Experience 11.5—Discipline Role Play

GOALS

The goals of this structured experience are to:

- ◆ Provide practice to participants in dealing with sensitive employee disciplinary issues.

MATERIALS

- ◆ Handout 11.7—Discipline Role Play Introduction Handout for participants

- ◆ Handout 11.8—Supervisor's Role for participants

- ◆ Handout 11.9—Employee's Role for participants

TIME

- ◆ 30 minutes

INSTRUCTIONS

1. Find a location in which a supervisor's office can be simulated for role-play exercise if possible.

2. Read the introduction of the role play to participants.

3. Distribute Handout 11.7, 11.8, and 11.9 to the participants selected to play the supervisor and employee roles.

4. Have the participants begin their discussion on this issue as if it were a real-life situation between a supervisor and an employee.

5. When the role play is complete, ask one of the participants playing the role of the Supervisor to review out loud the seven points that were to be covered during the exercise by the supervisor.

6. Ask participants playing the role of the employee if she felt that these points were clearly addressed during this session.

7. Review the importance of ensuring these types of points are addressed by a supervisor during a counseling session such as this.

DEBRIEF

Discuss the issue of administering discipline for absenteeism from both the supervisor's and employee's perspective in such a situation as presented in this role play. Ask the group how they feel about the fairness or justification of disciplining an employee for things that may not be directly under their control. Or, on the other hand, can this amount of absenteeism be permitted to go on without being addressed? Conclude the lesson by reflecting that often a supervisor must address issues that may not always seem fair, but this is still part of a supervisor's responsibilities.

Before concluding the activity, explain that in a real-life situation, such as the one in this role play, the employee should be advised that she should contact Human Resources to see if these absences might be covered by the organization's leave policies or the Family Medical Leave Act or other programs. Also suggest it would be a good idea for participants to contact their own Human Resources departments for guidance on these programs.

Structured Experience 11.6—Documentation Role Play

GOALS

The goals for this structured exercise are:

- ◆ To give participants practice in creating documentation.

- ◆ To create documentation about a meeting involving a supervisor and an employee having attendance problems.

MATERIALS

- ◆ Handout 11.10—Role Play Script—Supervisor's Part for participants

- ◆ Handout 11.11– Role Play Script—Employee's Part for participants

- ◆ Handout 11.12—Role Play Documentation Example for participants

- ◆ Paper and pencil/pen for each participant

- ◆ Simulated office environment for role play (two chairs in front of room will suffice)

TIME

- ◆ 30 Minutes

INSTRUCTIONS

1. Explain that in this lesson, two participants will enact a role play involving a supervisor and an employee who is currently having an absentee problem.

2. Ask for volunteers (or select participants) to play each of these roles.

3. Distribute Handouts 11.10, 11.11, and 11.12 to appropriate participants.

4. Provide a copy of the role-play script to the participant playing the part of the employee and the participant playing the role of the supervisor. Note that each script is designated for each of these roles, but understand that each script is exactly the same. The main difference is that the speaking part for each role is highlighted in lightly shaded grey to keep each role player focused on her role.

5. Instruct the group watching the role play that they are to document this meeting as if each participant was the actual supervisor providing this counseling to the employee and as if it were their meeting.

6. Instruct the role players to conduct the counseling session, which should only take a few minutes to complete. Once completed, ask the role players to join the rest of the group and ask everyone to create their documentation of this meeting. Allow enough time for everyone to complete this assignment.

7. After everyone has completed their documentation, ask for volunteers (or just ask certain participants) to share what they wrote down to create a record of this counseling discussion between a supervisor and the employee. Give several participants a chance to share their documentation, noting any additional points that may have been included by each subsequent volunteer.

8. Display or distribute a copy of Handout 11.12, which is a suggested example of how this discussion might be best documented.

9. Make sure you highlight the following points in your review of this example documentation:

   a. Date—It is important the correct date of the meeting be included on the document for future reference of when this meeting occurred.

   b. Time—Recording the actual time of the meeting provides additional background that may be useful in the future when this document is reviewed again, such as if the meeting was early or late in the day, how the meeting may have related to other events occurring on that same date, the frame of mind that the employee may have been in during the meeting, and so forth.

   c. The first sentence of the document itself states that the supervisor called the employee into his office to discuss her absenteeism. This establishes where and why the meeting was held.

   d. Describing the employee's behaviors gives a future reader of the document insight into the employee's attitude and mood during the meeting. Instead of just describing the employee as being upset, the document further elaborates exactly what behaviors were observed during the meeting, thus supporting the supervisor's perception about the employee during the meeting. This makes this observation more of a fact than an opinion. The document also makes the point that the supervisor avoided being brought into an argument by the employee. Again, this is an example of a statement in this documentation that could be used to dispute a possible claim made later by the employee that the supervisor was argumentative with him during the meeting.

e. The document captures the accusation that the employee made concerning the treatment of her by the supervisor. The document goes on to deny that this accusation is true and records what was said to the employee in response.

f. The point that the employee tried to make about not being paid was recorded as well as the supervisor's response that there are still costs to the company when she is absent.

g. The document also makes clear what the consequences could be of future absences by the employee. It records that the organization's attendance policy was discussed and in fact a copy of the policy was provided to the employee.

h. The document records that the employee was offered assistance by the supervisor and was referred to Human Resources to see if his absences might be covered by a company-sponsored program or by any regulations such as the Family Medical Leave Act (FMLA).

i. Finally, it is documented that the employee stated she understood what the supervisor had reviewed during the meeting but that she still appeared upset, again possible useful information at a later date. By further describing her attitude toward the issues discussed during the meeting and commitment (or lack thereof) to improving her absentee problem in the future, there is more information to use later as needed.

j. The last sentence states that the meeting lasted about 10 minutes. This information could be useful if the employee claims the supervisor had her in the office for an unreasonable amount of time.

DEBRIEF

Ask participants how they feel this documentation example could be helpful, particularly if the absenteeism with this employee continues in the future. This documentation could be very useful in the event of future problems with this employee's absenteeism.

Conclude the lesson by again emphasizing it is important for supervisors to create thorough documentation concerning significant events that occur in the workplace. As shown in this example, the documentation doesn't have to be extensive, but has to cover the important points that occurred. In this role-play example, the documentation was only a page long, but provided all of the pertinent facts that may need to be reviewed at a later date.

Note: Please see Content Module 9.32 for more information on creating effective documentation and consider reviewing or presenting it prior to this lesson.

Structured Experience 11.7—Performance-Improvement Process Plan

GOAL

The goals of this structured experience are to:

◆ Demonstrate the use of a performance-improvement process plan and why it is necessary to address poor job performance and provide a structured way toward improvement for the employee.

MATERIALS

◆ Handout 11.13—Performance-Improvement Process Plan (chapter 11)

◆ Handout 11.14—Performance-Improvement Process Plan (chapter 11)

TIME

◆ 45 minutes

INSTRUCTIONS

1. After discussing the need to sometimes address an employee's poor job performance in a formal manner (Content Module 9.34), use the slide *Reasons for Performance Problems.ppt* (online materials) and continue the instruction using the following material.

2. Explain that sometimes poor performance may be just a matter of the employee being in the wrong job. Addressing poor performance may be a matter of finding a better job fit to match the person's abilities and talents.

   ◆ Motivation might also be the basis of the problem. In other words, the employee has the ability to do the job, but isn't motivated for whatever reason to do the job correctly.

   ◆ Another possible reason for poor performance is ability. As a supervisor trying to deal with an employee's poor performance, it is important to understand if the basis of the problem is motivation or ability. If it is motivation, a performance-improvement process plan could be the answer to the problem and be successful. If it is a matter of ability, however, a performance-improvement process plan would be far less likely to succeed. If the employee can't do the job, then all the coaching in the world won't correct the problem. It is important to keep in mind that a performance-improvement process plan should only be introduced if there is a chance it can be successful. Otherwise it will be a waste of time and frustrating to both the supervisor and the employee.

◆ Sometimes an employee can't perform a job because she hasn't been properly trained or provided the resources necessary to do the job correctly. If this is the case, then these issues should be addressed and might also be included in the performance-improvement process plan.

◆ It is also possible that you may have a job that realistically can't be performed to the standards expected by you or the organization. In today's world of consolidations and cutbacks, it is possible that the job is too much for any one employee to realistically be able to perform. You need to examine the requirements of the job to ensure it is designed in such a manner that it should be able to successfully be performed by the employee.

◆ Finally, challenge participants to think about if they themselves may be a factor in an employee's poor performance. This could be caused by past problems, personality conflicts, or other working relationship problems that might exist between a supervisor and an employee.

3. Next, discuss when to use a performance-improvement process plan as follows:

    ◆ After the organization's normal performance appraisal and counseling process has not yielded acceptable results

    ◆ After coaching and counseling the employee concerning poor performance has not been successful. Emphasize that a performance-improvement process plan is typically used as a last step before termination for poor performance. This is something that should be told to the employee and will be addressed later on in this lesson.

4. Stress that a PIPP should be supported by documentation of prior poor performance, as poor performers typically challenge you on the facts concerning their performance, and tend to blame others or the system.

5. It is critically important that the responsibility for performance improvement must be placed on the employee—not the supervisor. If the supervisor does all the work during this process, it will ultimately not help the employee. This is the time the employee needs to prove that she can perform the job satisfactorily.

6. Throughout the process, a supervisor needs to keep discussions "behavior based." In other words, the employee needs to hear exactly what she is expected to do to better perform the job. If the employee is better able to understand and even visualize what is expected, she will be much more likely to make the desired changes in her behavior. Telling someone that she needs to change her attitude or improve her working relationships with others is too vague.

7. Confronting poor performance is not easy and is usually uncomfortable, but if you deal with the facts, keep it behavior based, and provide descriptive examples of the problem, the experience usually flows much smoother and may be better received.

8. When presenting a PIPP to an employee, a number of key points should be emphasized so everyone (especially the employee) understands what will happen going forward.

   a. The employee needs to understand that she must improve her performance during the time this process is in place, which is typically two to three months.

   b. Failure to reach an acceptable level of performance in all deficient areas as identified in the PIPP will likely result in the employee's termination.

   c. The employee must make progress toward reaching acceptable performance levels in all deficient areas during this time period or her employment will be terminated before the end of this process.

    d. Perhaps most importantly, upon successful completion of this PIPP, the employee must sustain this level of acceptable performance on her own. As a supervisor, you should make it clear that you will not be willing to repeat this process in the future, as successful completion of the process will demonstrate the employee does have the ability to do the job and any future performance problems will be considered a matter of lack of motivation on the employee's part.

9. Advise participants that as the employee's supervisor, they should be available to help the employee achieve the goals of the PIPP. Again, however, it is important for the employee to realize that she must accept primary responsibility for the success of this plan.

10. The PIPP presented in this lesson consists of six components presented in a chart format:

    ◆ Performance problems (describes the current performance problems)

    ◆ Performance goal (what are the deliverables and expectation of the employee)

    ◆ Support (the assistance that the supervisor will provide to the employee during the process)

    ◆ Timetable (the timeline established for the employee to meet in addressing the performance issues)

    ◆ Follow-up dates (times which the supervisor and employee will meet and review the progress the employee has made)

    ◆ Results (the expected performance and measurement criteria)

11. Distribute a copy of Handout 11.13 to participants, which is a blank copy of a PIPP document. Review each of the six components of the plan. Note that the dates at the top of the plan are important. The first date to be recorded is the time period that this performance-improvement process will be in place. The next date requested is the

initial meeting date when the plan is first presented to the employee. The next dates to record are each follow-up meeting dates the supervisor is planning as part of this process. It is critically important that any commitments made by the supervisor to the employee are followed up on. If not, the process will not be as effective.

12. Next, distribute a copy of Handout 11.14 , which is a completed initial PIPP for a fictional employee: I.M. Lowperformer.

    a. Review how each of these six components of the plan are addressed. Note that this is the first meeting between the supervisor and the employee, so there are no results (unacceptable, accceptable, or improving) listed. These should be completed in each subsequent follow-up meeting held with the employee. Also point out that in this case, the supervisor is planning on meeting with the employee every two weeks during this process. The stated goal during this initial meeting should be that the employee achieves an acceptable rating for each of the deficient areas as described on the plan document. Goals should be expressed in terms that are measurable and able to be expressed quantitatively (in other words, goals expressed numerically such as *zero unexcused absences* or *95 percent completion by end of month*). Failure to achieve this goal should lead to the employee's discharge unless there are mitigating reasons that might lead the supervisor to extend this performance-improvement process timeframe. In addition to completing this form or simply adding to the initial form if in electronic format, the supervisor can attach any documentation as needed to support the performance-improvement process and results.

  ### *DEBRIEF*

Conclude the lesson by commenting that if a manager does a good job managing poor performance, one of two things will happen:

1. Goal is achieved. The performance will be improved and there is a win/win result.

2. The manager has helped support a defensible and documented case for termination.

In either case, you have addressed the poor performance and brought it to resolution. This is much more desirable than simply allowing poor performance to go unaddressed or without consequence. Following such a process as this not only documents poor performance and efforts to help an employee improve her performance, but also it eliminates excuses for poor performance or the claim by an employee that "I was never told what was expected of me!" It is also the fairest way to deal with employee performance problems.

Again remind the group that a process such as the one described in this lesson is not the answer to every employee performance problem. It should only be utilized when there is a reasonable expectation it can be successful in improving an employee's poor performance. In some cases, such as when the employee doesn't have the ability to perform the job satisfactorily, other alternatives should be considered to deal with this type of problem, such as reassignment to a different job, layoff, or termination of her employment. Before making any decision to place an employee on a PIPP or discipline up to and including discharge, remind participants that they should seek the advice of their Human Resource or legal department in their organization.

Structured Experience 11.8—Performance-Improvement Process Plan Role Play

GOALS

The goals of this structured experience are to:

♦ Allow participants to practice the Performance-Improvement Process Plan (PIPP).

♦ Gain experience from both the employee and supervisor point of view.

MATERIALS

♦ Handout 11.14—Performance-Improvement Process Plan for participants

♦ Handout 11.15—PIPP Role Play Background-Supervisor for participants

♦ Handout 11.16—PIPP Role Play Background-Employee for participants

♦ A private area for each two-person team to conduct the role play

TIME

♦ 30 minutes

INSTRUCTIONS

1. This lesson would work best if followed by Content Module 9.34, which goes into more detail about the design and implementation of a PIPP. Facilitator should consider first presenting that lesson before introducing this lesson.

2. Facilitator should familiarize herself with the handouts, especially the roles of the supervisor and employee in the role play, to appreciate the dynamics that may occur as participants play these roles.

3. Begin the lesson by introducing it as a role play involving an employee having a performance problem. Explain that each participant will play either the role of the supervisor trying to coach this employee to improve her performance or the role of the employee having the performance problem.

4. Explain that in the role play, the supervisor is going to present to the employee a PIPP designed to address the performance problems the employee is currently experiencing.

5. Either assign or ask participants which part they would like to play in the exercise.

6. Once determined, provide a copy of the appropriate role-play background information to each participant.

7. Distribute a copy of either Handout 11.15—PIPP Role Play Background-Supervisor or Handout 11.16—PIPP Role Play Background-Employee for participants.

8. Give participants a chance to review their role plays.

9. Provide a private area for each two-person team to conduct their role play.

10. Monitor each group to see their progress in completing the role play; the supervisors review the entire PIPP with the employee and develop an action plan based on this document going forward. Note that because this is the initial meeting between the supervisor and the employee, no evaluation of "meets requirements," "improving," or "unacceptable" is listed on this PIPP. During each subsequent meeting, such an evaluation on each deficient performance area would be listed on this PIPP form.

11. Once everyone has completed the role play, reconvene as a group and ask participants to discuss their experiences during this lesson. As a prompt, you might ask those playing the role of the supervisors to go first, explaining the challenges they may have experienced when presenting this plan to the employee.

12. Next ask participants playing the role of the employee how they felt the role play went and if they understood what was required of them in the future. Ask if they understood what the consequences might be for not meeting the goals presented in the plan and if as a result they would work toward addressing these performance issues.

13. Emphasize that the objective of a PIPP is to help the employee understand exactly what is expected and the possible consequences for not reaching these goals. By utilizing such a plan, this should be very clear to everyone involved in the process.

  ### *DEBRIEF*

Discuss the fact that in the employee's role-play background, there were instructions that this person wasn't in complete agreement with what was to be presented to her on the PIPP. Ask the group how significant a factor this might be in the actual implementation and results of such a plan. Expect to hear comments that if the employee isn't committed to the success of the plan, the likelihood of its success will be significantly less. Part of the challenge of any supervisor presenting such a plan to an employee is to help that person understand the seriousness and eventual consequences of not accepting ownership for the success of the performance-improvement process.

Structured Experience 11.9—Performance Appraisal Role Play

GOALS

The goals of this structured experience are:

◆ Groups of three participants act in a role play where each is assigned one of the following roles: supervisor, employee, or observer. Each role is given specific instructions and background information concerning their responsibilities during the lesson. After each role play is completed, the observer should provide feedback to the person playing the role of the supervisor as well as those playing the employees. Participants could also take turns playing each role as time permits.

MATERIALS

◆ Handout 11.17—Background Data Sheet—Supervisor's Role

◆ Handout 11.18—Background Data Sheet—Employee's Role

◆ Handout 11.19—Observer's Role-Play Responsibilities

◆ Simulated office environment for the role plays to take place

TIME

◆ 45 minutes

INSTRUCTIONS

1. Explain that this role play requires a minimum of three participants to play the parts of the supervisor, employee, and observer. Time permitting, the roles for three individuals could be rotated among participants to give everyone an opportunity to experience each of the responsibilities. For each of the role plays, background information is provided that describes the situation and role each individual is to assume. The observer will be asked to complete a checklist to help provide feedback to the participants after the exercise is completed.

2. Set up a simulated office setting in which a supervisor and employee could conduct a performance appraisal in private. This could be accomplished by simply utilizing a part of the training room separate from other participants or even utilizing unoccupied offices, an available conference room, or any other private area.

    ♦ Distribute Handout 11.17—Background Data Sheet—Supervisor's Role, Handout 11.18—Background Data Sheet—Employee's Role, Handout 11.19—Observer's Role Play Responsibilities to individuals chosen for role play, according to their assigned roles.

3. Set the scene for this role play by explaining the following:

    The scenario for this role play is general in nature. In other words, the work setting and details of the position being evaluated are not specifically identified. You may find it helpful to utilize your own work setting and examples in the roles that each of you will play in this exercise. Feel free to customize this role play as much as you need in order to adapt it to real-life examples that provide you most comfort and familiarity.

    For purposes of this role play, envision a work environment that has been very busy lately due to a number of reasons, but most significantly due to increased business. As a result, everyone's workloads have increased. This has caused a number of employees to have difficulty in adapting to these increased demands. The employee who is being evaluated today has always been regarded as a very good worker but lately has been having some difficulty getting along with her co-workers and working as a member of the team.

    Recently the concepts of employee engagement have been introduced into the workplace and employees have been given more decision-making and problem-solving ability. In this engaged environment, employees have needed to work more closely together, as they are accepting more and more responsibility for both operation of their work area and are becoming more accountable for the actions and decisions concerning their jobs.

    The supervisor has tried a number of different approaches to help employees adapt to this new working environment. It has been an equally difficult adjustment for the supervisor to ensure the work is performed in a quality manner that meets the customer's requirements. In many ways it was easier under the old system, when everyone's roles were more clearly defined. The supervisor told the employees what work they were to do and made most of the decisions concerning how the work was to be performed. The employees performed the work as they were directed and typically had little or no input into how it was to be done. In an engaged work environment, the supervisor must help employees make decisions for themselves concerning how to do their jobs and guide them through the process of becoming more accountable for their work. Most of the employees have adjusted reasonably well to these changes. However, there are some individuals that are experiencing a number of problems with this new working environment, as is the case with the employee being appraised today.

Overall, the quality of the employee's work has not significantly changed, but her attitude about work has become of increasing concern to the supervisor. The supervisor has had several other employees comment on difficulties they have encountered working with this employee. It is evident the annual performance appraisal such as the one to be conducted today will serve as a starting point and some kind of ongoing day-to-day coaching strategy needs to be developed.

4. Immediately after each role play is completed, the observer should provide feedback to the participants concerning how well the objectives of the exercise were met and give suggestions on how they might improve their performance in future real-life performance appraisal sessions. Also, allow discussion from the participants playing the roles of supervisor and employee about what occurred during the exercise and the challenges and effectiveness of the session had it been in real life.

5. Time permitting, have participants change roles and repeat the role plays.

KEY POINTS

◆ Groups of three participants act in a role play where each is assigned one of the following roles: supervisor, employee, or observer. Each role is given specific instructions and background information concerning their responsibilities during the lesson. After each role play is completed, the observer should provide feedback to the person playing the role of the supervisor as well as those playing the employees. Participants could also take turns playing each role as time permits.

◆ To give participants practice and experience in conducting a performance appraisal.

DEBRIEF

Ask participants how effective they feel their role play was in helping this employee improve her performance in the future. Ask those playing the role of the supervisor and employee what they learned from participating in this role play and how they may be able to conduct better performance appraisals in real time in the future. Also, give observers an opportunity to provide comments on what they noted during the role plays that could be beneficial for the group to hear in order to help them perform this challenging supervisory responsibility.

Discuss how important it is to receive accurate feedback concerning job performance from your supervisor and how it can potentially improve future performance if done effectively. Ask the group what they believe makes the difference between going through the "motions" of performance appraisals and providing meaningful information that can help an employee improve her performance.

Conclude the lesson by discussing the importance of follow-up to a performance appraisal. Explain that one of the most important aspects of a performance appraisal is the follow-up which may need to take place after the appraisal has been completed. This follow-up may need to be on a regular or intermittent basis between the supervisor and the employee depending on the situation. Many times this follow-up is referred to as performance coaching, which is typically more frequent than more formal feedback processes. This type of coaching designed to support a performance appraisal helps both the employee and supervisor stay focused throughout the year on the goals and objectives established during the annual or semiannual performance appraisal.

It also gives the employee the opportunity to receive regular feedback on how she is progressing toward the goals established during the performance appraisal rather than deferring this feedback until the actual appraisal occurs.

Structured Experience 11.10—Synergy

GOALS

The goals of this structured experience are to:

◆ Demonstrate how groups of individuals working together are more successful than employees working alone through the use of a brief quiz.

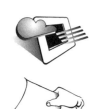

MATERIALS

◆ PowerPoint presentation *Synergy.ppt* (in the online materials)

◆ Copies of Handout 11.10—Synergy Trivia Quiz for participants

◆ Pencil/pen for each participant

◆ Space enough for participants to meet and work together in small teams

TIME

◆ 10 minutes

INSTRUCTIONS

1. Introduce lesson by displaying the slide *Synergy.ppt,* which defines the concept of *synergy:*

   Synergy
   Synergy is the blending of different human skills, talents, and experience to produce a total effect greater than the sum of the individual team members' skills, talents, and experiences alone. With synergy, $5 + 5 => 10$.

2. Explain that synergy is one of the basic building blocks of employee engagement.

   Synergy is what makes working together such a powerful force. When you have synergy, the whole is greater than the sum of the parts. Teams can accomplish what individuals working independently cannot accomplish.

3. Synergy is what enables groups to accomplish more than individuals. Synergy allows a group of 10 people working as a team to accomplish much more than 10 individuals, or even much more than 10 people working independently could achieve! Synergy is what drives employee engagement, making the concept so powerful at work.

4. It is through the collective knowledge, experience, and insights of team members that synergy allows the group to perform better than they could as individuals working independently.

5. Distribute a copy of Handout 11.10—Synergy Trivia Quiz to each participant and ask each person to take a few moments to complete it. Instruct participants not to share their answers with the other participants at this time.

6. After everyone has had a chance to complete the quiz, ask participants to form small groups of three to five people with those sitting closest to them. Instruct each small group to complete the quiz as a team, coming to consensus on each answer to decide on a team answer for each question. Ask each team to record their team's answers in the space provided on the quiz.

7. Next, reveal the correct answers to the Synergy Trivia Quiz as highlighted below:

   1. Who won the 1960 baseball World Series?
      A—Pittsburgh Pirates

   2. What actress has won the most Academy Awards during her career?
      C—Katharine Hepburn

   3. Who was the fourth president of the United States?
      D—James Madison

   4. What is considered to be the coldest place on earth?
      C—Antarctica

   5. In what state is the Grand Canyon located?
      A—Arizona

6. Who was the first U.S. astronaut to fly in outer space?
    D—Alan Shepard

7. What was the first Beatles number one hit in the Unted States?
    A—"I Want to Hold Your Hand"

8. How many pints are there in a U.S. gallon?
    B—8

9. If you were an octogenarian, how old would you be?
    B—80–89 years old

10. If you were in a dark room and reached into a drawer containing an equal number of single blue socks and single red socks, how many would you have to pull out of the drawer to get a matched pair?
    B—3

    Ask participants to record the number of correct answers each person had on their individual score and then their team's score and compare.

8. Ask by a show of hands who had a better score on the quiz working as a member of the team than they did as an individual. Expect that all or most of the participants will raise their hands.

 DEBRIEF

Ask participants how the concept of synergy could be utilized more often in their workplace and with their employees. What would be the benefit of increasing the amount of synergy in their workplaces and how could this increase employee engagement?

Structured Experience 11.11—Creating a Team Project Plan

GOAL

The purpose of the structured experience is to:

◆ Demonstrate how a project plan helps everyone on the team understand her role and responsibilities.

◆ Demonstrate ways that a complete project plan also helps team members stay organized and focused on their objectives and goals.

MATERIALS

◆ PowerPoint presentation *Project Plan Example.ppt* (in the online materials)

◆ Handout 11.21—Project Plan Example (chapter 11)

◆ Handout 11.22—Completed Project Plan (chapter 11)

TIME

◆ 20 minutes

INSTRUCTIONS

1. Begin the lesson by explaining how important it is for a team to create a project plan.

2. Explain that a project plan helps everyone understand what her responsibilities are as a member of the team. The project plan also helps track the team's progress toward its goals and highlights when people may be falling behind schedule. Keeping this project plan updated and current is important for everyone to know the progress and future challenges for the team.

3. Present the slide *Project Plan Example.ppt* or distribute Handout 11.21—Project Plan Example to participants and explain this is an example of a template for a project plan that can be used or adapted to organize your project team members' roles and responsibilities. Review each of the parts of the plan and emphasize their importance.

The first column lists and thus documents each individual goal established by the team.

It is important these goals be constantly in front of the team so everyone can stay focused on them. Next, the team member or members responsible for the goal are listed; again this serves as a constant reminder of who is responsible for this goal. The next column asks that the deliverable or deliverables for each goal be described. This lets everyone know what is expected to be done or delivered to complete this goal. The next column asks for a measure to be developed that can quantify as much as possible the achievement of each goal. Examples of goal measures will be provided in Handout 11.22. Finally the due date for the goal is listed, as well as a status of how far this goal is currently toward completion, and these are in the last two columns of the plan.

4. Display the second slide in the *Project Plan Example.ppt* slide set or distribute a copy of Handout 11.22—Complete Project Plan.

5. Review some of the details outlined in this completed project plan. Ask participants how the specifics listed in the project plan would be helpful in keeping the team focused on these responsibilities and moving forward with the work of the team toward completing the project.

DEBRIEF

Conclude the lesson by explaining that this project plan should be updated and reviewed during each team meeting or sent out as regular updates to team members, which will help keep everyone focused on the team's progress toward its goals. This way, each team member understands what follow-up responsibilities she has to complete and by when. This keeps everyone on track and contributing to achieving the team's overall goals and objectives. Another suggestion would be to also send these updates to others sponsoring or supporting the team. This can serve as a good communication tool concerning the progress of your team to these key stakeholders.

Handout 11.1—Rumors

THE RUMOR

There is an unconfirmed report that a major reorganization is about to be announced in the organization sometime during the next few weeks. According to reliable sources, several new top executives are being brought in and there is speculation that there could be a major shuffle in the current management team as part of this restructuring, involving cost reductions of 20 percent over the next 18 months. It is not clear what these cost reductions are going to involve at this time, but it could mean a number of current programs being slashed, eliminated, or changed. There might even be an early retirement package being offered to those who qualify for it with enough years of service.

There are going to be mandatory meetings held next week and information sent to employees' homes announcing these major changes. No one is supposed to know this information except a few top company officials at this time until the announcement is made, so this information should be kept very confidential.

Handout 11.2—Spending Time With Employees

What percentage of your working time do you spend interacting directly with those who report to you?

_____

_____

_____

Draw in a pie chart format what percentage you currently spend in the circle below.

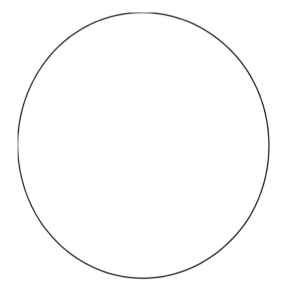

Is this the right amount of time?

Handout 11.3—Conflict Strategies

1. Win/Win Strategies

   Supervisor: John and Frank, I wanted to talk to you both concerning how you two have been having a problem working together lately and to come to some kind of resolution concerning this problem. Would that be ok with both of you?

   John: Yeah, sure.

   Frank: Sounds ok to me.

   Supervisor: Let me start by asking both of you to explain what the problem is between you two. John, why don't you go first and tell me what is going on from your perspective?

   John: Well, I just don't appreciate Frank making changes to my work without telling me first. When he does this, sometimes I don't find out until days later, and it causes problems for me because I am working under the assumption that nothing has been changed. This has caused me to have to redo a lot of work recently when I am already struggling to stay on schedule.

   Supervisor: Ok, Frank, can you comment on what John just brought up?

   Frank: Yes, John, first I just want to tell you that I am not intending to make your job any more difficult than it already is. I appreciate all the things you have going on right now and how hard it is to manage everything you have to do. I admit that I have made a couple of changes to things you have previously worked on, but that was only because I had knowledge of other things that you may not have been aware of that were important to what you were working on. I just went ahead and made these changes when you were gone, intending to bring you up to speed on why they were necessary, but never got a chance to do this before you got back and saw the changes for yourself. I do want to tell you that they were necessary or I wouldn't have made them, and I am sorry that I wasn't able to tell you first.

   John: I am not disagreeing the changes weren't necessary or correct—just that I didn't know they had been made.

   Frank: Again, I apologize that I didn't make sure you knew about them. I am just so busy myself that I forgot to tell you or thought that I would when I saw you next time.

   Supervisor: Ok, I think we all have a better understanding about how and why this occurred. What can we do to prevent this problem from occurring in the future?

Frank: Well, I could set up a procedure that automatically notifies John when any changes are made relating to what he is working on and explaining the reason for the change. Also, I could set it up so that John gets the same updates that I receive so he will know when these types of changes are made. That way he'll know right away about the changes going forward and not be working on old information, and I don't have to try to remember to tell John about each change every time they occur, which has been more frequently lately. I think such a system could be put in place pretty easily.

John: That would be great. There have been many times when I simply didn't know about these types of updates in the past. Receiving these in real time in the future would prevent many problems and rework for me.

Supervisor: Sounds like we have a good solution that will benefit everyone and prevent this type of problem from occurring in the future. Thanks to both of you for being willing to openly discuss this issue and work toward a solution acceptable to each of you.

2. Win/Lose Strategies

Employee: I would like to talk to you about the assignment you recently gave me. I don't think it's fair that I get stuck with this work when other employees don't do half the things I do. There should be some way to make sure that everyone pulls their weight around here, not just me all the time.

Supervisor: I am not going to discuss other employees with you or their workloads. I believe that I am always fair in giving out assignments with everyone. The assignment I just gave you is part of your job, not other employees', and I expect you to get it done. If you have any questions about the assignment, I will discuss it with you; otherwise you need to get to work on completing this. Do you have any other questions?

Employee: No, I guess not.

3. Lose/Lose Strategies

Employee: I would like to talk to you about some of the problems I am still having concerning my job. It still isn't any better than the last time I talked to you about these issues. If things don't get any better, I am just going to have to quit and find another job, which is too bad, because I would like to keep working here.

Supervisor: Well, I don't really know what else I can tell you or do about it. We have already talked about it several times and I don't have a solution to your problem. I suppose if things aren't getting any better, then maybe you had better move on to another job if that's what you want to do. However, I would hate to see you leave because you do a good job here.

Employee: Well, I guess that's what I am going to have to do.

4. Lose/Win Strategies

Supervisor: I see that you have been late for work again this morning. This is the fifth time that you have been late since the last time we talked about this not that long ago. I told you at that time this needed to improve, but obviously it hasn't. No one else who works for me has nearly as many problems getting to work on time as you. I told you before, if this continues, that you would receive a disciplinary notice, and that's what I called you into my office this morning to discuss with you.

Employee: Please just give me one more chance. I promise you that I will stop being late so much. As I told you before, I can't help it sometimes. I know it is against the rules and other employees get upset when I am late and they have to cover for me. I just can't afford to get another discipline on my record or it could cost me my job, which I do need to hang onto right now. You'll see, it will be different this time. I really mean it!

Supervisor: Ok, I will let it slide this one last time. But remember, if you have any more tardiness or unexcused absences, you will receive discipline and whatever consequences may come with it. Do you understand?

Employee: Yes, thank you, and I won't let you down this time.

Handout 11.4—Supervisor Role

SUPERVISOR'S ROLE

As you know, these two employees do not get along very well, and this situation has existed for a number of years, although as you understand it, they were actually friends at one time long ago. Each employee has the potential of contributing to the success of the entire team, but only if they can get past this conflict they have with one another, as it has the potential of interfering with the teamwork in your entire group. This is something you should remind each of these individuals as you conduct this coaching session with them.

As supervisor in this conflict role play, encourage each employee to express to one another what she feels is the real reason for their conflict. Encourage them to develop areas of agreement and common goals or objectives. Each employee should seek feedback from the other on how they could improve their relationship and make commitments to change her behavior to help achieve this goal.

Handout 11.5—Employee A

Instructions to person playing employee A in this coflict role play:

You are upset that you have to work more closely with this other person. You feel that things were just fine the way they have been for the past few years when the two of you only occasionally had to have contact with each other. Your issue with the other person is that she was constantly trying to tell you how to do your job. The other person just can't seem to understand that her way of doing things may not be the best way to perform the job. No one else's opinions or ideas seem to count or matter to this individual. Every time the two of you try to work together, it always seems to end up in a contest to see who can do things better.

At one time, the two of you were friends and enjoyed one another's company. However, the other person's competitiveness ruined your friendship and relationship. You still have respect for the other person's ability and wish that you could work better together as part of the team. You believe if you both could get along, your combined efforts could really help the group's efforts. However, as long as this other person has this attitude, you don't believe you two can ever work well together effectively again.

Handout 11.6—Employee B

Instructions to person playing employee B in this conflict role play:

You are upset that you have to work more closely with this other person. You feel that things were just fine the way they have been for the past few years when the two of you only occasionally had to have contact with each other. Your issue with the other person is that she was constantly trying to tell you how to do your job. The other person just can't seem to understand that her way of doing things may not be the best way to perform the job. No one else's opinions or ideas seem to count or matter to this individual. Every time the two of you try to work together, it always seems to end up in a contest to see who can do things better.

At one time, the two of you were friends and enjoyed one another's company. However, the other person's competitiveness ruined your friendship and relationship. You still have respect for the other person's ability and wish that you could work better together as part of the team. You believe if you both could get along, your combined efforts could really help the group's efforts. However, as long as this other person has this attitude, you don't believe you two can ever work well together effectively again.

Handout 11.7—Discipline Role Play Introduction

In this role play, a supervisor is conducting a disciplinary counseling session with an employee concerning an absentee problem. As a supervisor, one of your greatest challenges and most difficult responsibilities is in issuing discipline to employees. However, even though this is one of the most unpleasant tasks you must perform, discipline when necessary is also one of your most important responsibilities. Not enforcing the rules by allowing employees to violate them is not fair to those who follow them. But this often puts a heavy burden on a supervisor to have to enforce these rules and issue discipline to employees.

Background Information

The employee who is being talked to today has had an absentee problem for the past 18 months. Before that time, she would occasionally miss work, but not to the extent that it has been recently. When at work, the employee does a good job and is a contributing member of the team. One of the problems with this person's frequent absences is that when she is not at work, it disrupts the entire work group. The supervisor has spoken informally to this employee on a number of occasions during this time period about the excessive absences and each time was given a full explanation why the absence occurred and was assured that the problem would be corrected. The employee has mentioned that she is having a number of problems in her personal life at this time that are causing the absentee problem. Regardless of the reason and no matter how legitimate the reasons, however, the employee's absences cause many difficulties for everyone else at work, and some kind of action needs to be taken to address this problem.

Handout 11.8—Supervisor's Role

As explained in the background information, the employee you are to talk to today has an absenteeism problem that began about 18 months ago. Following each absence, you met with the employee and asked why she had missed work. The reasons for these absences have varied, including personal illnesses, sick children, car problems, personal business, funeral, and so forth. You have previously told the employee after the last absence that if she missed any additional time, you were considering issuing formal discipline. The situation today is that the employee is returning to work after again missing time from work.

Because this employee has worked for you for a number of years without having an absenteeism problem, you don't understand why all of a sudden she seems to have so much trouble coming to work. This is something that you want to explore during this meeting. Because the reasons for these absences have varied to such an extent, you do not know if there is any one problem in this person's life or a number of factors causing these absences. You have told all of those who work for you if they ever had anything that they needed to discuss with you, you would always be available for them. You are not sure that there isn't something else happening in this employee's life that might be the cause of these absences and you are also not sure how to approach this subject with her. You have asked her in the past if there was any reason for these absences that you should be aware of or if you could provide support or guidance in helping correct this problem. The employee has indicated there might be something going on in her personal life but hasn't been very specific or interested in discussing this issue, so you are unsure if this is an issue where you could refer the employee to HR or to the Employee Assistance Program.

Due to the excessive nature of these absences, you have prepared a first-level disciplinary action to be presented to the employee today. You will explain to her that if this absenteeism continues, further discipline may result. You expect the employee to object to this discipline, stating that she doesn't feel it is fair for her to receive discipline for a situation that couldn't be prevented or controlled.

The following are the most important points that you plan to stress to this employee during the disciplinary counseling session:

1. State the problem and why it needs to be corrected.

2. Give the employee the opportunity to give her side of the story before a final decision on the action to be taken is made.

3. Explain the significance of any discipline issued today and its impact on the person's employment.

4. Review what discipline would result if these absences continue in the future.

5. Offer any support or help the person may want or need to correct her absentee problem.

6. Ask for a commitment from the employee to correct this behavior.

7. End the session by summarizing how important it is for the employee to be at work each day and the problems that are caused when she is absent. Again offer support and assistance to help in correcting this problem.

Handout 11.9—Employee's Role

As explained in the background information for this role play, you as the employee have missed a lot of work during the past year and a half. When asked the reason for these absences, your answer should be that you have had a number of things happen in your and your family's lives during this time period. You feel there has not been much you could do to prevent these absences, as each one was for a different reason and all of them legitimate. You might want to express your feelings to your supervisor that you don't feel it is fair you should receive discipline for absenteeism when there wasn't anything you could do about missing this much work. Your supervisor may ask if there is some problem that you need outside help to handle which is causing these absences to occur. You are not sure this is something you are comfortable talking to your supervisor about at this time.

You have had other employees complain about the problems that are created for them when you miss work. You realize that others have to work harder to get the job done when you are gone. You are concerned about this and are committed to modifying this behavior for the benefit of your co-workers and the organization. You try to work hard to perform your duties to the best of your abilities and you do not want this problem to negatively affect your job or working relationship with your co-workers.

Handout 11.10—Role Play Script—Supervisor's Part

Scene: Supervisor brings a disgruntled employee into his office to discuss excessive absenteeism.

Date: Today

Time: Now

Supervisor: Come on in and have a seat. How are you doing today?

Employee: (snarling) Ok, I guess.

Supervisor: I've asked you to meet with me today because I want to discuss your attendance lately. In reviewing your record, I noticed you have been missing a lot of time, in fact quite a few days over the past few months.

Employee: (coming into meeting with a negative/defensive attitude) Look, don't give me that grief! You've been picking on me ever since I started working for you. I don't see what the big problem is anyway, I am here most of the time, at least as much as most other people around here. Anyway, what I do on my own time and why I'm off work is my own business and I don't get paid anyway when I'm not here.

Supervisor: I agree that what you do on your own time is not my business. However, how much time you miss from work is my concern. I called you to my office in hopes that we might find a way to improve your work attendance. But if you don't want to discuss these things with me today that is your decision. However, I do want to make sure that you understand the following concerning your attendance. First, we have an attendance schedule policy that everyone is expected to follow. I am giving you a copy of this policy that is in the current employee handbook for your reference. Your benefits continue when you are off from work, so there is still an expense to the company when you are gone. We also have to replace your position when you are absent, often on an overtime basis, costing the company additional unplanned expenses. And finally, any continued absences can result in disciplinary action unless there is an improvement. Do you understand?

Employee: Yeah, I guess so.

Supervisor: Ok, that's all I wanted to discuss with you today. If there is anything I can do to help you improve your performance, let me know. I also want to inform you that your absences might be covered by a company policy such as our short-term disability program or the Family Medical Leave Act or FMLA. You should contact Human Resources for more information on these programs or regulations.

******End of Role Play*****

Handout 11.11—Role Play Script—Employee's Part

Scene: Supervisor brings a disgruntled employee into his office to discuss excessive absenteeism.

Date: Today

Time: Now

Supervisor: Come on in and have a seat. How are you doing today?

Employee: (snarling) Ok, I guess.

Supervisor: I've asked you to meet with me today because I want to discuss your attendance lately. In reviewing your record, I noticed you have been missing a lot of time, in fact quite a few days over the past few months.

Employee: (coming into meeting with a negative/defensive attitude) Look, don't give me that grief! You've been picking on me ever since I started working for you. I don't see what the big problem is anyway, I am here most of the time, at least as much as most other people around here. Anyway, what I do on my own time and why I'm off work is my own business and I don't get paid anyway when I'm not here.

Supervisor: I agree that what you do on your own time is not my business. However, how much time you miss from work is my concern. I called you to my office in hopes that we might find a way to improve your work attendance. But if you don't want to discuss these things with me today that is your decision. However, I do want to make sure that you understand the following concerning your attendance. First, we have an attendance schedule policy that everyone is expected to follow. I am giving you a copy of this policy that is in the current employee handbook for your reference. Your benefits continue when you are off from work, so there is still an expense to the company when you are gone. We also have to replace your position when you are absent, often on an overtime basis, costing the company additional unplanned expenses. And finally, any continued absences can result in disciplinary action unless there is an improvement. Do you understand?

Employee: Yeah, I guess so.

Supervisor: Ok, that's all I wanted to discuss with you today. If there is anything I can do to help you improve your performance, let me know. I also want to inform you that your absences might be covered by a company policy such as our short-term disability program or the Family Medical Leave Act or FMLA. You should contact Human Resources for more information on these programs or regulations.

******End of Role Play*****

Handout 11.12—Documentation Role Play Example

Date: March 3, 20_ _

Time: 8:45 A.M.

Subject: Counseling meeting with _____ on her absenteeism

I called _____ to my office to discuss her absenteeism. She appeared to be upset and raised her voice several times during our conversation. She said she felt I didn't like her and accused me of picking on her since she has been working for me. I stated that I had no negative feelings about her and that I treat everyone I supervise fairly and equally regardless of anything that may have happened in the past. She also stated that she doesn't get paid when off of work so it wasn't really any of the company's business if she misses work.

I didn't argue with her about these points, but reminded her that I was concerned about her absenteeism that was currently at a higher rate than acceptable according to company's attendance rules. I also reminded her of the attendance policy and gave her a copy of the latest update to that policy. I also reminded her that her benefits continue to be covered while she is off and that she has to be replaced, sometimes with an employee working overtime, when she is gone. I also informed her that any future unexcused absences could result in further discipline, up to and including discharge. I closed the meeting by asking if she had any questions or needed any additional information.

I told her that I sincerely hoped that she would improve her attendance in the future and provided the telephone number for the company's Employee Assistance Program provided by an outside organization who specializes in helping employees with any personal problems they might be experiencing that could interfere with their jobs. I also suggested that she should contact Human Resources if she felt that any of the absences would be covered under the company's Short-Term Disability Program or possibly the Family Medical Leave Act (FMLA).

She stated that she understood what I told her, but still appeared to be upset when leaving my office. The meeting lasted about 10 minutes.

Supervisor's Signature

_____

Handout 11.13—Performance-Improvement Process Plan

Name:

Dates of Plan: _____ to _____

Dates of Meetings:

Initial

Meeting Date: Follow-up

Meeting Date: Follow-up

Meeting Date: Follow-up

Meeting Date:

Completed by

_____

Table 11–1

Performance Problem(s)	Performance Goal	Support	Timetable	Follow-up date	Results • Meeting Requirements (MR) • Improving (I) • Unacceptable (U)

Handout 11.14—Performance-Improvement Process Plan

Name: I. M. Lowperformer

Dates of Plan: May 1, 20___ to July 31, 20___

Dates of Meetings

Initial Meeting Date: April 30, 2___

Follow-up Meeting Date: May 15, 2___

Follow-up Meeting Date: June 1, 2___

Follow-up Meeting Date: June 15, 2___

Final Meeting Date: July 1, 2___

Completed by

_____

Date: April 30, 2___

Table 11–2

Performance Problem(s)	Performance Goal	Support	Timetable	Follow-up date	Results • Meeting Requirements (MR) • Improving (I) • Unacceptable (U)
Not calling on right customers/ spending too much time and money on wrong customers	Create list of top 20 customers in territory.	Work with Regional Sales Mgr.	Due May 7	May 7	
Missing appointments, not following up with customers and deadlines	Create and submit within 7 days a monthly visit schedule for each account. Make appointments with each customer at least 1 week in advance. Submit plan by end of prior month in future to supervisor.	Use Top 20 list. Review plan w/ Regional Sales Manager by 3rd day of month	Due May 7	May 7	
Lack of confidence by others concerning your dependability Too many missed deadlines and commitments unmet	Respond to all customer inquiries, complaints, issues, requests, etc. within 2 business days. Ensure all follow-ups completed 100%. Inform supervisor of all such contacts.	Regional Sales Mgr. R&D Tech. Services Sales Group	Immediately	May 14	
Failure to keep supervisor informed on critical information relating to accounts	Zero surprises to supervisor concerning customer issues. Call/email supervisor at least 3 times/week with customer contact communication. Respond to all vmx's/emails within 24 hours.	Superv. Go-Help Desk VMX Support	Immediately	May 14	

Handout 11.15—PIPP Role Play Background (Supervisor)

SUPERVISOR

In this role play, you are meeting with an employee who has had a history of poor performance over the past several years. Unfortunately, for a variety of reasons, this poor performance has not been adequately addressed in the past. This individual has only recently begun reporting to you and this is really the first time to your knowledge that her poor performance has been addressed in such a way. Prior to this meeting, you reviewed with this individual her poor performance during the performance review for last year. You have also counseled this employee on a number of performance issues during the past several months that you felt were not acceptable. Unfortunately, this person's performance continues to be at an unacceptable level and must be addressed utilizing a performance improvement plan. You are expecting this to be a difficult meeting.

Your purpose during this meeting should be to communicate to this employee what you are dissatisfied about concerning her performance, the goals you expect her to achieve, the support available, timetables, follow-up dates, and how performance will be measured, as well as the consequences for not meeting the objective of this plan. All of these factors are part of the PIPP that you have prepared for this meeting.

You expect that this employee will have difficulty accepting responsibility for the results of her performance. As you have heard in the past, this employee will try to place blame on others for her low sales. She will particularly focus blame on her last supervisor as well as the other salespeople who she works with, claiming lack of teamwork and cooperation. As this individual has worked in the business longer than you, she will try to use this fact to intimidate you and make you feel as if you don't know the "way the business is really run."

During the role play, you need to listen to this individual, but make sure that she also hears what you have to say. Your ultimate goal must be to have this individual assume responsibility for results of this performance-improvement plan. She will try to move responsibility for as many things as she can to you. You need to prevent this from happening. You want this employee to provide you with a weekly call sheet so you are satisfied that she is spending her time most effectively. You expect resistance on this issue as well.

It is critical that the employee leaves this meeting understanding that she is in serious performance trouble and her job is on the line. You need to schedule a follow-up meeting with her as described in this plan.

Handout 11.16—PIPP Role Play Background (Employee)

EMPLOYEE

You have just gotten a new supervisor who doesn't seem to "know the ropes" about how this business is run. In fact, you have been in the business considerably longer than her. Over the past several months, your new supervisor has been giving you a lot of grief about your performance. She isn't satisfied with the way you are doing your job, despite the fact that it has been perfectly acceptable for all these years with your other supervisors. She mentioned a number of issues during your recent annual performance evaluation meeting and has sent you a number of "nasty" letters and emails concerning the way you do your job. You have tried to ignore these things, but it seems that she is getting more serious about these issues. Your new supervisor has complained about the accounts that you have been calling on and how much time and entertainment expense you spend with certain customers. She doesn't seem to understand that these have been good accounts for many years, even though they may not be buying as much as they used to. They also are good friends of yours that you don't want to offend and possibly lose future business when the economy and business gets better.

You feel that if your supervisor wants these other companies to be called on more frequently, she needs to get someone else who has the time to call on them. You are going to tell her this if it comes up during your upcoming meeting. You also believe that she will bring up the fact that you have missed a few appointments with potential customers that she wanted you to call on. You knew that this was just a waste of time and decided that you could better spend your time on your "regular accounts."

You have tried to get business with most of these companies in the past and know that you are never going to be able to outbid the competition. You just can't understand why she can't seem to understand this. Besides, if the company would only reduce the price to be more competitive, you might feel that these calls were worthwhile. Also, you never get any support from R&D on answering these customers' objections to our products. Until these issues are addressed, as far as you are concerned, it is just a waste of time to even call on these people. You should tell your new supervisor this during the meeting.

But the thing that bugs you the most is that this new supervisor wants to know what you are doing every minute of every day. You are afraid that you are going to spend so much time doing this that you won't have any time left to sell anything! You are simply going to tell her that it isn't practical for you to report everything you do to her.

Your goal is to be able to keep things just as they are today concerning the way you do your job. The way you see it—if it has been good enough for all these years, it should be good enough for the new supervisor. You plan on telling her that.

Handout 11.17—Background Data Sheet—Supervisor's Role Play

(To be distributed to participant playing supervisor role.)

SUPERVISOR'S BACKGROUND INFORMATION

In appraising this employee's performance, your first objective should be to determine how the introduction of employee engagement in the workplace may be influencing her attitude about work. During the appraisal, you need to explore with the employee what is negatively influencing her performance and what can be done to begin to correct this problem. Some suggestions might be to provide any training that might be available and appropriate to help the employee adapt to the new work environment and to develop stronger interpersonal skills for working as a member of a team. The employee being appraised does have the potential to someday be promoted to a position of more responsibility but must first develop the skills necessary for becoming an effective member of the team at work.

In developing an action plan for the employee, you need to consider some kind of ongoing coaching program which can serve to provide support and feedback on a regular basis on her performance. You as the supervisor must make sure that the employee's overall work performance in its entirety is reviewed during the session and not just address this single weakest performance factor. The employee has continued to perform her job in a quality manner and has been very dependable in attendance, meeting work deadlines, learning new tasks, and finding innovative new approaches to solving problems on the job.

Your overall objective should be to reinforce those aspects of the job that the employee has been performing well, have her accept and acknowledge the fact that she is having a problem working in the new engaged work environment, and help develop a plan to improve this deficiency. As this is the first annual appraisal that the employee has had since these changes were introduced and her problems began, you might expect her to be somewhat defensive about this feedback. The employee may try to bring up other people's performance as the reason why she is having difficulties. You will need to make decisions concerning how appropriate it may be to discuss other people's performance during the performance evaluation as it relates to this employee's work and how much of the appraisal session needs to be directly focused on her own actions.

As part of your new role and responsibilities as a supervisor in this type of work environment, you must help employees learn to resolve problems and conflicts they have with one another as much as possible and help employees grow and accept greater levels of responsibility, not only for their own actions, but also for the results of the team.

In this performance appraisal form, you should consider addressing the following as the most important requirements of the employee's job to be evaluated and list these on the form shown below:

- Job skills and knowledge
- Quality of work
- Teamwork
- Adapting to change
- Working relationships
- Personal development

Once you have completed the performance appraisal form and thought about what you intend to review with this employee, ask her to come to your office and begin the role play.

PERFORMANCE APPRAISAL FORM

Performance areas to be reviewed:

Rating

1. _____

Unacceptable	Marginal	Good	Excellent
1	2	3	4

Action Plan:

2. _____

Unacceptable	Marginal	Good	Excellent
1	2	3	4

Action Plan:

3. _____

Unacceptable	Marginal	Good	Excellent
1	2	3	4

Action Plan:

4. _____

Unacceptable	Marginal	Good	Excellent
1	2	3	4

Action Plan:

5. _____

Unacceptable	Marginal	Good	Excellent
1	2	3	4

Action Plan:

6. _____

Unacceptable	Marginal	Good	Excellent
1	2	3	4

Action Plan:

Supervisor's Overall Comments:

_____

_____

_____

_____

Overall Rating:

Unacceptable	Marginal	Good	Excellent
1	2	3	4

Handout 11.18—Background Data Sheet—Employee's Role Play

(To be distributed to participant playing employee role.)

As the employee being appraised today, you feel that you have done a good job during the past year despite the many changes that have occurred in your workplace recently. There are a number of problems you want to point out to your supervisor about other employees who are not "pulling their weight" in this new work environment that has recently been introduced. Even though you believe that engaging employees is a good thing, you are still thinking that many of the changes that have been made are not working out very well. You want to point out that there are several other employees who are taking advantage of the freedom they now have. You are concerned that your performance evaluation is going to be negatively affected by these changes and will feel a little defensive if it is brought up during your appraisal today. You want to ask your supervisor why they can't just go back to the old system when everyone understood the rules and what their role and job was supposed to be.

You are concerned that you are not getting credit for your job knowledge and ability. There was a time before these new concepts were introduced at work when you were considered one of the very best employees in your work group and the person everyone came to for answers to the problems they could not solve by themselves. However, now you feel that no one is listening to you anymore. Whenever there is a problem, someone calls for a team meeting and they start a "brainstorming" session in which everyone contributes their ideas as a group concerning what should be done to solve problems at work. It seems to you all they are doing is wasting a lot of time in meetings writing down everyone's ideas and suggestions when all they really have to do is ask you what should be done. After all, this system worked well for many years until this new engagement way of doing things came into the workplace. You are at a point where you are not even bothering to offer your opinions even when you see mistakes being made by others.

You hope to get a chance to talk to your supervisor about advancement opportunities that might be available to you in the future. You feel that if you were just able to get a chance to be promoted, you could really reach what you are capable of achieving. In fact, you have several suggestions for your supervisor about how the work could be better organized and distributed if she will only listen to what you have to say. Several of these ideas involve providing better training for new employees that significantly increases their understanding of the operation and makes them more productive in a much shorter time. You would even be interested in helping provide this training for future new employees.

Despite all the problems you have been experiencing lately, you still want to see the company be successful and do a good job. You would like to improve your performance and again be regarded as a top-performing employee. You are hoping that your supervisor can give you some guidance today on how you can resolve the current problems you are experiencing and get back on track to being what you believe you can be at work.

Handout 11.19—Observer's Role Play Responsibilities

(To be distributed to participant playing observer's role.)

EVALUATING SUPERVISOR'S ROLE

As an observer, you are asked to evaluate how well both the supervisor and employee covered the main points of the role play. Mark "yes" or "no" concerning how the participant playing the supervisor role accomplished the following objectives and be prepared to provide this feedback to her:

Yes___ No___   Did the supervisor provide (or simulate) a private office environment for the performance appraisal free from interruptions and distractions?

Yes___ No___   Did the supervisor have a completed performance appraisal form to be reviewed with the employee?

Yes___ No___   Did the supervisor have an overall plan for discussing the employee's performance with objectives and goals to be achieved?

Yes___ No___   Did the supervisor explore what might be negatively affecting the employee's work performance and suggest corrective actions to address these problems?

Yes___ No___   Did the supervisor recommend training to help the employee improve performance and work more effectively as a member of the team?

Yes___ No___   Did the supervisor ensure that the employee's total performance was reflected in the appraisal and not just the negative aspects of the person's performance?

Yes___ No___   Did the supervisor recognize the positive aspects of the employee's performance as well during the appraisal period?

Yes___ No___   Did the supervisor allow the employee to express her frustrations and help her deal with these emotions in an understanding manner?

Yes___ No___   Did the supervisor offer assistance to the employee in dealing with the problems she was experiencing?

Yes___ No___   Did the supervisor encourage the employee to focus on her own performance rather than that of others?

Yes___ No___   Did the supervisor give the employee feedback concerning promotional or advancement opportunities the employee could realistically expect in the future and what development lessons for her that should be explored?

Yes___ No___   Did the supervisor establish any follow-up plans with the employee to reinforce goals developed during the appraisal?

OBSERVER'S ROLE PLAY RESPONSIBILITIES

EVALUATION EMPLOYEE'S ROLE

As an observer, you are asked to evaluate how well both the supervisor and employee cover the main points of the role play. Mark "yes" or "no" concerning how the participant playing the employee role accomplished the following objectives and be prepared to provide this feedback to her:

Yes___ No___   Did the employee express her frustration with the new employee engagement approach that has been recently introduced in the organization?

Yes___ No___   Did the employee try to blame her problems on co-workers not pulling their weight and taking advantage of the new freedom they have been given?

Yes___ No___   Did the employee express concern that her appraisal would be negatively affected because of these changes?

Yes___ No___   Did the employee express concern that she was not getting credit for the positive aspects of her job performance?

Yes___ No___   Did the employee express concern that her perception was that no one was listening to her anymore?

Yes___ No___   Did the employee ask about advancement opportunities that might be available for her?

Yes___ No___   Was the employee receptive to the supervisor's attempts to find out what was causing the employee's problems with her co-workers?

Yes___ No___   Did the employee accept suggestions that the supervisor gave to try to provide assistance to the employee in improving her performance?

Yes___ No___   Did the employee accept the fact that she shares in the responsibility for improving her performance and must help accept responsibility for this improvement?

Yes___ No___   Was the employee receptive to any planned follow-up on the supervisor's part to continue to focus on improving her performance on an ongoing basis?

Yes___ No___   Did the employee respond to this performance appraisal meeting in such a way that you feel she would improve her performance in the future as a result?

Handout 11.20—Synergy Trivia Quiz

Table 11–3

Synergy Trivia Quiz	Your Answer	Team's Answer	Correct Answer
1. Who won the 1960 baseball World Series? a. Pittsburgh Pirates b. NY Yankees c. Chicago White Sox d. NY Mets			
2. What actress has won the most academy awards during her career? a. Elizabeth Taylor b. Ingrid Bergman c. Katharine Hepburn d. Julia Roberts			
3. Who was the fourth president of the United States? a. John Adams b. Thomas Jefferson c. George Washington d. James Madison			
4. What is considered to be the coldest place on earth? a. Siberia b. North Pole c. Antarctica d. Cleveland			
5. In what state is the Grand Canyon located? a. Arizona b. Utah c. Nevada d. Colorado			
6. Who was the first U.S. astronaut to fly in outer space? a. John Glenn b. Gus Grissom c. Neil Armstrong d. Alan Shepard			
7. What was the first Beatles number one hit in the U.S.? a. "I Want to Hold Your Hand" b. "Please Please Me" c. "Love Me Do" d. "From Me to You"			

Table 11–3 cont'd

8. How many pints are there in a U.S. gallon?
 	
  a. 4
  b. 8
  c. 12
  d. 16			

9. If you were an octogenarian, how old would you be?
 	
  a. 80 years old
  b. 80-89 years old
  c. 90-99 years old
  d. Over 100 years old			

10. If you were in a dark room and reached into a drawer containing an equal number of single blue socks and single red socks, how many would you have to pull out of the drawer to get a matched pair?
 	
  a. 2
  b. 3
  c. 5
  d. 6			

Scoring	Number of correct answers _____	Number of correct answers _____	

Handout 11.21—Project Plan Example

Table 11–4

	Goal	Team Member(s) Responsible	Deliverable	Measure	Due Date	Status
1.						
2.						
3.						
4.						
5.						
6.						
7.						
8.						

Handout 11.22—Completed Project Plan

Table 11–5

	Goal	Team Member(s) Responsible	Deliverable	Measure	Due Date	Status
1.	Design customer survey on proposed new product	Steve Smith Juan Hernandez	Design survey for team's approval	Team's agreement on survey design	3/1	First draft presented 3/1
2.	Meet with marketing department on survey plan	Kevin Jones K. Chen	Final survey presented to marketing department	Marketing department's approval of survey	3/15	Survey approved 3/7
3.	Send survey to customers	Benita King Shandra Bellimi	Identify customers to participate in survey and send to them	Customers receive survey before new season beginning in May	4/1	Surveys sent out 3/21
4.	Analyze survey data	Carlos Santee	Review and analyze data from survey results	Develop report on customer response to changes	5/15	Report developed before 5/15
5.	Recommend actions based on survey results	Kathy Brown Mishear Cosenza	Propose response to customer feedback based on data analysis	Present plan based on customer response to marketing department	5/22	Meeting held with marketing department 5/20
6.	Implement Actions	Singh Mennigash	Develop implementation plan	Implement plan	6/1	Plan implemented 6/1
7.	Evaluate Results	John Black Sue Yu	Collect data concerning implementation plan	Develop implementation report	7/1	Report completed 6/25
8.	Present results to VP of Marketing	All	Prepare presentation for VP	Presentation to VP of Marketing	7/15	Meeting scheduled 7/15

◆

Using the
Online Materials

Open the webpage www.astd.org/coachingemployeeengagementtraining in your
web browser.

Content of the Website

The website that accompanies this workbook on coaching employment engagement training contains
three types of files. All of the files can be used on a variety of computer platforms.

- ◆ **Adobe.pdf documents**—These include handouts, assessments, training instruments, and
  training tools.

- ◆ **Microsoft Word documents**—These text files can be edited to suit the specific circumstances of organizations and to fit the precise needs of trainers and trainees.

- ◆ **Microsoft PowerPoint presentations**—These presentations add interest and depth to
  many of the training activities included in the workbook.

- ◆ **Microsoft PowerPoint files of overhead transparency masters**—These files make it
  easy to print viewgraphs and handouts in black and white rather than use an office copier.
  They contain only text and line drawings: there are no images to print in grayscale.

Computer Requirements

To read or print the .pdf files on the website, Adobe Acrobat Reader software must be installed on
your system. This program can be downloaded free of cost from the Adobe website, www.adobe.com.

To use or adapt the contents of the PowerPoint presentation files on the website, Microsoft Power-Point software must be installed on your system. If you just want to view the PowerPoint documents, you must have an appropriate viewer installed on your system. Microsoft provides downloads of various viewers free of charge on its website, www.microsoft.com.

Printing From the Website

TEXT FILES

You can print the training materials using Adobe Acrobat Reader. Just open the .pdf file and print as many copies as you need. The following documents can be printed directly from the website:

- Handout 11.1—Rumors (chapter 11)

- Handout 11.2—Spending Time With Employees (chapter 11)

- Handout 11.3—Conflict Strategies Role Play (chapter 11)

- Handout 11.4—Supervisor Prompt (chapter 11)

- Handout 11.5—Employee A Prompt (chapter 11)

- Handout 11.6—Employee B Prompt (chapter 11)

- Handout 11.7—Discipline Role Play Introduction Handout (chapter 11)

- Handout 11.8—Supervisor's Role (chapter 11)

- Handout 11.9—Employee's Role (chapter 11)

- Handout 11.10—Synergy Trivia Quiz for participants (chapter 11)

- Handout 11.11—Role Play Script—Supervisor's Part (chapter 11)

- Handout 11.12—Role Play Script—Employee's Part (chapter 11)

- Handout 11.13—Role Play Documentation Example (chapter 11)

- Handout 11.14—Performance-Improvement Process Plan (chapter 11)

- Handout 11.15—PIPP Role Play Background—Supervisor (chapter 11)

- Handout 11.16—PIPP Role Play Background—Employee (chapter 11)

- Handout 11.17—Background Data Sheet—Supervisor's Role (chapter 11)

◆ Handout 11.18—Background Data Sheet—Employee's Role (chapter 11)

◆ Handout 11.19—Observer's Role Play Responsibilities (chapter 11)

◆ Handout 11.20—Team Award Presentation (chapter 11)

◆ Handout 11.21—Individual Recognition (chapter 11)

◆ Handout 11.22—Project Plan Example (chapter 11)

◆ Handout 11.23—Completed Project Plan (chapter 11)

◆ Assessment 10.1—Communicating Assignments Quiz (chapter 10)

◆ Assessment 10.2—Conflict Comfort Zone Self-Assessment (chapter 10)

◆ Assessment 10.3—Complaint-Handling Quiz (chapter 10)

POWERPOINT SLIDES

You can print the presentation slides directly from the website using Microsoft PowerPoint. Just open the .ppt files and print as many copies as you need. You can also make handouts of the presentations by printing two, four, or six slides per page. These slides will be in color, with design elements embedded. PowerPoint also permits you to print these in grayscale or black-and- white representations. Many trainers who use personal computers to project their presentations bring along viewgraphs, just in case there are glitches in the system.

Adapting the PowerPoint Slides

You can modify or otherwise customize the slides by opening and editing them in the appropriate application. You must, however, retain the denotation of the original source of the material; it is illegal to pass it off as your own work. You may indicate that a document was adapted from this workbook, written and copyrighted by Peter R. Garber and published by ASTD. The files will open as "Read Only," so before you adapt them, save them onto your hard drive under a different filename.

Showing the PowerPoint Presentation

The following PowerPoint presentations are included on the website:

◆ Project Plan Example.ppt

◆ Characteristics of an Engaged Team Player.ppt

◆ Types of Difficult Team Members.ppt

- Team Leaders Responsibilities.ppt

- Definition of Consensus.ppt

- Deciding When Teams Can Be Effective.ppt

- Potential Reinforcers.ppt

- Coaching Performance Tips.ppt

- Types of Feedback.ppt

- Levels of Feedback.ppt

- The 5 Ws of Documentation.ppt

- 2 Basic Rules about Managing Performance.ppt

- 5-Step Performance Correction Process.ppt

- A Coaches Goal.ppt

- Employees' Reactions to Complaints.ppt

- Complaint Handling Steps.ppt

- Conflict Comfort Zone Matrix.ppt

- Conflict Management Matrix.ppt

- Conflict Strategies.ppt

- Causes of Conflict at Work.ppt

- Is Conflict Always Bad.ppt

- Following Directions.ppt

- Basic Supervisory Principles.ppt

- 14 Commitments for Effective Coaching.ppt

- Phrases That Kill Ideas.ppt

- 5 Levels of Listening.ppt

- ◆ Coaches Communication Model.ppt

- ◆ The Importance of Communication.ppt

The presentation is in .ppt format, which means that it automatically shows full screen when you double-click on its filename. You can also open Microsoft PowerPoint and launch it from there. Use the space bar, the enter key, or mouse clicks to advance through a show. Press the backspace key to back up. Use the escape key to exit a presentation. If you want to blank the screen to black as the group discusses a point, press the B key. Press it again to restore the show. If you want to blank the screen to a white background, do the same with the W key. Table A-I summarizes these instructions. We strongly recommend that trainers practice presentations before they use them in training situations. You should be confident that you can cogently work through them. If you want to engage your training participants fully (rather than worry about how to show the next slide), become familiar with this simple technology before you need to use it. A good practice is to insert notes into the *Speaker's Notes* feature of the PowerPoint program, print them out, and have them in front of you when you present the slides.

Table A–1 Navigating Through a PowerPoint Presentation

KEY	POWERPOINT "SHOW" ACTION
Space bar *or* Enter *or* Mouse click	Advance through custom animations embedded in the presentation
Backspace	Back up to the last projected element of the presentation.
Escape	Abort the presentation.
B *or* b B *or* b *(repeat)*	Blank the screen to black. Resume the presentation.
W *or* w W *or* w *(repeat)*	Blank the screen to white. Resume the presentation.

Carliner, Saul. *Training Design Basics*. Alexandria, VA: ASTD, 2003.

Kemp, Jerrold E., Gary R. Morrison, and Steven M. Ross. *Designing Effective instruction* (2nd edition). Upper Saddle River, NJ: Prentice-Hall, 1998.

Kirkpatrick, Donald L., and James D. Kirkpatrick. *Evaluating Training Programs: The Four Levels* (3rd edition). San Francisco, CA: Berrett-Koehler Publishers, 2006.

Knowles, Malcolm S., Elwood F. Holton III, and Richard A. Swanson. *The Adult Learner* (5th edition). Houston, TX: Gulf Publishing Company, 1998.

Tobey, Deborah. *Needs Assessment Basics*. Alexandria, VA: ASTD, 2005.

About the Author

◆

Peter R. Garber is the author of over 50 books and training products on a wide variety of Human Resources and business topics. He has worked as a Human Resource professional for over 32 years and is Manager of Employee Relations for PPG Industries, a Pittsburgh-based manufacturing company. He is also an adjunct faculty member at the University of Pittsburgh, where he teaches leadership courses using much of the materials included in this book. *Coaching Employee Engagement* is based on Mr. Garber's extensive experience over the years in leading organizational change and employee engagement. Mr. Garber is married, has two grown daughters, and lives in Pittsburgh.

Index